LONDON
BOULOGNE

LEMNOS

PRETORIA
KIMBERLEY   HARRISMITH
BLOEMFONTEIN
RONDEBOSCH

Margaret Macdonald

FOOTPRINTS SERIES
Edited by Suzanne Morton

The life stories of individual women and men who were participants in interesting events help nuance larger historical narratives, at times reinforcing those narratives, at times contradicting them. The Footprints series introduces extraordinary Canadians, past and present, who have led fascinating and important lives at home and throughout the world.

The series includes primarily original manuscripts but may consider the English language translation of works that have already appeared in another language. The editor of the series welcomes inquiries from authors. If you are in the process of completing a manuscript that you think might fit into the series, please contact her, care of McGill-Queen's University Press, 3430 McTavish Street, Montreal, QC H3A 1X9.

Margaret Macdonald
Imperial Daughter

SUSAN MANN

McGILL-QUEEN'S UNIVERSITY PRESS   Montreal & Kingston • London • Ithaca

© McGill-Queen's University Press 2005

ISBN 0-7735-2999-3 (cloth)

Legal deposit third quarter 2005
Bibliothèque nationale du Québec

Printed in Canada on acid-free paper that is 100%
ancient forest free (100% post-consumer recycled),
processed chlorine free

This book has been published with the help of a
grant from the Canadian Federation for the Humanities
and Social Sciences, through the Aid to Scholarly
Publications Programme, using funds provided by
the Social Sciences and Humanities Research Council
of Canada.

McGill-Queen's University Press acknowledges the
support of the Canada Council for the Arts for our
publishing program. We also acknowledge the financial
support of the Government of Canada through the
Book Publishing Industry Development Program
(BPIDP) for our publishing activities.

Library and Archives Canada Cataloguing
in Publication

Mann, Susan, 1941–
Margaret Macdonald : imperial daughter /
Susan Mann.

Includes bibliographical references and index.
ISBN 0-7735-2999-3

1. Macdonald, Margaret Chisholm.
2. Military nursing.
3. World War, 1914–1918—Medical care.
4. Canada—Armed Forces—Medical personnel—
Biography. 5. Nurses—Canada—Biography. I. Title.

UH347.M23M35 2005
355.3'45'092
C2005-902864-5

This book was designed and typeset by studio
oneonone in Sabon 10.2/13

Contents

Illustrations

Preface

Nursing Sister Clare Gass introduced me to Margaret Macdonald. The encounters were brief and neither of them hinted at this book. The first occurred in September 1915 when Gass recorded in her diary Macdonald's visit to her hospital in France. The second was in May 1999 when my work on the Gass diary led me, through the intermediary of Gass's niece Elizabeth Anderson, to Macdonald's niece and nephew, Mairi Macdonald and Ronald St John Macdonald in Halifax. At that point my interest was limited to any Macdonald papers that might shed light on Clare Gass. There were none, and I went on my way. But unbeknownst to me, the Macdonalds began to ponder on their aunt's untold story.

Before *The War Diary of Clare Gass* was published in 2000, Ronald Macdonald suggested that I undertake that story. Because of the paucity of personal papers, I resisted until the teaching of a new course on women and the First World War at the University of Ottawa opened my eyes to the broad implications of a story such as Macdonald's. She personifies the point at which gender intersects with the overlapping contexts of ideology, structure, and institution in the late nineteenth and early twentieth centuries. Imperialism, feminism, bureaucracy and scientific management, medicine, the military, higher education and careers for women, and the professionalization of nursing – all of these were part of her life, and each can be seen in a slightly different light because of her participation in them. Her story could still, in fact, be told from that somewhat abstract perspective, but along the way I unearthed enough material to allow me – without losing sight of those themes – to keep the focus on Macdonald herself. Hence this biography.

Lest the reader be concerned, this is neither a commissioned nor an official biography. Ronald and Mairi Macdonald and their sister Elizabeth Podnieks of Toronto were enormously helpful in sharing with me the contents of their memories and their cupboards, but they carefully maintained their family's discretion as I shaped the results of my research into this narrative. I thank them for challenging me with this five-year jigsaw puzzle, of which neither the contours nor many of the pieces were discernible at the beginning.

Here is the story of a woman whose Scottish, Catholic ancestry, colonial Canadian upbringing in rural Nova Scotia, and professional nurse training in New York led her onto the world stage of imperialism and war – an unusual place for a woman at any time, and Macdonald made the most of it. She nursed in the Spanish-American War, the South African War, and in Panama, and became matron-in-chief of Canada's military nurses in the First World War. The way she approached the avenues open to her, the doors she herself opened, others' expectations of her, and the demands she placed on herself and her nursing colleagues are all reflected in the subtitle, Imperial Daughter. She was a woman with a taste for power. She was a Canadian and she had read her Kipling.

Many people have helped me in the detective work of extracting Macdonald from the privacy of her family and the forgetfulness of history. The bibliography and notes at the back of this book reveal my indebtedness to archivists and archives in Canada, Britain, and the United States. The person I want specifically to acknowledge here is Kathleen Mackenzie, the archivist at St Francis Xavier University, who was so very obliging during my visits there. In the notes, too, are the names of numerous individuals who happily provided information about Margaret Macdonald. Among them in particular is Father Gregory MacKinnon of Antigonish, former president of St Francis Xavier University. He first took me to the Macdonald home and gravesites in Bailey's Brook. As we poked around the tombstones, he told me so much that he had gleaned from his mother, Margaret's cousin. In Bailey's Brook on other occasions, I encountered the same "highland hospitality" that newspaperman Joseph Howe had commented on in the 1830s. Neighbours Wilma Burke, Dougal and the late Carmie Macdonald, John Verhagen, Catherine Anderson (of nearby

Avondale), Helen and Donald Brown, Don Butler, and Bernard MacDonald all opened their doors and their recollections without requiring the pinch of snuff that Howe had offered his hosts. Instead, I offer this book, an account of one of the "D.D. Macdonalds," in the hope that they recognize some of it and enjoy it all.

Closer to home, thanks are also in order. Véronique Décarie and Sigrid Schlichtig in Montreal, with whom I try in vain to write fiction, both read the manuscript and offered useful comments from their non-historian's perspective. McGill-Queen's University Press, whose editorial, production, and marketing staff are such a delight to work with, produced Carlotta Lemieux to edit the manuscript. What a treasure! And in Ottawa, where my daughter Britt-Mari and her family housed and fed me so well during numerous research trips, I want to assure my small granddaughter Hannah that I do not in fact live at the national archives.

SUSAN MANN
Montreal, April 2005

Abbreviations

AMSM	Army Medical Services Museum, Aldershot, England
ANS	Army Nursing Service
BEF	British Expeditionary Force
CAMC	Canadian Army Medical Corps
CEF	Canadian Expeditionary Force
CGH	Canadian General Hospital
CNA	Canadian Nurses' Association
CNATN	Canadian National Association of Trained Nurses
CSH	Canadian Stationary Hospital
DGAMS	Director General, Army Medical Services (Britain)
DGMS	Director General Medical Services (Canada)
DMS	Director of Medical Services (Canada)
LAC	Library and Archives Canada
MCM	Margaret Clotilde Macdonald
MFC	Macdonald Family Collection
MFS	Macdonald Family Scrapbook
NARA	National Archives and Records Administration, Washington, USA
NSA	Nursing Sisters' Association of Canada
NSARM	Nova Scotia Archives and Records Administration
OC	Officer Commanding

PAMC   Permanent Army Medical Corps
QAIMNS   Queen Alexandra's Imperial Military Nursing Service
RCAMC   Royal Canadian Army Medical Corps
SFXA   St Francis Xavier University Archives, Antigonish, Nova Scotia
TFNS   Territorial Force Nursing Service
TNA   The National Archives, London, England
VAD   Voluntary Aid Detachment
VMS   Vie Macdonald Scrapbook

Margaret Macdonald

ONE

A Regular Little Trump

Bailey's Brook, Pictou County, Nova Scotia
26 February 1873, 7:00 A.M.

Another girl, tiny and energetic, a sister for Marcella and Adele. What do the parents think as they greet this latest addition to their household? That God has indeed blessed them? It would be an appropriate thought for devout Scots Catholics – they are members of the Bailey's Brook mission from Arisaig and close friends of Bishop John Cameron of the diocese of Antigonish. The father, forty-six-year-old Donald St Daniel Macdonald, is doubtless pleased that his long-delayed desire for a family is taking form and that his wife is coming through the birthing well. Still, girls are a costly investment and the profits largely intangible; he will have to look to his affairs. He may also be thinking that this small bundle is just the right birthday present for the young mother, Mary Elizabeth Chisholm. Mary will be twenty-four the next day and is exhausted, glad perhaps just to be alive. She knows of many who don't pull through. But does she feel a little disappointed as she regards the new baby? She seems able to produce only girls, even though she is the one daughter in a family of boys. Well, there will be more children to follow if her mother Flora is any example. (Flora had her last baby at the same time as Mary's first.) Five of Flora's, however, died in infancy, another cause for anxiety. But this one seems healthy enough – just that small red mark on her left arm. Donald St Daniel

("D.D.") solemnly records the name of his new daughter in the family New Testament: Margaret Ste Clothilde Elizabeth Macdonald.

Eventually, ten such names were recorded in the Macdonald's Bible. A boy did appear two years after Margaret, but he was not right from the start. The family's reputation for intense privacy – still strong in 2004 – may have dated from this boy's seven-year existence, which is noted only in the Bible, in D.D.'s brief family record, and on a tombstone placed years later in the tiny cemetery, east along the road from home. Two more girls followed, chipper and lively like the three older ones, before a healthy male child appeared in 1880. For a while it seemed that Ronald St John might be the only boy, for a sixth girl was born less than two years later and then a boy who died before even acquiring a name. But two more lads appeared in 1886 and 1889. Of the eleven babies born in twenty-one years, nine survived to adulthood: six girls and three boys. As late-nineteenth-century families go, this was fairly typical, perhaps somewhat favoured. Well might Margaret inscribe on her mother's tombstone in 1927: "A loyal and courageous wife. A dear and devoted mother."[1]

In other respects, too, the family was typical. Along with most Nova Scotian Scots, both parents could trace their ancestry to the Scottish Highlands. The Macdonalds hailed from the west coast, south of Skye; their Canadian descendants remembered the region in their eventual choice – and misspelling – of Moydart as a name for their Bailey's Brook home. That house, likely more commodious than any ancestral abode, began in the 1860s as an expandable two-story white clapboard house, with a black sloping roof, dormer windows, and deep red trim. As it grew with the family, it acquired lawns and cultivated gardens, the whole domain still visible today. Back in the much wilder regions of the western Highlands of Scotland, the Macdonalds' line could be traced through Clan Ranald as far back as anyone could care to count. Their religion they attributed to the possible presence of St Columba in Moidart in the sixth century. With this tradition and faith, Macdonalds fought Bonnie Prince Charlie's losing battles in the mid-eighteenth century; one of their descendants raised a monument near Bailey's Brook in the 1930s to three local veterans of the defeat at Culloden.

This same brooding past was also part of the Chisholm heritage. The Chisholms came from Glen Affric near Strath Glass, on the eastern side of the Highlands above Loch Ness. To the Scottish Catholic mix the Chisholms added some French ancestry, dating from the "auld alliance" of Scotland and France in the late middle ages. None of this heritage provided much security for either family in the English-dominated Scotland of

Moydart House, Bailey's Brook

the late eighteenth century, and although neither family was forced out, it seems that both the Macdonalds and the Chisholms were among the earliest of the hundreds and then thousands of their compatriots who headed west across the Atlantic. D.D.'s grandfather, Angus Macdonald, arrived in Pictou in 1790, when there were only eight Catholic families there and only another twenty in the Merigomish district to the east. Angus had a land grant in his pocket, part of his discharge from the British navy, in which he had served for some fifteen years – originally under duress (having been plucked from his fishing boat and "pressed" into service) and subsequently with considerable aplomb. He chose his land in eastern Pictou County, inland about two miles from Northumberland Strait: an uncleared spot on the east side of Bailey's Brook. Meanwhile, Chisholms had found their way to Antigonish Harbour and thence to Marydale, east of the South River and south of St Andrew's. As the two families settled in and the area developed, the Chisholms were among the Catholic majority of Antigonish County while the Macdonalds, although surrounded by Catholics in Bailey's Brook, were in the minority in the largely Scots Presbyterian population of Pictou County.[2]

How did a Macdonald and a Chisholm meet, much less woo and wed, when they lived in communities forty miles apart, in different counties, at a time of uncertain communication? Although D.D. and Mary were two generations out of Scotland, they differed in age by twenty-three years. To account for their meeting, a family tale and a genealogy intertwine, each giving credence to the other. Apparently, when D.D. was much younger, he had been in love with one Flora MacIntosh who, according to a Chisholm family genealogy, was born in Lismore, just north of Bailey's Brook, closer to the sea. She and D.D., who were six months apart in age, would certainly have attended the same church, perhaps even the same school in the 1830s. The family story then offers two possibilities: that D.D. proposed to Flora and was turned down or that he left the area to work and returned to find Flora marrying another. Either way, the genealogy has Flora, not yet twenty-one, taking as husband a man twelve years her senior, William Archibald Chisholm from Marydale. As a millwright who built gristmills and then sawmills along the South River in the district around St Andrew's, Chisholm was much more established than the twenty-year-old D.D., who was just beginning to think about going into business rather than farming. His consolation for losing Flora – so the story goes – was to lay claim to her first daughter "if she'll have you," Flora reportedly cautioned.

It is hard to imagine D.D.'s fancy not being taken by any other young woman over the following years. But the tale has it that there was an interlude of twenty years before he met and was smitten by "someone special" at the wedding of a mutual acquaintance – perhaps a relative of D.D.'s – in St Andrew's. The someone special was Mary Elizabeth Chisholm, who was enjoying her first social outing since returning from the Notre Dame convent school in Arichat on southeastern Cape Breton. The nineteen-year-old Mary and forty-two-year-old D.D. were married in November 1868. Her parents could be assured of their daughter's well-being, for D.D. was by then a well-established merchant and an increasingly large landholder at Bailey's Brook.[3]

D.D. brought his bride to a rural farming community in a landscape that still has the look and feel of Scotland. Highland-style mountains mark the area to the south, with lower hills to the east and west. In between, a broad undulating valley slopes gently towards the sea to the north. From the slightest height of land, the whole can be seen, expansive yet containable – promising. If the land were flatter, it would be a "strath" (flood plain) of the brook that runs through it; if it were narrower and the brook straighter, it would be a "glen." The stream itself rises among the springs

D.D. Macdonald

Mary Chisholm Macdonald

of the mountains and picks up numerous tributaries as it tumbles and then meanders towards the sea at Lismore, where John Baillie first settled in the 1780s. The brook has lost much of its intensity over the years, but it was once a lively little river navigable by small craft for a short stretch at its mouth and attractive to spawning salmon.

On both sides, the tangle of forest and brush that greeted the first Macdonalds gradually gave way to fine farmland "bearing various crops ... exhibiting various signs of good or bad husbandry, according to the taste or information of their possessors."[4] These possessors – Macdonalds, MacGilvrays, MacKinnons, MacLeans, MacDougalds – carved out parcels of land fronting onto the brook, an essential source of fresh water. Catholics all, they built a school (1818) before they built a church (1834), and they had their children instructed in practical matters, in the Scottish values of reticence, honour, thrift, and industriousness, and in the Roman Catholic faith. They all spoke Gaelic. "Here you may go into a dozen of houses, without finding as much English as will suffice to tell you the Road; but you will find lots of genuine Highland hospitality," remarked the newspaperman and soon-to-be politician Joseph Howe on rambling through Bailey's Brook in 1830. He happily partook of a "bannock of oaten meal" and "a bowl of unskimmed milk" in return for "a pinch of excellent snuff."[5] Whether this repast was shared with four-year-old D.D. Macdonald is unknown, but Joseph Howe became his lifelong political hero.

Bailey's Brook is hard to find in the twenty-first century, and Joseph Howe's account adds to the Brigadoon flavour of the place. Only three small highway signs orient a modern rambler, two from the shore road along Northumberland Strait and one from the inland Trans-Canada Highway as it traverses mountain glens between New Glasgow and Antigonish. But how do travellers know when they have arrived at Bailey's Brook? No signpost, no village, no church, no school, no shop, no marker on the brook hints at a once-thriving community. Indeed, another few hot days of summer and the brook itself could disappear. On its eastern bank, on the north side of the gravel road that crosses the brook from west to east, sits the Macdonald home, now yellow with white trim, unidentified and untended. Farther east, about a mile and a half away, a tiny cemetery confirms the presence of Macdonalds in these parts.

In the other direction, barely a quarter of a mile beyond the house, where the gravel road meets a paved road – which is only slightly more travelled and leads north to the shore road or south to the highway – a more modern marker attests to the presence of at least one of the Macdonalds. An angular piece of granite, looking rather like a tombstone, with an engraved bronze plaque on it, solemnly declares in the language of Historic Sites and Monuments that a remarkable woman was born near here: Margaret C. Macdonald. What the plaque does not reveal is that she spent the first twenty and the last twenty-five years of her life here in Bailey's Brook. Nor does it record the views of local passers-by with long roots in the community. According to them, Margaret would not have approved of the monument. She was too much of a "lady" to care for the fuss and publicity. It seems that she wore her celebrity lightly. As for strangers, in the unlikely event that any pass this way, they would be more inclined to say "Margaret who?"[6]

To turn a highland lass in rural Nova Scotia into a lady required parental determination of uncommon magnitude. Both D.D. and Mary possessed this determination, and D.D.'s general store, established in Bailey's Brook in 1851, increasingly provided the means. The business prospered as the area's only source of imported goods from Halifax, Montreal, the United States, and Britain – everything from buttons to salt, sugar and tobacco, shoe nails, caps, writing paper, fine cloth, and all manner of farm accoutrements. The store also served as the only outlet for farm products, small and large – from butter packed in tubs made by local Mi'kmaq to four-footed animals – all heading for the lumber camps of New Brunswick or Cape Breton, or the towns of Antigonish, New Glasgow, or even Halifax. Everyone in the community passed through D.D.'s store (on the south side of the road, just up "Rory's" hill, east of the family home) for their purchases, sales, and news. Everyone depended on D.D.'s supply routes, which he was always interested in expanding, even eventually going into shipbuilding. He was the community's link with the outside world.

When times were good, everyone prospered, the Macdonalds a little more so. When times were bad, everyone depended on D.D.'s credit. He extended the credit only so far and then demanded payment, if not in cash then in kind, first in cattle and then in land. Maps of the time register D.D.'s ongoing acquisition of land, and they also reveal the location of public services such as the schoolhouse and post office, both of them on his land. In case anyone missed these manifestations of a laird-in-the-making, one only needed to look at the Macdonald farm itself, with its ever-expanding white clapboard house, enlarged as necessary to fit the growing family but also beginning to show signs of a certain grandeur. "One of the best cultivated farms in the Township with a homestead second to none," D.D. recollected with pride.[7] The census takers of the time confirmed his view, noting his status as "merchant" decade after decade, when everyone else in the locality was a "farmer." They also recorded, as of 1881, the presence of two live-in female servants; a decade later there were stable and shop hands as well, two young men classed as servants. The D.D. Macdonalds were on their way to material and social prominence.

In 1905, shortly before his death, D.D. listed all the agricultural and household "firsts" he had brought to the area: the first mower, first double-seated riding wagon, first grain separator, first steel heating range, first hot-water furnace, first concrete cellar floor, first riding plough, and – the sure sign of middle-class ambitions for his daughters – the first piano. It came from New York, and like the hot-water furnace it was still the only one in 1905. D.D. Macdonald also "provided a classical education for 8 of his children." Although he did not claim this as a first, it undoubtedly was, especially for the daughters, in a rural farming community where only primary schooling was available locally. D.D. concluded his list with the fact that he owned "the only fireproof safe in Township" – an indication of the care and probably shrewdness with which he handled his money. He kept an eye out for (and contributed to) agricultural, technological, and commercial progress, and he did not stint his family. The children were to be comfortable, cultured, and educated.[8]

In the early 1900s when D.D. was well into his seventies, he invested in a small-craft boat harbour at the mouth of Bailey's Brook. "Were I ten years younger," he wrote to his daughter Margaret, who by then was in South Africa, "I would have a lobster Factory there fully equipped with good accommodations for bathing etc., as the situation is lovely – it would be a nice and attractive resort during hot weather." He contented himself with the boat harbour, proud of the political connections that had facilitated the investment.[9] In his sixties, he had already ventured into fishing, lumbering, shipping, and shipbuilding, much of it with J.W. Carmichael, a prominent New Glasgow businessman who later became a Liberal senator. Meanwhile, D.D. kept on expanding his farm holdings, as well as the scope and contents of his general store. Goods coming to and going from the store passed in wagons along the road at least twice a day when in the late 1870s the railway from New Glasgow to Cape Breton got as far as Avondale, five miles southwest of Bailey's Brook. Over the years, D.D. had also acquired a number of public positions, most of them bearing a tinge of Liberal patronage but all of them attesting to his prominence and sense of public duty: justice of the peace, postmaster, commissioner of schools, commissioner for giving relief to insolvent debtors, and, most lucrative of the lot, vendor of intoxicating liquors.[10] By 1905, however, he was beginning to slow down. "Now into his eightieth year," he conceded, "old age with its infirmities has arrested his ambition."[11] Nonetheless, the result of it all was status and wealth for all to see. At his death in 1906 he was reported to be "one of the wealthiest men in eastern Nova Scotia ... honoured and respected throughout both counties [Pictou and Antigonish]." The only one of his daughters mentioned by name in a press obituary was Margaret C. Macdonald, who was then in Panama.[12]

Margaret's mother, as befitting a nineteenth-century rural wife, is much less visible. She was fifty-seven when her husband died, and just as she had done since their marriage in 1868, she continued to run the household well into the 1920s. Mary Elizabeth Chisholm had brought a fine and unusual education to her marital home and was known later in life as a "woman of strong character and very marked individuality."[13] She encouraged such traits in her children, and they show up prominently in Margaret. Mary also fostered in her children a lifelong acceptance and simplicity of religious belief, beginning with prayers when they were so young that they could barely talk. She engaged them, necessarily, in the multiple tasks of a farm household, a household that in her lifetime never had electricity and only gradually acquired such conveniences as running water and an indoor toilet. She assigned them responsibilities in the vegetable garden and hen house, and looking after the younger children. She sent them off berry picking with a word of caution about the bears in the mountains. And she seems not to have minded if they stopped off for a swim in one of the waterfall-fed pools in the hillside. She taught the girls to sew, the material for their dresses being ready to hand in D.D.'s store. Also, as soon as they could count, she had them helping out in the store. But she didn't expect them to stay there. Her educational ambitions for the children were as strong as her husband's. Mary was the one, however, who made sure that they were dressed and ready for school, although it was D.D.'s name, along with that of other men, that appeared on contracts engaging a teacher for the local school (who was always a man until the very late nineteenth century).

The Macdonald children and the other young scholars – aged from about four to sixteen, judging from a contemporary photograph – followed a curriculum specified by the parents: reading, spelling, writing, arithmetic, English grammar, geography, and mathematics. Occasionally the parish priest would drop in unexpectedly and test the children, not on their religion but on their scholastic progress. He then rewarded them with a half-day holiday, and they would happily rush outdoors, probably only to be cornered and assigned yet another task by Mary, who could see the school from the Macdonald home.[14] Her children seem to have been quick and keen scholars, so much so that the parents – especially Mary,

Six Macdonald children among the "scholars," Bailey's Brook, c 1890

perhaps, given her own convent education – began to think of sending them elsewhere as soon as they outgrew the local schoolhouse. But in the meantime she filled their home with kindness, gaiety, music, dancing, books, and food a-plenty. There was nothing dour about this Scottish Canadian household (photographs of the time not withstanding). Mary's kindness and gaiety were self-generated, the music and dancing a collective activity, the books imported and devoured en famille around the dining-room table, the food locally and domestically produced under Mary's watchful eye and busy hand.

Her generosity extended beyond her own large family. She offered "unbounded hospitality" to all visitors, permanent hospitality to the orphaned daughter of a cousin, and a welcome each summer to the motherless children of her brother Joseph Chisholm.[15] Besides relatives and neighbours from the community, the visitors included politicians, priests, and business people. They all came calling – and, given the distances, they often stayed. Meanwhile, in this intellectually stimulating household, the conversation bubbled around world events, national and provincial politics, and local happenings. The politics were Liberal. One of Mary's early adjustments to marriage had been to relinquish the Conservative allegiance of the Chisholms.

In 1906 when D.D. died, all the Macdonald children except for fifteen-year-old Donald Duncan ("the kid") were adults, and six of the nine were away from home. The eldest, thirty-six-year-old Marcella, ("Cell") had not wandered very far. Married to James Macdonald from Cape Breton, who had now taken over D.D.'s general store after helping him with it for more than fifteen years, Cell was in fact Mary's closest neighbour. They could glimpse each other's houses and send the grandchildren running across the fields from Cell's Egnaig Cottage (named for the Moidart locality in Scotland that had spawned the Macdonalds) to Mary's Maple Villa, a name which, like the family, moved up in the world to become Moydart sometime after 1911. The second daughter, thirty-four-year-old Adele ("Dell") was farther away, both geographically and spiritually. She had been a teaching nun since 1896 with the prestigious (and dowry-requiring) Congrégation de Notre Dame in Montreal, the same community of nuns that had taught Mary at Arichat in the 1860s. The fourth daughter, twenty-nine-year-old Florence ("Floss"), the one girl with a university education (BA, St Francis Xavier, 1897), was also in Montreal preparing for the same religious vocation.

The third daughter, thirty-three-year-old Margaret ("Maggie"), followed a path of her own, and it took her far. Like the nuns she was single, but unlike them she was out in the world. As a nurse in Panama in 1906, she was the farthest away of all Mary's children, and her letters home were all the more welcome. Mary and her fifth daughter, twenty-seven-year-old Mary Ann ("Vie") who never left home, watched for Margaret's letters avidly and extracted material for the growing pile of family scrapbooks. The first of Mary's sons, twenty-five-year-old Ronald ("Ronnie"), the sixth child, was off in British Columbia, practising medicine in Rossland after taking his degree at McGill University. His younger sister Catherine ("Kate"), twenty-four, was temporarily still at home. Her future husband, Dr D.J. McMaster, not yet on the scene, was in Cape Breton, where Ronald later encountered him in medical practice in Inverness and subsequently introduced him to Kate. Nineteen-year-old William ("Bill"), the second son and eighth child, was in Halifax studying law at Dalhousie. With "the kid" Donald, still in school at Bailey's Brook, Mary could account for them all with considerable pride. Most of them were away exercising their versions of parental ambition beyond the Brook, but they always returned, for weekends or longer vacations, and Mary's white frame house always welcomed them.

The only peculiarity among her children, discernible in 1906 and confirmed later, was a tendency not to marry. Of the nine children, only four married: two of the six girls and two of the three boys, both of the boys when well into middle age. The sons may have been following a paternal example in that D.D. had married late and four of his five siblings did not marry at all. Or they and their sisters may have been placed beyond the local marriage market with that piano, their classical education, books, and connections. Consequently, they were also outside the family, church, and community functions that provided the nineteenth-century props for encounters and courtships. Among none of the Macdonald children does there appear to have been anything like the romantic tale that brought their parents together.[16]

And what of Maggie? Did she as a child stand out in that family? In the nineteenth-century record, children are even more difficult to locate than their elusive mothers, and it is hard to avoid reading back from the adult to the child. Her later military file reveals a small woman, 5 ft. 3 in. and 115 lb., blue eyed ("the bluest eyes you've ever seen")[17] and brown haired. An old photograph confirms the supposition of a petite child with fair hair on its way to being brown. The birthmark on her left arm was sufficiently large in adulthood to have a military doctor note it in 1914, so it must have been increasingly visible in childhood, though the clothing of the time would have rendered it inconspicuous.[18] Most likely, her adult traits of energy, quick-wittedness, and practicality were discernible in the small Macdonald child; they are rarely the products of education. She later listed a sense of humour and a good digestion among the prerequisites for a woman entering public life.[19] They too imply a healthy, outgoing child. But she was a girl in a family staking its place in the rural middle class, and the options for her future were very limited. She could teach, she could become a nun, she could marry, or – family circumstances permitting – she could stay at home. Maggie did none of these. She had neither the temperament nor the calling of her sisters Adele and Florence. Indeed, she considered a "religious point of view" too narrow for observing, much less participating in, the world,[20] though her religious faith never wavered. Nor did her independence, which is probably what kept her from marriage.

Were there any childhood hints of nursing as a future occupation? Might she have been particularly sensitive to the unfortunate lad born next to her in line who died at age seven when she was not yet ten? If so, she disclosed none of it to a romantic wartime reporter who was searching for the born nurse. What she may have said, and certainly what the reporter chose to record, was that she had "preferred to play with sick dolls, was interested in the ailments of all the dependants about the place, and was not bowled over by the sight of a gory nose."[21] As a youngster

Maggie, age eight

she would certainly have observed local women tending the sick in the neighbourhood. But she is not likely to have known about nursing as a profession until she was at least in secondary school. Medicine was of course a male preserve, so the fact that one of her maternal uncles was a doctor and her younger brother Ronald was to become one could not serve as models for her.

For a bright Catholic girl, daughter of ambitious parents who valued education, secondary schooling necessarily meant a convent. And given the distances, going to a convent school meant being a boarder. By the time Maggie was ready for such schooling, likely in the mid-1880s, Stella Maris Convent had opened in Pictou, thirty miles west of Bailey's Brook and thus much closer than its sister school at Arichat, where Maggie's mother had been a pupil. An advertisement for the latter school in 1884 reveals the program of study that Maggie probably followed at Stella Maris: "Under the direction of the Sisters of Congregation of Notre Dame, the Course of Instruction comprises French and English languages, Writing, Arithmetic, Bookkeeping, Algebra, Geometry, Geography and the Use of Globes, Ancient History, Rhetoric, Botany, Philosophy, Chemistry, Music, Vocal and Instrumental, Drawing and Painting, every kind of Useful and Ornamental Needlework, and in general all the branches of a complete female education."[22]

Margaret's two older sisters had gone to Stella Maris, Marcella at age eleven for seven years, and Adele at thirteen for two years.[23] So Maggie, who was eleven in 1884, would have been there for some of the same time as her siblings. They would have helped her with the routine, easing the initial strangeness for a young girl away from home for the first time. The school year was long – from the first of September to mid-July, with breaks at Christmas and perhaps at Easter – so Maggie learned early to be away from her family for long periods. She also became used to living in an all-female setting, strictly regulated by a hierarchy of women. From her sisters she probably heard who were the favourite nuns and which the least interesting subjects. She later showed an aptitude for French and geography; perhaps the "use of globes" at Stella Maris caused her to dream of future travel. In any case, she fared sufficiently well academically that the family began to look farther afield for future studies. She had no inclination to interrupt her studies, as Adele had done at fifteen, to attend Normal School in Truro and become a primary school teacher (and subsequently a nun). Nor did she seem to have the social flare of Marcella, who spent some time between her schooling and marriage being "one of the leading belles of the County."[24] She did, however, follow Marcella by doing her final schooling with the Sisters of Charity at Mount St Vincent Academy in Halifax.

The parents' choice of Halifax and the Mount for their first and third daughters' further education is intriguing. Halifax was a long way from Bailey's Brook: five miles by road to the train at Avondale, twenty miles by train to New Glasgow, another forty miles to Truro, and a further sixty into Halifax, the total trip a day's journey in the late nineteenth century. Nova Scotian young people went greater distances than that, well into the "Boston States" for factory or domestic employment, but such occupations were by now beneath the Macdonalds. Their daughters' education was not only a value in itself but also a contribution to the family's social standing. In Halifax, two convent schools vied for the well-bred daughters of established and aspiring families. Sacred Heart Convent, in the south end of Halifax, was older and, in the eyes of many, more prestigious; daughters of the Catholic elite were schooled there. Mount St Vincent Academy, on the northern outskirts of the city in Rockingham on Bedford Basin since 1873, was newer and, in the eyes of some, a bit of an upstart. The Sisters of Charity had come to Halifax from New York in 1849 to educate the poor, but with the expansion of their teaching and the growth of their community they had branched out into fee-paying education as a means of supporting their new mother house and novitiate. One result was competition with Sacred Heart for the daughters of the well-to-do, and another entailed clashes with the bishop of Halifax in the late 1870s. The clashes caused such a stir that when the sisters appealed to Rome, the Pope asked his favourite eastern-Canadian conciliator, Bishop John Cameron of the neighbouring diocese of Antigonish, to arbitrate the dispute. Part of the solution was to sever the link between the Sisters of Charity and the Halifax diocese (a link which the sisters disputed) and to attach them directly to the papacy with Bishop Cameron exercising the Pope's jurisdiction.[25]

Cameron's oversight of the Sisters of Charity and the Mount lasted less than three years, but he may well have given the nod to the Mount when his good friends the Macdonalds were contemplating further schooling for their daughters in the late 1880s. For some reason the family overlooked Mount St Bernard – established in Antigonish in 1883 by the Congrégation de Notre Dame – as an option for Margaret, although Adele went there and so later did Florence. While Margaret was at Mount St Vincent Academy, the Macdonalds came to have an even closer connection with the school. In 1891 Margaret's maternal uncle Joseph Chisholm married Frances (Fanny) Affleck, and Fanny's older sister Annie was married to John Thompson, attorney general of Nova Scotia in the late 1870s; Thompson was adviser to the Sisters of Charity during their dispute with the bishop of Halifax and advisee of bishop Cameron in matters ecclesiastical. Yet another sister of Fanny's, Johanna Affleck, was a nun with the Sisters of Charity.[26] Margaret's link to the Mount thus combined all manner of Nova Scotian family, class, political, and religious interests.

Like her schooling at Stella Maris, Margaret's time at the Mount has left very little trace. As she set off for Halifax, probably in late August 1890, she had every intention of keeping track of her activities, for she inaugurated a scrapbook with the carefully printed words: "Maggie C. Macdonald Mt St Vincent Academy Bedford Basin Halifax N.S." But she then devoted most of its pages to her later and more unusual experiences in New York City.[27] The Mount itself lost its records in spectacular fires over the years, so Margaret's scholastic career is more than shadowy. In all

Mount St Vincent Academy

likelihood, she followed a program similar to that at Stella Maris, with more advanced studies in the liberal arts. For such studies she had considerable flare, winning a silver medal for overall excellence and prizes in mythology, geography, French and/or Christian doctrine when she left the Mount in 1892.[28] She made lasting friends while there, especially Florence Kelly, who went on to New York with her and then into the military during the First World War. She clearly stood out among her peers. Her new Aunt Fanny reported glowingly to Maggie's mother on the eighteen-year-old schoolgirl: "Maggie came in last Saturday – I was so glad to see her. I am not surprised that the sisters at the Mount think so much of her – she is a regular little trump and I have taken a great fancy to her."[29]

In their enthusiasm, the sisters may well have had a religious or secular vocation in mind for Maggie. They would certainly have reinforced her family and convent lessons in service and dedication. At the Mount, she would have learned the history of the Sisters of Charity, both local and farther afield. She would have been aware of their nursing of sick immigrants on McNab's Island at the entrance to Halifax harbour in 1866 and their more recent involvement with the Halifax Infirmary.[30] She probably learned something about the religious sisters – and other women – nursing in the Crimea in the 1850s and in the American Civil War in the 1860s. She certainly knew of Florence Nightingale: her scrapbook contains a newspaper drawing of Nightingale's departure for the Crimea in 1854. She may also have known of the much more recent though considerably less numerous presence of nurses on the Canadian prairies during the Northwest Rebellion of 1885. Whether any of this was at the time directing her towards nursing is unknown, but it must have been opening her eyes to horizons broader than matrimony. Sometime in the year after leaving the Mount – during which she spent some but not all of her time at Bailey's Brook[31] – she made her decision to train as a nurse in New York.

Persuading her parents to agree could well have taken a full year, for both nursing and New York would have caused them consternation. One family story has Maggie defying her father and going off against his wishes, even being disowned by him. A variant on this story was D.D.'s refusal to allow her to train as a nurse in Canada and hence her opting for an American school. Another version has Maggie in fact fulfilling, via nursing, a thwarted paternal ambition to be a doctor.[32] The latter is the more likely, for Margaret's letters to her father from nursing school in New York reveal no tension; quite the contrary, they are loving and glowing descriptions of every detail of her work, in response to his keen desire to know everything. Just as telling is D.D.'s will, written in 1903, ten years after she went to nursing school. In it he bequeathed to her the largest single sum of money. She was special to him.

Margaret's letters to her mother have a different flavour, full of reassurances about her health and well-being. Mary obviously worried about Margaret's proximity to sick people in a large city hospital. They must all have debated the pros and cons for months before she sallied forth. Among the pros were inclination, independence, work, and income, with service and duty added for ballast. In a Catholic family, secular nursing was perhaps the closest calling to becoming a nun. But the major impediment would have been lingering questions about the propriety of middle-class girls working as nurse-servants in urban hospitals. At the time, these institutions cared mostly for the desperately poor and still relied largely on a labour force of untrained working-class women. The good folk of Bailey's Brook had probably never seen a hospital, much less been in one, and they may have feared that Margaret was going down in the world even as she went out into it. For her part, Margaret knew of hospitals in Halifax, but she would not have been a patient there, much less a worker.

While she was in Halifax, however, an article in a popular magazine may have attracted her attention. Author Sophie Hensley, a young writer from Nova Scotia living in New York City, interviewed Canadian nurses there and wrote about their training and practice for the *Dominion Illustrated Monthly*. She listed the seven hospitals with training schools for nurses, one of which was New York City Hospital "(formerly Charity)," a name bound to resonate with Margaret. The training regimen, Hensley reported, was "all much the same": twelve-hour days of ward duty, followed by lectures from doctors on physiology, anatomy, materia medica, and obstetrics, quizzes by the lady superintendent, and examinations twice a year. In effect, the student nurses gave their labour to the hospital – Hensley called it "service" – in return for two years' training, along with board and lodging. They supplied their own uniforms but did receive eight dollars a month for expenses. Once trained, they could earn as much as twenty to twenty-five dollars a week in private-duty (home) nursing while sharing living arrangements with a few other nurses in "furnished rooms somewhere in a nice, though not expensive, locality." Hensley was enchanted with a particular Canadian nurse and described her in a fashion that would appeal to middle-class readers: "One of those delightfully independent women who are self-sufficient and self-supporting, without losing anything of the charm of an essentially womanly woman."[33] If Margaret knew of this article, one could imagine her showing it to her parents with the firm remark, "There I am. That's what I want to do."

However, she was barely nineteen when the article appeared. The New York nursing schools had an age requirement of twenty-one, and at least one of them insisted on twenty-five. Moreover, Canadians were flocking to these schools, so much so that one school had to impose a quota lest the "daily applications from all parts of Canada" swamp Americans.[34] Obviously, many young women were searching for a legitimate way of leaving home, and there were not enough Canadian training schools to meet the demand. Nearest to Bailey's Brook was the Victoria General Hospital in Halifax, which had just begun its nursing school in 1890. Farther away was the Montreal General whose training school only acquired real substance that same year. Even farther away was Toronto General Hospital's school of nursing. But all these institutions were Protestant, and this may have had a bearing on Margaret's choice – though, in fact, not until 1892, in Toronto, could she have found a Catholic nursing school that did not require her becoming a nun.[35] Not that the New York schools were Catholic; they were merely larger, more established, and drew from a greater number of applicants.

The New York City Hospital (formerly called the Charity Hospital) where Margaret eventually went had no links to the Sisters of Charity, despite its name. It was a thousand-bed public hospital under the jurisdiction of New York's Commissioner of Public Charities and Corrections, and it provided free care for the city's poor. Along with a number of other hospitals and a prison, it was on Blackwell's (now called Roosevelt) Island in the East River, a short ferry ride from midtown Manhattan. Complete with a nurses' "home," an important ingredient of a good training school,[36] the setting may have been considered appropriately safe for proper young women. Of more immediate significance to Margaret Macdonald was the fact that its training school was prepared to let her in under age. "If you can come at once," the acting superintendent wrote to her in Bailey's Brook in late September 1893, "there is a vacancy for you, if not there will be none for three months."[37] In a flurry of excitement, Margaret, aged twenty years and seven months, packed her bags and was in New York "on duty in Ward 1" six days later.[38]

She was just the kind of student that ambitious American nursing schools were looking for. Since the 1870s they had been building their own prestige and that of their hospitals with the creation of a different kind of ward worker. On the way out were the uneducated and untrained working-class women for whom hospital work was the institutional equivalent of charring, laundry work, or domestic service. On the way in were refined young women of the rural and small-town middle class, well-educated, well-disciplined daughters of professionals, farmers, tradesmen, and businessmen.[39] In short, they were the Margaret Macdonalds of the late nineteenth century. In England, it took Florence Nightingale most of her post-Crimea lifetime to convince her contemporaries that this was the nurse of the future – even with her own specially designed training school at St Thomas' Hospital, London, since 1860. In the United States, numbers alone suggest that the Americans absorbed her ideas faster: 15 nursing schools in 1880, most of them initially modelled on St Thomas's, with 157 graduates; twenty years later, 432 nursing schools with 3,456 graduates.[40] All of them were producing the "new nurse," a woman who was capable of keeping accurate reports on patients and was punctilious in her obedience, cleanliness, and order. Only with such nurses could doctors introduce "a system and science in the treatment of the sick."[41] Margaret Macdonald was part of this trend. The year her school had opened, in the summer of 1875, with "twenty-two girls from 'good families,'" the chief of the medical staff had claimed that their presence "eliminated fighting and swearing and ... brought improvements in the food service, cleaner wards, and a more cheerful atmosphere to the entire hospital."[42] By the time Margaret, "a young lady of most excellent character,"[43] came along in 1893, she could count on working in a cheery, efficient, clean, and well-run hospital while living in a nurses' home with some fifty to sixty other young women much like her.[44]

By the 1890s, her nursing supervisors were increasingly interested in the professional status of nurses. They were proud of running their institutions on military yet familial lines, demanding and enforcing contemporary Nightingale values of hierarchy, duty, and discipline. "The organization of a training school is and must be military," Lavinia Dock, assistant superintendent of nurses at Johns Hopkins Hospital, told an international audience during the Chicago world's fair in 1893. "It is not and cannot be democratic. Absolute and unquestioning obedience must be the foundation of the nurse's work, and to this end complete subordination of the individual to the work as a whole is as necessary for her as for the soldier."[45]

Women trained to such standards would be able to carve a professional notch for themselves in the expanding world of hospital and public health care. To assist them, nursing leaders such as Louise Darche, Macdonald's superintendent at New York City Hospital, began planning longer programs of study and a standardized curriculum, all intended to "shift the balance from service to education."[46] They also persuaded their peers to form professional organizations in order to lobby for state registration of nurses so that the public could distinguish between a trained and an untrained nurse, the qualified and the unqualified, the professional and the amateur. If they still talked of nursing as women's work – indeed, they used this language precisely to make a professional space for women – they no longer thought of it as a woman's natural calling. Nursing now required extensive knowledge, disciplined training, and professional organization. Although the models for these ideas all came from the contemporary male world, they nonetheless provided certain women with the wherewithal to stake a huge claim in the world of work.

Into this setting Margaret Macdonald stepped with great glee. Her weekly letters to her family from nursing school – fifteen of which have survived from her first year – bubble with enthusiasm about the work, the learning, the head nurses, the doctors, her student colleagues, her patients, and even herself. "I am more in love with the place every day and am so glad I came here," she wrote to her "dearest Papa." "If I were home for a day I don't believe I could talk of anything but the Hospital for I'm so crazy about it all."[47] The nursing school's combination of doing and learning appealed to her. Through the various stages of her training, which involved two years' service in all the different wards of the hospital, she mastered nursing methods mostly by practising them. She also learned things that surprised her:

I never knew until lately that Phthisis (consumption) was catching, did you? We keep everything so well carbolized that there is scarcely any danger. The patients have spit-cups by their beds and in those we always keep a solution of carbolic. If they spit on the floor or blankets (and they do on the sly) then it dries and the germs fly around and that's how a person can catch it. I try to change the sheets of my phthisis patients every day also their clothes and keep the beds, stands, etc well carbolized. So I am sure not to get it. Anyhow, I think if a person is in a good healthy condition there is no danger whatever. What I am particularly [word missing] of is this, If I get a pin scratch or cut of any kind on my hands there is so much danger of getting a bad disease if anything gets in the cut. However, we have all kinds of preventives and disinfectants so I'll be careful.[48]

Among the bad diseases still prevalent was smallpox. The student nurses were all vaccinated against it shortly after their arrival at nursing school, and Macdonald's "took" so fiercely that she told her parents only after the worst of the reaction had passed.[49] By then she was sure of her immunity, but she reassured the family nonetheless: "You have doubtless seen by the papers that our Island is quarantined just now. One of the male Nurses is down with Small Pox. You need not be the least bit alarmed for we are all right. They never come near us or anything like that."[50] Three months later she explained in more detail when the disease reappeared: "Several cases of Small Pox have broken out in the Hospital principally on the male side though. In Ward 2 females there is a suspected case so the Nurse there is isolated for three weeks – not allowed to come near us or even leave the Ward. There is a boat calls here and takes away all contagious diseases to North Brothers Island … No one is allowed to go off or come on the Island for the next three weeks. All the Doctors and Nurses are quarantined. It is rather annoying not being able to get over to the City for so long."[51]

Less alarming to her parents was her introduction to surgery, with the thorough disinfection required in operating rooms. "Sometimes, I think it [the scrubbing, boiling, sterilizing] all nonsense but then there is always so much danger of germs getting into the wound." Her lack of knowledge about surgery made her feel awkward, even though her first task was merely to mop a surgeon's brow.[52] Gradually she took part in more intricate operations. None of them upset her; she was not the least bit squeamish and passed on the details to her father: "We had a Laparotomy in our Ward last week and I saw it. After making the incision the Dr. put his hand in and took out part of the intestines. He cut away a Hernia and sewed up the intestines in two or three places. It is great fun watching those things."[53]

Her enthusiasm appears to have made Macdonald into a prize pupil. Her superiors soon spotted her work as good, efficient, and quick. Accordingly, they gave her more of it, moving her to the postoperative side of a ward from the less demanding admissions side. "You must not think I find it hard," she reassured her father, "for even though the work was twice or three times as hard I wouldn't leave. It's just lovely work."[54] To her mother she confided, "It may give you a little pleasure to know that all the Head Nurses I have worked under speak very highly of me. They say I do my work perfectly and I think, myself, they trust me a good deal more than they do some juniors. It is very satisfactory to me to know that my efforts to do the best I can are appreciated. Of course, all this I am just saying to *you*."[55] By April of her first year, Margaret had progressed from successful probationer to junior and then senior nurse. She had stints of night duty, and unlike some of her colleagues she enjoyed that too. She also worked occasionally in New York hospitals that did not have nursing schools and contracted with those that did for the services of student nurses. On the academic side, she absorbed increasingly sophisticated lectures in anatomy, physiology, materia medica, diseases, surgery, obstetrics, hygiene, and sanitation.[56]

When off duty Margaret had just as much fun. She and Flo Kelly, the friend from Mount St Vincent, decorated their shared room, making it the "prettiest in the house."[57] In the parlour of the nurses' home they entertained visitors, including some men friends. They were a jolly pair, always on the lookout for humour and romance. They amused themselves by filling in hospital forms with their own versions of patients' conditions: "Margaret Crazy Macdonald," a seventeen-year-old bartender in a "gossip factory" had "collided with a schooner" and was now being brought by ambulance from Harlem Prison with a diagnosis of "Alcoholic Insanity"; twelve-year-old "Marguerite Macdonald" from Ward 5 operating room was being transferred to the "Insane Asylum" with a diagnosis of "Run down from over work on night duty" and instructions to treat her with milk punches.

In the scrapbook where Maggie stored these missives, she also kept track of the romance in her life. There were bits of pink ribbon, a tiny floral bouquet, some valentines – one with a charming description of her:

"Fair she was, oh, witching fair / Eyes a-brim with merry folly / Heigh ho! But Margy's cheeks / Were redder than the holly"; and one entire page is filled with all the possible variations of the name of a young doctor and then her own, Miss Meg Macdonald, spelled out three times.[58] None of this did she recount to her family. Instead, she told them about the ferry trips that she and Flo made to New York, where they visited family friends, gazed at elegant homes, and watched people on the grand avenues. They had their pictures taken, went to the theatre and museums, tried out various Catholic churches in the city, and they shopped. (Having helped out as a child in her family's rural store Margaret watched her money carefully and the shopkeepers critically.) She also followed politics, though was unable to decide, as a Liberal in Canada, whether she was a Republican or Democrat. The fact that women could not vote does not seem to have aroused her curiosity.

The combination of good fun and hard work produced a knowledgeable, sprightly, and dedicated young woman. Years later, as matron-in-chief with the Canadian military, she insisted on the same recipe for her nurses. In the 1890s she was already proud of the speed with which she assimilated methods, practice, and new situations. The more interesting cases challenged her, and she was not intimidated by doctors or patients; she could be quite firm with the latter and even a bit sassy with the former. She also cast a critical eye on things around her, from druggists' habit of keeping patients' prescriptions to doctors writing in unintelligible Latin. She ignored the snide remarks that some of her classmates made about her religion, yet she made equally biting remarks about what she saw as an overemphasis on money by the Catholic churches in New York: "You can't go into a church but the priests are talking of collections."[59]

She had a high sense of morality and was a bit prudish, but she applied neither to the cases she was treating. An abortion was the same to her as a hernia or an amputation. Nothing seems to have rattled her, though the telling of it caused some anxiety at first. "I hope to goodness you burn my letters," she instructed her father three weeks after her arrival in New York, "for they are not fit to be seen. I am ashamed of the things I write but still, I know you would like to hear of them."[60] Clearly, she was struggling with the discretion and innocence expected of a proper young Victorian woman, particularly about bodily functions. But she could justify speaking of syphilis, hemorrhages, passing a catheter, or drawing fluid from a stomach by her father's keen desire to know. Not surprisingly, given her background and earlier schooling, she took to the hierarchical nature of the hospital, and she increasingly liked to be in charge.

On graduation in the late spring of 1895, this eagerness for leadership was not immediately rewarded. Had it been, Macdonald would have stayed on at New York City Hospital or gone to another as one of a handful of supervising or head nurses on their way to becoming a superintendent of a nursing school.[61] A number of Canadians had forged just such a path to considerable prominence in American nursing, among them Louise Darche of New York City Hospital and Isabel Hampton of Johns Hopkins. Instead, Macdonald took the more usual route of private-duty nursing in New York City. At the time, far more people had their nonsurgical ailments tended to at home than ever went to hospital, and the wealthier hired private nurses. To obtain such work, nurses had to have good connections with city doctors in order to be recommended to patients. Macdonald's scrapbook has seven pages of doctors' calling cards. She also had her name listed with major medical supply stores, and above all, with her own hospital's registry of graduate nurses. There, for a ten-dollar annual fee, she kept the registry agent informed of her availability for work, and she agreed not to accept prices lower than $21 a week for ordinary nursing cases, $25 a week for obstetrical or contagious cases, and $4 a day to nurse adult males.[62] Such registries were among the original purpose of alumnae associations, which were just beginning to be formed in the 1890s. Macdonald was sufficiently proud of her nursing school to take on an executive role with its alumnae association in 1898.[63] While in training, she had boasted to her parents about the prominent showing that the New York City nurses' school had made at the world's fair in Chicago.[64] Now she counted on that prominence and her own skill to provide her with steady work.

She certainly found work, for she was in New York until the early autumn of 1904, except for two significant absences when she was in South Africa. Steady work, however, was another matter. Macdonald was one of an increasing number of trained nurses in New York, and the number soon became too large for the city's population of just over three million. Only people with a reasonable income could afford a private nurse, and even they might choose an untrained and therefore cheaper attendant for their sick family members. Moreover, the need for a nurse varied with the seasons; illness blossomed in winter and tapered off in summer, except when a particular disease, such as cerebrospinal meningitis in 1893, chose those months to strike hard.[65] Some nurses deliberately limited their employment by specifying ailments or conditions such as contagious diseases or obstetrical cases that they would not treat.[66] But even if they could afford to be choosy, all private-duty nurses had to put up with the inherent disadvantages of the work: the isolation, the whims of employers, and the status (or lack thereof) in a family where a temporary nurse was usually resident. And in between cases, there was the constant hunt for new work, perhaps even new lodgings, with the attendant financial insecurity.

Later in life, Macdonald acknowledged but dismissed the difficulties. "No one appreciates more than I do the disadvantages of private nursing," she told a graduating nursing class in 1920. But she went on to argue its opportunities, and one can only assume that she had appreciated them in the 1890s: "It is an education in itself. It greatly enlarges and broadens one's vision and serves to develop a deeper and more sympathetic understanding of the problems of life," to say nothing of the possibilities for travel or even of romance.[67] How much of either came Macdonald's way during her years in New York is unknown, and she may well have been romanticizing her earlier life. That life included several changes of address in New York – at least three in 1896 alone – perhaps suggesting their proximity to different jobs (or the different jobs themselves), more compatible flatmates, changing finances, or her own restlessness.[68] Until she found her niche in the military, she was always ready to undertake something new.

While in New York she also engaged in district nursing. This early aspect of public health provided free nursing assistance to the poor in their homes. To the nurses, it offered more stability and a bit more independence but less choice than private-duty nursing. In such work Macdonald was an employee of a private philanthropic agency and she went wherever the need arose. This could take her into awkward and even dangerous situations, but it had the advantage that she was treating beholden patients who might be more tractable than their middle- or upper-class counterparts. Certainly, the work allowed the nurse more "independent judgment and autonomy"; with fewer doctors involved in district nursing, she "had to use the force of her personality to obtain patient compliance, her own ability to improvise procedures, and her own judgment as to what kind of care should be provided."[69] Work like this would be very appealing to Macdonald. She seems not, however, to have been taken by the contemporary reform impulse of such people as Lillian Wald, who was just two years into her work with the Nurses' Settlement House on Henry Street in the Lower East Side when Macdonald came into the nursing workforce.[70] Macdonald may have wanted to change her own world – this desire had taken her out of Bailey's Brook in the first place – but she showed no eagerness to change the world at large. Rather, she appears as

Meg, age twenty-three

a down-to-earth woman, intent on living an independent life. Nursing gave her the means to do just that. She was twenty-two years old when she began to earn her own living. How grand that was, and in "such an attractive place" as New York City.[71]

Within three years, however, she was looking for something more. The minute the Spanish-American War broke out in April 1898, Macdonald – and fifteen hundred other nurses – deluged the American government with earnest entreaties to be allowed to nurse soldiers. The "regular little trump" from Bailey's Brook wanted to go to war.

TWO

A Yen for Wars

During the Second World War, when it was acceptable to be enthusiastic about warfare, Margaret Macdonald confided her "yen for wars" to a group of nursing graduates. Whether she was recruiting for the army or merely reminiscing, she was clearly longing to be back in the thick of things. She claimed to have "followed" as many wars as she could over her lifetime and only regretted having been considered too young for the Boxer Rebellion in China, and now too old for the present conflict.[1] Without the age restrictions she would happily have added those two to the three she did manage to follow: the Spanish American War, the South African War, and what she later termed "the first great war."[2] She thus became a military nurse in an age of imperialism; even her civilian employment in Panama had military overtones. To all of her activities she brought the enthusiasm of an imperial daughter as she forged a place for women in man-made conflicts.

For a woman with a yen for wars, she chose a perfect time to live. Between her birth in 1873 and her death in 1948, some forty serious armed conflicts scarred different corners of the globe, two of them of unprecedented extent and viciousness. All of them arose from disputes over territory, resources, and power but those involving Europeans and their allies had the additional emotional magnet of imperialism. In its

British guise, the imperialism of the late nineteenth century had a quasi-religious flavour, lending urgency to the civilizing mission of English-speaking peoples. Theirs was the "white man's burden" to carry superior political and social mores to the lesser peoples of the world. All the latter had to do was relinquish territory and resources (and the Royal Navy was never far away should there be any hesitation) and in return they would be uplifted by British political, educational, religious, and familial practices. From the British point of view it was all eminently reasonable. And thanks to science and literature, music, and the daily press, it was increasingly popular – so popular indeed that it could affect colonials of British stock all around the world. It could stir the English-speaking United States of America to concoct a version of its own, and it could turn the heads of Highland Jacobites in Pictou County, Nova Scotia.

Although much of imperialism can be analysed as male fantasy,[3] there was ample scope for female participation. Whether as part of the ideology or in reality, white British women acquired considerable public importance through imperialism. Ideologically, they represented civilization: they were the model for colonized peoples to emulate; they were the standard by which subject races were deemed elevated, modern, advanced. As "mothers of the race," their biological function, still considered the only real one for women, took on political significance. Unless they produced and nourished healthy children (preferably male), no imperial venture, whether naval, commercial, or political, could flourish. Moreover, without their willingness to travel to foreign parts to accompany their husbands, the men might stray into debauchery. Single women also had a role to play. As "intrepid adventurers," women such as Mary Kingsley were as much an oddity in Africa as they were in England, but they demonstrated all the values held dear by imperialists: strength, courage, discipline, propriety, command, and curiosity. Their far more numerous missionary sisters added the religious dimension: sacrifice, succour, and proselytism. When the focus of imperialism became increasingly military at the turn of the twentieth century, high-spirited and dutiful young women took another route to public service – that of the army nurse.

Before she even thought of being an army nurse, Margaret Macdonald had all the characteristics of an imperial daughter. In her outpost of empire in Bailey's Brook, she acquired military values from her father, who had been an officer in the pre-Confederation militia in Pictou County. From him too came the imperial commercial tenet of free trade, which had caused D.D. Macdonald to oppose Confederation in the 1860s and to support the Liberal Party thereafter. D.D.'s traditional ties were firmly

British, though this had its contradictory elements for a family that was both Scottish and Canadian. Yet the odd mixture of defiance and deference created an imperial bond of uncommon durability, one that Margaret herself demonstrated as a daughter to her family and to the "motherland." Both ties required her to be dependent and obedient, subordinate and disciplined, domesticated to the service roles of helpfulness and cooperation, and faithful to a religion of hierarchy and authority. Yet these same ties gave her room to demonstrate all the opposite characteristics. In both the domestic and the imperial setting she had the scope to exercise her own power and authority, to determine her own way of living, to travel, compete, acquire status – and go to war. It is small wonder that she blossomed into a materfamilias when she was in charge of Canada's military nurses in the First World War. Even less surprising is that she would turn on doubting relatives during the dark days of the Second World War and snap, "One thing you can be sure of – there's *sure* to be an England."[4] Above all, an imperial daughter is steadfast.

Military nursing was not yet a career option for her in the 1890s. The British army, both at home and abroad, still relied heavily on untrained male orderlies – and even on the wives of some of the men – to care for sick or wounded soldiers. A few professionally trained nurses began to be hired for military hospitals in Britain as early as the 1860s, and the Army Nursing Service was officially formed in 1884 as a civilian, not military, body; but the numbers remained tiny until after the South African War. As part of the British presence in India, the Indian Army Nursing Service was formed in 1886, and by 1893 it had the largest number of professional military nurses anywhere, all of fifty-two.[5] Only with the shock of disease as the major killer of British troops during the South African War did military authorities belatedly recognize the need for more and better nursing – and therefore trained women. As for the United States, there were no military nurses at all when Macdonald was at nursing school. The three thousand contract nurses with the northern army during the Civil War (few of them professionally trained) had all disappeared with the end of hostilities. And they did not reappear for the Spanish-American War at the end of the century until it became clear that disease rather than warfare was killing the soldiers.[6] Meanwhile in Canada, where a tiny permanent military force of just under nine hundred and a larger, part-time militia of thirty-five thousand were still under the overall command of a British officer (and where British troops themselves were still present in Halifax and Esquimalt) no military nurses existed.

Macdonald's first taste of military nursing came in the summer of 1898.

By then she had been doing private-duty and district nursing in New York City for three years, with the occasional summer visit to Nova Scotia. Those visits, sometimes with a nursing chum in tow, broke the routine, filled the slow summer months when jobs were scarce, and anchored her ties to family and home. Still, there was nothing doing in Bailey's Brook for a professionally trained, independent young woman. New York always called her back. But in April 1898 a highly unusual job prospect appeared: nursing for the American army as the United States began exercising its own imperial muscle in the Spanish-American War. Macdonald was among the first to apply. She had to content herself, however, with having her application "on file for future reference in case of need," for in late April the surgeon general foresaw "no necessity for the employment of trained female nurses" and made it clear that in any case "no female nurses will be sent to Cuba or to hospitals on the Gulf Coast" because of the prevalence of yellow fever.[7] Both predictions were short-lived as fever of all hues overtook the soldiers, whether in Cuba or in the badly sanitized camps on the mainland.

Nevertheless, it was August before Macdonald received a contract. In the interim she no doubt followed the fortunes and misfortunes of the war as the United States quickly dislodged Spain from a military presence in the Caribbean and the Pacific. Given her own background and temperament, she was likely caught up in the popular excitement over the display of American power. Cuba, Puerto Rico, Hawaii, the Philippines, Guam – all were "liberated," controlled, or directly annexed as a result of the United States' winning the war within four months. Was she enough of a strategist to see the implication for the construction of the Panama Canal? Or was she too busy lobbying the competing groups who offered to guarantee properly trained and impeccably recommended nurses for the American army? The Daughters of the American Revolution, the American Red Cross, the Sisters of Charity, the more recently formed Associated Alumnae of Trained Nurses, and eventually the surgeon general's office in the person of Dr Anita Newcomb McGee all had a hand in sorting and promoting the nursing applications.[8]

Macdonald's turn, like that of most other nurses, came at the end of the war. She may have done as others did and simply showed up at an army camp when the demand for nurses suddenly soared. With the end of the war on 12 August 1898, the interest of the press and the public turned from the glory of victory to the sorry state of American soldiers. Those in Cuba in particular were diseased, famished, and badly housed. Hasty plans were made to bring them home and to isolate them in makeshift camps, far from an urban population that was fearful of contagion.[9] Camp Wikoff at Montauk Point on the far northeastern tip of Long Island was one such camp. Like the others, it had a large general hospital to care for the worst cases of yellow fever, dysentery, typhoid, starvation, and dehydration. With a combination of penny-pinching and common sense, the army realized that these cases required skilled nursing care as much as medical attention, and trained female nurses were thus in high demand. On 18 August, eleven days after the opening of Camp Wikoff, Margaret Macdonald was there, ready to sign a contract on the spot. At thirty dollars a month and with "one ration in kind per day," transportation and medical attendance while on duty,[10] and free tented accommodation, she was better off than in New York.

Yet conditions were fairly chaotic at first. The speed of construction and the arrival of more soldiers than expected, combined with political bumbling and administrative incompetence, meant that the camp was in a shambles.[11] Macdonald's arrival coincided with the first wooden floors for the tents, piped water, even decent food.[12] She clearly was prepared to make the most of it, and this attitude as well as her competence must have been evident to the military administrators. In short order she was "Head Nurse in a Ward of fifty beds" in charge of "two sometimes three nurses ... and three to five orderlies." And she was prescribing and dispensing medicines on her own judgment.[13] Even at its largest, the hospital at Camp Wikoff had only 40 doctors, so some of the 10,000 patients in the seven weeks of the camp's existence were bound to be turned over to the more enterprising of the 329 nurses.[14] Macdonald was one of them and she revelled in it. "I am having a perfectly delightful experience," she wrote her mother, "and would not have missed it for anything."[15]

In mid-September, as the number of patients dwindled at Camp Wikoff, Macdonald sought another kind of military nursing experience – serving on the hospital ship *Relief* that transported ailing and wounded soldiers from Cuba and the gulf ports to New York. Whether or not she actually achieved this is unclear. Her father later claimed that she did, when he urged Canadian government officials to accept her as a military nurse for service in South Africa.[16] But she herself never listed the *Relief* among her experiences; nor did the U.S. Government when she asked years later for an official statement of her war service.[17] What is clear is that the senior officer of the ship did not require her services as of 16 September and told her to report to Camp Wikoff, all transportation paid.[18] She may have gone back there but, if so, it was only briefly, for three days later in New York City she annulled her contract "at her own request" and was "paid in full $32.00."[19] She then resumed her round of private duty nursing.

This was tame compared to military nursing. Serving an individual or a family paled in comparison to serving a country or a cause. In the military, Macdonald had much clearer status than in a household, where she was neither relative nor servant. In a private home she worked in isolation, whereas in the army she had professional colleagues in abundance; also, her hours of work were far more regular. Moreover, an army hospital was full of variety, whereas a household with a single patient could be quite tedious. In fact, work in an army hospital more closely resembled nurses' training. It offered breadth, discipline, expectations, and organization. Macdonald had thoroughly enjoyed her nursing training, and she could thus settle very easily into army structures. There she need not worry about living arrangements, for the army provided both food and shelter. Although she had to supply her own uniform during the Spanish-American War, later the military would furnish that too.

Later, too, Macdonald experienced one of the great attractions of army life: travel. Purposeful travel was so much more satisfying than the maid-nurse-companion kind of travel that a wealthy invalid might offer. And in the army one could be sure that there were no "women's diseases" to tend to; pregnancy and childbirth were, quite literally, left at home. Having once declared that "babies are not very interesting subjects,"[20] Macdonald may well have been glad to be free of such work. As a corollary, in the military she had the opportunity of working almost entirely with men. The sick and wounded soldiers at Camp Wikoff had surprised her with their patience and gratitude[21] (in contrast, presumably, to the demanding women she had encountered in private homes). In a household, authority remained with the employer; in the army, some small portion of it devolved onto the nurse. Few other settings in the late nineteenth century allowed women this type of power. In the hope that there might be other such opportunities, Macdonald took the American oath of allegiance,[22] maintained her private nursing contacts, and kept her eye out for war.

She did not have to wait long. Within a year, war in the Far East and war in South Africa caught her attention. The Boxer Rebellion, brewing in China since 1897, became so dangerous to foreigners living there that an international force was sent to China to help quell the uprising. Nineteen nurses were dispatched from the United States.[23] Macdonald later claimed that at the age of twenty-six she had been too young to go, but she may have been engaging in a bit of retrospective rhetoric, for she was in fact in

South Africa when the American nurses were in China. It is possible that they were being recruited in the autumn of 1899 when she was still in New York and that with her Spanish-American War experience and her membership in the American Red Cross she had hoped to be among them. This might explain why she seems not to have applied for service in South Africa with the Canadian contingents until December 1899, two months after the initial flurry and choice of candidates.

The flurry was occasioned by the Canadian government's decision to send troops to South Africa to assist Great Britain in its conflict with the Boer republics north of the British Cape Colony. Whether Great Britain actually needed Canadian assistance is another matter, but the display of imperial solidarity was certainly comforting to the British, and although politically fraught in Canada, it was emotionally welcome there too. Macdonald and her family in Bailey's Brook would have shared English Canadian enthusiasm for the war and been part of the popular pressure on the Liberal government of Sir Wilfrid Laurier for a military contribution. D.D. Macdonald, with his ear always to the political ground, would have known of the likelihood of sending soldiers. If soldiers, then perhaps doctors, and if doctors, then possibly nurses too. This indeed occurred in October 1899, when four nurses and one doctor went to South Africa with the first contingent of Canadian soldiers. D.D. must have kept his daughter in New York informed, for when she was home for Christmas she received acknowledgment of her application.[24] Her father then vouched for her credentials directly to Laurier's minister of finance, the Nova Scotian William S. Fielding, who passed them on to the minister of militia, another Nova Scotian MP, Frederick W. Borden.[25] Two weeks later Margaret was on her way.

She was not the only nurse with political connections. Some, indeed, topped hers. Of the initial four who had departed for South Africa in October 1899, Georgina Pope was the daughter of William Henry Pope, newspaper owner, politician, and one of Prince Edward Island's fathers of Confederation. Her brother Joseph was one of the highest ranking federal civil servants in Ottawa.[26] Eleven years older than Macdonald, Pope had also trained in the United States; she was the first selected from the almost two hundred nursing applicants. This gave her seniority over the first group of nurses and subsequently over Macdonald when the two of them were together as part of a third group sent in 1902, with Pope at its head.

In 1899 the second nurse chosen had political connections almost as good as those of Pope. Sarah Forbes of Liverpool, Nova Scotia, had a doctor father and a lawyer brother, both of whom had been Nova Scotian members of parliament. The brother had given up his seat in 1896 to allow Fielding an easy by-election passage to the House of Commons. His compensation came within the year in the form of a county court judgeship. And in 1899 a bonus arrived for his sister Sarah when she was selected as a nurse for South Africa. She had professional connections with Georgina Pope, having worked under her at Columbia Hospital for Women in Washington.[27]

Elizabeth Russell of Hamilton, the third of the initial nurses chosen, also had Liberal Party ties. While her own military experience in the Spanish-American War (on the *Relief* and in the Philippines) would certainly have distinguished Russell from other applicants, her doctor father's active Liberal politics and prominent position as medical superintendent of the Hamilton Asylum for the Insane no doubt helped.[28] The political links of Minnie Affleck, the fourth nurse chosen, are more obscure. Her home in Middleville, Ontario, and her work at the Ottawa Children's Hospital place her far from the seafaring Afflecks of Nova Scotia, but the name is so unusual that there may be a connection. If so, it would link her to very prominent people indeed, albeit Conservatives: Lady John Thompson (Annie Affleck), then living in Toronto; and Mrs Joseph Chisholm (Fanny Affleck), whose husband was a law partner of Robert Borden in Halifax and the uncle of Margaret Macdonald.

The explicit or implied favouritism of these appointments continued with the second group of nurses. Along with Macdonald, at least one other of the four chosen to go to South Africa in January 1900 with the second contingent of soldiers had an influential background. Marcella Richardson, a graduate of the same nursing school in New York as Macdonald, was the only westerner among all the nurses. She came from Regina where her father, Hugh Richardson, was the senior judge in the Supreme Court of the North-West Territories. In fact, he had presided over the trial of Louis Riel in 1885.[29] Less evident are the political connections, if any, of Margaret Horne of Montreal and of Deborah Hurcomb of Ottawa, the senior nurse of this foursome. Hurcomb was superintendent of the Perley Nursing Home in Ottawa at the time, and this may have given her access to women who counted in the capital and even to the prominent Conservative businessman George Perley, whose family had provided the nursing home.[30] At a time when no military and few other official channels in Canada could document a nurse's qualifications, these informal networks provided an assurance of the nurses' ability and propriety. It would be well into the First World War before this manner of personnel planning began to be questioned.

In the meantime, the British government was not quite sure what to do with the Canadian nurses. According to English law, British troops could only be "attended by surgeons registered [in the] United Kingdom and nurses belonging to [the] army reserve."[31] No such reserve existed in Canada as yet, nor was there any suggestion that Canadians should join the British army reserve. Macdonald and her nursing companions were thus freelancers who signed a one-year contract with the Canadian government. The initial plan, in a war in which most plans went awry, was that the Canadian nurses would tend only Canadian soldiers. But this assumed a stable setting for the Canadians or reliable train links from the front to the base as well as an easy means of ensuring that sick and wounded Canadians got to the same hospital. None of this could be guaranteed in an increasingly guerrilla war that had no fixed front and where the railway lines were frequently sabotaged. While a doctor might be nearby during a pitched battle or even accompanying soldiers on a scouting venture into the South African veldt, this was not the case for nurses. Neither British nor colonial nurses were to be anywhere near troops in the field. They were stationed at base hospitals, all British, to which the Canadians were attached for varying lengths of time. Like their male compatriots, the Canadian nurses came under British army authority once they were in South Africa, and the army quickly realized that legal restrictions on their use had to be jettisoned.

Margaret Macdonald set out for South Africa in mid-January 1900 on a four-week voyage from Halifax. She and her shipmates on the *Laurentian* were part of an expanded Canadian contribution to a war that was going badly for the British. While military losses were an affront to imperial power, the medical losses, particularly from disease, were shocking. Like the Americans in their recent war with Spain, the British learned the hard way of the need for skilled nurses. As the result of a public outcry in Britain, followed by a royal commission of inquiry through 1900, the number of British nurses in South Africa rose from in forty in November 1899 to one thousand a year later.[32] For the four Canadian nurses aboard the *Laurentian*, emotions would have been running high. Pride, anticipation, anxiety all swirled within a heightened sense of duty and service. The women were being allowed into the male world of warfare, high adventure, and world politics. They were well aware of a sentiment, put in words to Macdonald two years later, that as nurses they were embarking on "the noblest work that women may do for 'King and Empire.'"[33] In 1900 it was "Queen and Empire," and this must have given them an additional thrill.

Besides, it was grand fun. Macdonald, Hurcomb, Horne, and Richardson were the only women on a ship carrying 360 men, most of whom were in the Royal Canadian Field Artillery. Known as "nursing sisters," with all the religious and familial connotations of the term, the women had the equivalent rank of lieutenants, so their social encounters were limited to the officers; but even among them they were a distinct minority.[34] Unlike the soldiers, whether officers or other ranks, the nurses had no military duties to perform on board ship. But they must have taken the opportunity to learn a few military ways. Macdonald and Richardson would certainly have shared their American army nursing experience with the other two, and they all may have pored over military manuals; and if they did not actually attend the drill and lectures imposed on the soldiers,[35] they likely picked the officers' brains on such matters over a meal or during a promenade or an evening's entertainment.

Years later Macdonald admitted that it had taken her some time to fathom military ways,[36] and when in 1914 she was in charge of a hundred nurses aboard the *Franconia* she had lectures specifically designed for them. Presumably, she felt the lack of such training in 1900. The nurses were not even able to learn by doing, for they were expressly prohibited from nursing on board ship except in "serious cases of illness or injury."[37] On the *Laurentian*, the only such cases occurred among the 263 horses that were being transported to South Africa, and all the nurses could do for them was feel some pity – along with some curiosity when the carcasses were heaved into the sea, and relief when a change of wind carried the stench of confined beasts elsewhere. Apart from the horses, everyone seems to have had a good time. The nurses were probably two to a cabin – the four nurses of the first contingent had all shared one on the much more crowded *Sardinian* when it sailed from Quebec at the end of October 1899.[38]

The nurses took their female presence seriously, serving tea on deck every afternoon at five and gracing the two dining tables of the officers' mess. As befitted Victorian shipboard etiquette, the women were accompanied at table by gentlemen whose position guaranteed both responsibility and respectability. Margaret Macdonald sat between the ship's Captain Eaton and Dr Ryerson, founding president of the Canadian Red Cross; Deborah Hurcomb, diagonal to Margaret, had Chaplain Cox on her left and Major Hurdman to her right. Scattered elsewhere around the tables, were the mere lieutenants, among them John McCrae, who was grumpy at first at the prospect of a chaplain and four nurses disturbing the masculine intimacy of the mess. But once the places were set, he had only the chaplain and two nurses to contend with at his fourteen-person table, and they quickly won him over. "Miss Macdonald," two down on the other side of the table from McCrae, was well within speaking and eyeing distance. Her lively personality and ability to speak "a little Gaelic" were bound to appeal to the affable McCrae, who referred to her a few months later as "a mighty good sort."[39] In the meantime, they all seem to have participated enthusiastically in the ship's social activities: the teas, concerts, deck games, promenades, long discussions of bad books in the ship's library (and quick decisions to toss the worst of them overboard), much letter writing, a brief stop at Cape Verde for fuel, and then the frolic and awe of crossing the equator. Only the rolling ship and the increasingly hot weather – and, during the last week, a scarcity of water – caused any difficulties.[40] By then fast friendships had been formed – McCrae, for example, copying from memory his poem "The Harvest of the Sea" into the front of a book that Macdonald used as a souvenir of the voyage.[41]

On arrival in Cape Town in mid-February the nurses parted company with the "gentlemen in kharki ordered south."[42] They had orders to report to the British principal medical officer, and over the following months they were posted to British hospitals at Rondebosch, Kimberley, Bloemfontein, and Pretoria. Intermittently, these postings crossed with those of their four nursing colleagues from Canada who had been in South Africa since the end of November. During the entire time, Macdonald corresponded with some of her male shipmates from the *Laurentian*, reported what she could of their activities in letters home, and met up with some of the men at Bloemfontein and Pretoria. Apart from Nursing Sister Horne, who was invalided out of South Africa in September, they all travelled back to Canada together in December.

At Rondebosch, just outside Cape Town, Macdonald's American military experience had her feeling right at home. Like Camp Wikoff on Long Island, No. 3 General Hospital was a brand new, tented hospital, hastily constructed to cope with the ever-increasing numbers of sick soldiers. Macdonald's nursing was therefore similar to that at Wikoff – more medical than surgical as she kept fevers down, watched for danger signs, and ensured that her patients were clean and as well nourished as supplies allowed. She seems not to have exercised any of the authority she had at Camp Wikoff; the British doctors and nurses among whom she worked, although grateful for the additional help from the colonials, were doubtful at first of its quality. In any case, when all eight Canadian nurses were at Rondebosch they had two "superintending sisters" among them – Georgina Pope and Deborah Hurcomb – and they in turn were subject to

No. 3 General Hospital, Rondebosch

Two Canadian nursing sisters (Georgina Pope at right) with a British
colleague, Rondebosch, 1900

the supervision of the English superintending sister, Sidney Browne. So Macdonald was just one of about twenty-five nurses in a six-hundred-bed hospital. They put in nine-hour days and slept in individual bell tents, which provided partial shelter from high winds and sandstorms but none from scorpions and snakes.[43]

Barely three weeks later, in the middle of March, Macdonald moved closer to the military action, having been posted to Kimberley. It took her two days by train to reach the diamond capital of South Africa (Cape Colony), which lay five hundred miles northeast of Cape Town. The town was emerging from a four-month siege by the Boers that had finally been broken by British troops in mid-February under the recent and more adept leadership of Lord Roberts. Hospital conditions at Kimberley were rudimentary, No. 11 General Hospital being an amalgam of a number of field hospitals around the town. It gradually took the form of a temporary hundred-bed hospital in the Masonic Temple. The four Canadian nurses of the *Laurentian* were on their own here, with the assistance of several British orderlies – in all their other postings they were "attached to, and under the superintendence of the English army nursing sisters."[44] Because the nurses were so few and the hospital so transitory, no accommodation was provided for them on site and they were billeted in a private home. As in Rondebosch, their patients were desperately sick soldiers, suffering from enteric fever (typhoid) and dysentery, diseases that were endemic in South Africa, but aggravated by military camp conditions, and much more deadly than the Boer guns. In spite of the danger of becoming ill themselves, Macdonald and her companions were "well," according to one of their shipmates from the *Laurentian*, who added: "Their zeal is not a whit abated by the dangers they have passed."[45]

The zeal may have diminished somewhat at their next posting, Bloemfontein. The town, about one hundred miles east of Kimberley, had been the Boer capital of the Orange Free State. By the time Macdonald, Hurcomb, Horne, and Richardson arrived there on 23 April, it had been in British hands for almost six weeks, and Margaret used the new designation Orange River Colony in her letters home. Supply lines to Bloemfontein were not always secure, and as a result the food and medical stores were meagre; nor was there sufficient good water. The army camps around the town were poorly located – a blunder that the medical officers blamed on Lord Roberts for not heeding their advice.[46] Consequently, bad sanitation facilitated the spread, to epidemic proportions, of the same diseases the nurses had treated at both Rondebosch and Kimberley: enteric fever and dysentery. Here, at No. 10 General Hospital, the Canadians encountered their "hardest work in the country" and barely held their own against the very worst of the four to five thousand cases in Bloemfontein. Both diseases attacked the intestines, with debilitating diarrhea, high fever, delirium, and, frequently, death. One of Margaret's soldier correspondents quipped to her, "This business of dying of enteric for your country is not what it is scratched up to be. (We have not got as much nerve as you girls and we funk.) There is nothing 'dulce' or 'decorum' about it."[47] All three of Macdonald's colleagues took sick, Margaret Horne seriously enough to be invalided back to the Cape and then to Canada via England.[48] Whether by luck or stamina, Macdonald herself remained healthy throughout her stay in South Africa.

Despite the heavy workload, nursing did not occupy all of her time. She attended to her religious obligations with mass every Sunday and confession on the first Friday of each month. And she met everybody who was anybody in and about Bloemfontein: "I see General Kelly-Kenny at Mass every Sunday – we see all the swells here. I met the Miss Roberts and they are the homeliest little old-maidish looking things that I ever saw. Lady Roberts is a fine looking old Dame. We had Mr Stanley (son of the ex-Gov. Gen. of Canada) here as a pt. I have met several officers of the 'Black Watch' that Dr. Chisholm raves so much about. It's awfully jolly meeting all these people."[49] Macdonald was always ready for some fun, and when Canadian officers from the *Laurentian* appeared in the vicinity they all had a grand time.

Among the soldiers camped outside Bloemfontein in late June was John McCrae. The two had not seen each other since February, but they had kept in touch. Macdonald had sent him "a parcel of chocolates, tobacco, novels and 'a hot water bag'"[50] and could now receive his thanks in person. She and Deborah Hurcomb, accompanied by "the parson" (propriety *oblige*), had tea on more than one occasion at the camp of D battery of the Royal Canadian Field Artillery, McCrae's unit. He wrote to his mother about the encounters and described the teas as "a form of entertainment far removed from the similar affairs of Canadian society but nevertheless ... very pleasant."[51] He and his fellow officers also visited the nurses at their hospital in the Dames Institute in Bloemfontein.[52] Margaret and "Jack" seem to have enjoyed at least two long evening conversations in early July before McCrae was ordered elsewhere. He then wrote to her, taking back much of what he had said – critical comment, it would seem, on war, politics, and religion – explaining that he was "not a skeptic, oh, no." He addressed the letter in Kipling style to "Her Ladyship in Khaki, Fair" and wondered how seriously he was to take her refusal to see him

"Her Ladyship in Khaki, Fair"

again until he had exchanged his "North West Canadian hat" for a proper military helmet. He added, "We are not likely to meet again in S.A., perchance never," yet he told her the time of departure of his troop train south, two days later.[53] Did she just happen to be at the station the very next day as McCrae and his men came into Bloemfontein from camp?[54]

In fact, they did meet again in South Africa. In early August their paths crossed for a few days in Pretoria, a place that Macdonald found not "as pretty as Bloemfontein but the surrounding district is much more so."[55] McCrae chose to take a three-day leave in the town, aware no doubt that

The Irish Hospital, on Pretoria's main square

the Canadian nurses – all seven of them – were there. Macdonald, Hurcomb, and Richardson had left Bloemfontein on 20 July and moved
another two hundred miles northeast into the Transvaal as British troops
continued their capture of Boer territory. Macdonald was so relieved to
see "something green again instead of the everlasting khaki-colored
veldt."[56] The other four Canadian nurses were already there, Pope and
Forbes having experienced severe conditions in Kroonstad since May,
while Affleck and Russell had endured the same at Springfontein.[57] The
Canadians all joined a larger group of British nursing sisters at the Irish
Hospital, a privately endowed institution located in the ornate Palace of
Justice on Pretoria's main square. At the hospital, which also served as the
nurses' living quarters, Macdonald and her colleagues welcomed John
McCrae, who came calling the day he arrived in the city and again the
next evening, still without a helmet. Whether her concern for his headgear
was one of safety or aesthetics is unknown, but it was the latter that
pleased McCrae when khaki helmets were finally issued to D battery at the
end of August.[58] By then he and his men were elsewhere, and Macdonald

did not see him again until the return voyage to Canada in December, though there are hints of an ongoing correspondence.

At the Irish Hospital in Pretoria, Macdonald had better nursing conditions than in her three other postings. The private nature of the hospital allowed it to turn some patients away,[59] so she worked more regular hours with more manageable numbers: one hundred and ten patients on night duty[60] and thirty-seven in a regular daytime ward, "with only one serious case."[61] Among her patients were several Canadians – "and a fine lot they are too!" – including a lad who had come on the *Laurentian* as a stowaway.[62] Total patient numbers of four to five hundred were a relief after the four to five thousand in Bloemfontein and made the nurses' work ... "not so heavy."[63] Macdonald's ward took in wounded as well as the still more numerous cases of typhoid and dysentery. Another difference from earlier postings was the hospital's plentiful supply of good water,[64] crucial in caring for ill soldiers. By this time, too, the Canadian nurses had become accustomed to English nursing practices, and the initial friction with the English nurses had subsided. Indeed, Macdonald seems to have made good connections with Ethel Becher, in charge of the nurses at the Irish Hospital at one point, who later became matron-in-chief in England. She was also friendly with one of Becher's "superintending sisters," Maud McCarthy, who headed the nurses of the British Expeditionary Force in France during the First World War.[65] Although hospital work in Pretoria kept Macdonald too busy to write an article for a home newspaper – "really it is next to impossible to collect one's thoughts when on active service"[66] – she was not overworked.

The easier nursing in Pretoria allowed her more leisure time. "We always have a few hours off in the afternoon and invariably go for a drive and to Tea afterwards," Margaret wrote one of her sisters. The drives – by horse, wagon, or carriage – took her through Pretoria and into the surrounding district. Everywhere she encountered "hedges & hedges of roses," flower-bedecked cottages, and air heavy with the scent of jasmine and orange blossoms. The teas had her in the company of Canadian or English officers posted in the area or of visiting English dignitaries, whose names she dropped casually to her family along with the fact that she had "fired several shots with a Lee Enfield rifle – all by myself too." The nurses hosted a tea once a week on the balconies of the hospital, a military band providing musical entertainment from the town square.[67] Given the exorbitant cost of everything in Pretoria, the teas were frugal affairs; butter, eggs, and biscuits were prohibitively expensive. Still, it was all very pleasant as the guests discussed week-old news from the *Bloemfontein Post*, the only paper that came into Pretoria. Macdonald is unlikely to have told her companions of the pro-Boer sympathies of one of her sisters: "It does make me mad," she grumbled to her father, "but I suppose she ought to [be] excused on the ground that nuns know nothing of the outside world and only look at things from a religious point of view."[68] For all her strong Catholicism, this was certainly not what Macdonald was doing in South Africa. When on duty she was engaged in serious military work; when off duty she had "very jolly times."[69] Among these was the "special night permit" she obtained to circumvent Pretoria's curfew and be out about town until midnight of 24 October, the festive eve of Britain's formal annexation of the two Boer republics, the Transvaal and the Orange Free State.[70] With their annexation, the war was assumed to be over.

At some point during her time in Pretoria, Macdonald appears to have had her first taste of military nursing under fire. Probably in October, she persuaded a reluctant army surgeon to allow her to assist at operations in what must have been a tented field hospital outside the town, an area still not entirely secure. During one such operation a Boer shell burst nearby and a piece of shrapnel struck her on the shoulder. Unperturbed, she continued her work until the operation was completed and only then sought medical attention for herself. The incident subsequently came to the ears of Lord Roberts, who complimented her for bravery. With a combination of modesty and pride, she accounted for her behaviour with the simple comment: "I am the daughter of a Highlander."[71]

By early November, the Highlander from Nova Scotia was packing up to leave. Her one-year service was coming to an end, and the hospital in Pretoria, now a unit of the British Army Medical Corps, was closing down. The Canadians all hoped that they would return home via England. It would be splendid to see London, the imperial capital, and perhaps, as Macdonald mentioned to her sister, pop over to Paris.[72] This did not in fact happen, but in the meantime she and her six Canadian colleagues took their first leave of the year with a trip into Natal, southeast of Pretoria. They visited Ladysmith, which had been besieged by the Boers just a year earlier, and the coastal town of Durban and then returned to Pretoria for the five-day train ride to Cape Town.[73] There they had a further wait at No. 1 General Hospital, Wynberg, before boarding the *Roslyn Castle* on 13 December with, among others, the same people who had been on the *Laurentian* eleven months earlier. Most of the men going aboard were somewhat the worse for wear because of last-minute binging in the city the night before.[74] The nurses had been far away from these revels, having been housed eight miles from the city centre, though propriety as well as geography would in any case have kept them from any such behaviour.

Once on board ship with more than eight hundred men, Macdonald and her six colleagues had some nursing duties, for enteric fever had followed the soldiers and claimed two of the twelve stricken men. Like the soldiers, the nurses may have been a bit weary, anxious to be home, more subdued than on the outward voyage. Even the cheery John McCrae, as secretary of the ship's social committee, could not arouse much enthusiasm except for the weekly concerts on deck.[75] War, it seems, is more fun to go to than to come from. Still, they would have been enchanted by the tumultuous welcome in Halifax when they disembarked on 9 January 1901. And then they scattered. Margaret Macdonald, in her "becoming costume of khaki with red trimmings ... rosy cheeks and bright eyes,"[76] may have been greeted in the city by her lawyer uncle Joseph Chisholm and his wife Fanny. From Halifax she would have gone by train to Avondale, where the handsome horse-drawn Macdonald carriage from Bailey's Brook fetched her home for a belated Christmas and New Year. With the family all agog over the experiences of their imperial daughter, she spent some weeks catching up on all their doings. She was still at home when the federal census taker stopped by on 31 March, for he recorded her as a member of the household. She may well have stayed there for the rest of the year, or perhaps she returned to New York to earn her living once again as a private-duty nurse. In either case, she would have been wondering "What next?"

Well she might ask that question. There were still no career possibilities for nurses in the Canadian military, nor would there be until 1906. However, a reserve Army Nursing Service was established in August 1901 as part of the ongoing reorganization of military medical services. All the eight nurses who had been in South Africa in 1900, plus two others, became the first members of this new force. With their militia status, they were an integral part of the military (although not permanent members) and could be called upon in any military emergency. Among the initial ten members, Macdonald's name appeared in seventh place, corresponding, it would seem, to the date of her appointment for service in South Africa and the length of time she spent there.[77] Since no duties were required of these members – any military activity on their part being on an "if and when" basis – the nurses continued their regular work. Wherever Macdonald was at this point, she let it be known that she was "anxious to go"[78] when another possibility for military service arose towards the end of 1901. However, her seventh place on the list of reserve nurses almost cost her the chance.

Conditions had not stabilized in South Africa in spite of the British victories in 1900. Guerrilla warfare continued in the former Boer Republics, and Britain had to send additional and replacement troops. The Canadian government offered to send more too. This time a fully equipped field hospital was to accompany the Canadian Mounted Rifles. Field hospitals at the time had no nurses officially attached to them, so the five nurses Canada offered to send as well were separate from it.[79] The imperial authorities agreed to the offer, and preparations were made in December for the Canadians to leave early in 1902. Before anything official had been settled, a Halifax newspaper published the names of five of the eight nurses who had been in South Africa in 1900 as volunteers willing to go again. Margaret Macdonald, Sarah Forbes (both Nova Scotians), and Georgina Pope were among them.[80] However, on a more official list of five names circulating within the ministry of the militia and including Forbes and Macdonald, Pope's name did not appear. Her brother Joseph, the under-secretary of state, assured the minister, Frederick Borden, that his sister was very much available for renewed service. So Borden now had six names for five positions, the additional one being the senior nurse from the first South African tour of duty and the one whose name was in first place on the Army Nursing Service list. The obvious solution was to drop one of the other five, the most likely being Margaret Macdonald, since she was lower on the Nursing Service list. But before Borden could sort things out, the names of the five (minus Pope) appeared in the press.

In a flurry of correspondence with Governor General Lord Minto over Christmas and the New Year, Borden, now under pressure to add yet another name along with that of Pope, urged Minto to convince the British government to accept eight nurses instead of the agreed-upon five. "I am very willing to assist Miss Pope," he told the governor general, "but not at the expense of hurting the feelings or injuring the reputations, as nurses, of the others."[81] In Borden's eyes, both Macdonald and Forbes would be publicly slighted if the governor general stood firm at five nurses – Macdonald by having her name removed, and Forbes by having to stand down as senior nurse. Nonetheless, he informed Forbes that she could not be the leader, and she obligingly "waived any right she might have [to seniority], in favour of Miss Pope."[82] The governor general was slow to acquiesce and even slower to elicit British approval for an increased number.[83] But by the end of January, eight Canadian nurses had formal approval to go. With Georgina Pope in charge, Sarah Forbes, Deborah Hurcomb, and Margaret Macdonald were joined by four newcomers: Eleanor Fortescue, Florence Cameron, Margaret Smith, and Amy Scott. They all boarded the *Corinthian,* a passenger liner, in Halifax on 27 January 1902 en route to South Africa via England.

This time the nurses did not accompany the troops. The two ships assigned to carry No. 10 Canadian Field Hospital and the 2nd Regiment, Canadian Mounted Rifles, did not have space for five nurses, much less eight. In any case, one of the ships, the *Manhattan,* had already left with half the troops before the nursing numbers had been finalized; the other, the *Victorian,* carrying the hospital and the remaining troops, left the same day as the *Corinthian,* 28 January. The *Victorian* could have done with nurses aboard, since measles and smallpox broke out among the soldiers.[84] It went straight to Durban, whereas the nurses took a much more circuitous route via Liverpool, London, Southampton, Madeira, and Cape Town, reaching Durban more than a week later. Because they were not on the same ship, the nurses did not develop the same close rapport with the officers that Macdonald and Hurcomb had known on the *Laurentian.* Macdonald's letters home from her second stint in South Africa reflect this lack of male Canadian companionship.

The nurses' voyage out emphasized their separateness. Because of their uniform and their destination, they were oddities among the civilian passengers of the *Corinthian.* But once they arrived in London, their colonial status added to their allure in the ten-day fête accorded them in the imperial capital. There Macdonald began her lifelong affair with London: "One could live there forever and see something new every day." There, too, she nourished her growing attraction for English high society, many of whose members were passengers with her on the next leg of the journey aboard the *Saxon,* another passenger liner, "a perfect palace of a boat," which took them from Southampton to Cape Town. "Lots of officers," a knight or two, and gentlemen wearing evening dress to dinner all charmed Macdonald, though she and her colleagues remained in uniform: "We do not change garb – which is a great blessing." A blessing too was the fact that the eight nurses got along "swimmingly," Miss Pope being "awfully nice" and Eleanor Fortescue, Macdonald's cabin mate, equally so. Florence Cameron kept them all amused, which can only have heightened Margaret's own sense of fun.[85]

This time, the eight Canadians remained together in South Africa in one place. They had hoped to be attached to the Canadian field hospital, and Macdonald assumed that the purpose of their being sent from Cape

Town to Durban on the hospital ship *Orcana* and then inland by train towards Harrismith was to catch up with the unit. She looked forward to working under Colonel Worthington, the hospital's commanding officer, whom she had met when she was in South Africa in 1900.[86] However, at Harrismith, almost two hundred miles northwest of Durban, the nurses were attached to the British No. 19 Stationary Hospital, and there they remained from the middle of March until the peace proclamation of 31 May brought a definitive end to the war. Meanwhile, the field hospital, in the wake of the Canadian Mounted Rifles, was initially at Newcastle, then at Volksrust, and then much farther inland at Klerksdorp in the Transvaal, where it divided into two sections, a mobile one close to the action of the Canadian soldiers, and a more fixed one at Vaalbank.[87] In Harrismith, therefore, the nurses saw few Canadians, either as patients or as medical colleagues, though Macdonald seems to have known something of the field hospital's movements.

In their half-tented, half-hutted hospital, staffed primarily by British nurses and doctors, the Canadian nurses acquired a reputation for fine teamwork. Even with their numbers down to six when Hurcomb and Cameron became ill, they relished the experience.[88] The 600 patients, a third of whom had enteric fever, kept them busy but not overwhelmingly so. Macdonald had time to joke with her 36 regular patients (occupying six tents); she got lost among the tents housing her 250 night-duty patients, sympathized with overworked and underfed orderlies, broke the rules to bring them extra food, kept on the right side of Georgina Pope for duty assignments, and obeyed her father's instructions to maintain her health and attend to her religious obligations.[89] In a letter to her twelve-year-old brother she recounted an incident with a severely ill patient who was just beginning to come round: "Sister, I have a *Crow* in my nose," the soldier had said. "He wanted to know if I could'nt get it out. I told him that in Canada people did'nt have Crows in their noses so that I did'nt know how to get at it. I do'nt know yet what he meant. When reporting to the Day Sister I told her and I suggested that he was having 'too much Croly' (that's the Doctor's name in that ward) but she never even smiled so my little joke was wasted. Some people are so dull ar'nt they?"[90] Macdonald herself was never dull. When off duty, she explored on horseback as much of the neighbourhood as possible, including guarded blockhouses. She visited a school in a concentration camp where young Boer children delighted her with their brightness and willingness to learn English – even to having pen pals in England – but she admitted fiercely to hating the Boers. Of the "kaffirs," South African blacks, she had some fun with their limited English and took their servant status for granted.[91]

In the few surviving letters to her parents, she maintained the same division of information that she had established during her nursing training. To her mother she described the weather, her clothing, and the state of her health; with her father she discussed political events and the progress of the war. She was as interested in lace for her petticoats and ostrich feathers for her hats as she was in the ongoing fighting. In April 1902 she sent her father a newspaper account of "the great gallantry of the Canadians" in an unnamed battle, likely that of Hart's River in late March. She also sent him a press account of the death of Cecil Rhodes, the premier of Cape Colony, and indiscreetly passed on her patients' scathing opinion of General Rundle, who had marched his men on rations of one pound of flour a day for ninety days. Her own opinion of the English she expressed when telling her father how the Seventh Dragoon Guards had wined and dined the Boer General Christiaan De Wet. Taken aback by this particular display of respect for the enemy, she clucked "Ar'nt the English tiresome?" As for a likely end to the war, the only sure way of knowing, she said, was by a reduction in the size of her hospital in early May, which meant the staff would soon be dispersed.[92]

The end of the war interrupted Macdonald's growing fascination for the military. At the age of twenty-nine, she had three stints of military nursing to her credit, and in all of them she had demonstrated skill, resilience, humour, and character. Many people could speak well of her. On the month-long return voyage from Durban to Halifax in July aboard the *Winifredian*, Macdonald was able to spend more time with the officers of the 2nd Regiment, Canadian Mounted Rifles, and No. 10 Canadian Field Hospital than she had had in South Africa. Six of the seven hospital officers were aboard, and she already knew at least two of them: Colonel Worthington, the commanding officer, and Lieutenant Lorne Drum, both of whom had been in South Africa in 1900. The missing officer, second-in-command Major Guy Carleton Jones, had been left behind in South Africa because of illness.[93] During the voyage, the nurses and officers would have shared their experiences and solidified their memories of the war. It is unlikely that they had as much to grumble about as the troops, who were dissatisfied with the food and dirt of the ship, though there may have been a general sense of letdown after a grand adventure.[94]

Although Margaret had been away only seven months, the folks at home were glad to see her back. For all the imperial ties of the Macdonald family, South Africa was very far away. She holidayed a while in Bailey's Brook, catching up with her family's doings. Her father, well into his seventies, was beginning to slow down. Sister Cell had a new baby, and her husband Jim was taking on more responsibility in D.D.'s store. Florence, at home between two teaching experiences in the United States, had not yet made the decision to follow her sister Adele into a career as a teaching nun. Stay-at-home bouncy Vie was as lively as ever, and younger sister Kate was home for the summer vacation. Two brothers were also home from school, Ronald from his McGill medical studies and Bill from St Francis Xavier. And of course there was the youngster, Donald (egging on his elders in lawn tennis matches on the family court). Among the gang as well was the young orphan cousin, Janet McGregor Macdonald, barely ten years old, who was full of admiration for the uniformed and well-travelled Margaret. To oversee the flurry of activity around Margaret's homecoming was her energetic mother Mary, proud of her brood and the well-run household that could accommodate them all. Like them, she wondered what this unusual daughter would turn to now.

New York of course beckoned. There Macdonald had friends and contacts. Private nursing was always an option. At some point in the next two years she did postgraduate training at Harlem Emergency Hospital in New York, either to acquire some specialty experience or to catch up with civilian nursing. Perhaps she had an administrative job in mind, in some nursing school, and felt she needed broader hospital experience. Or was she just occupying her time between private-duty nursing positions? Macdonald seems not to have been tempted, as was Georgina Pope, to apply for a matron's position in England with the newly constituted Queen Alexandra's Imperial Military Nursing Service.[95] Instead, she expected something in the United States to provide employment and satisfy her wanderlust. On the occasions when neither materialized, she appears to have returned to Bailey's Brook for comfort and sustenance. She was there, early in 1904, to receive the disappointing news that her lack of U.S. citizenship prevented her from joining the ten American nurses who were going off to assist Japan in the Russo-Japanese War. So sure had she been of the posting – she was, after all, a member of the Spanish-American War Nurses' Society that supplied five of the ten nurses – that she was on the brink of ordering uniforms.[96] However, later that same year, when she was back in New York, something closer than Japan and just as adventurous showed up. Early in September the chief clerk of the Isthmian Canal Commission wrote to Miss Macdonald inquiring whether she could accept a position as a nurse in Panama during the construction of the canal.[97] She could and did. Ten days later, she was on a ship, heading south.

Something about the grand purpose of the Panama Canal appealed to her. She liked being part of world events and sought them out, equipped with the only entrance qualifications permitted of a woman at the time:

her nursing training. That training gave her access to imperial ventures such as the American construction of the Panama Canal between 1904 and 1914. The entire project was designed to facilitate American defence, bolster American commerce, advertise American engineering prowess, and reveal American power. Backed by the American military in May 1904, the Panamanian government had ceded control of a ten-mile wide "Canal Zone" to the United States. With much of the enterprise managed like a military campaign, Macdonald would feel right at home. Army surveyors mapped the route across the Isthmus; army engineers designed the forty-mile construction through jungle, swamp, and rock face, necessitating huge locks to join an inland waterway on the height of land between Colon on the Caribbean side and Ancon on the Pacific. The army protected both ends of the canal route. Army service corps provided the model for housing and feeding up to thirty-eight thousand people, who came and went over the years from the United States, Spain, Italy, and the Caribbean islands. Of most significance to Macdonald, and indeed to the success of the entire project, was the presence of army medical personnel who kept the labour force relatively healthy in an area reputed for its devastating epidemics of yellow fever and malaria. Things that nurses had been trained in since the 1870s and that army doctors had only slowly recognized now became part of the American grand design. Cleanliness, sanitation, pure water, nourishing food, and skilled nursing care in modern hospitals were all crucial to the completion of the canal. Macdonald was part of that emphasis on public health, and she seized the fine connection between a nurse's work in a hospital ward, an unprecedented construction project, and the imperial ambitions of a modern state.

Within three days of being offered the job, she had signed her contract with the Canal Commission. In return for a year of nursing services at Ancon Hospital, she was to receive fifty dollars a month and free board, lodging, and laundry. Her passage to Panama – a seven-day trip from New York – would be paid, and if her work proved satisfactory her passage back to New York would also be assured. Should she fall ill, the hospitals of the commission would tend her at no cost. Each year of service earned her six weeks of paid leave, with return transportation provided; she would need only to pay the food costs of twenty-five dollars each way. Moreover, that same rate would apply to any members of her immediate family who wanted to come visiting. Promotion and pay raises were offered to good workers, and Macdonald received both in less than a year. She took her leave in July 1905, and before its expiry requested and received eight weeks more, without pay.[98] In late October 1905 she returned to Panama where she remained until mid-April 1906.[99] It was the longest period of continuous employment she had known since leaving nursing school in 1895.

During her stay at Ancon, the hospital expanded and modernized to fit the needs of a growing workforce. Originally constructed by the French during their abortive attempt at cracking the isthmus of Panama, Ancon Hospital was on a hill above Panama City, facing the Pacific Ocean. Consisting of a series of tile-roofed wooden buildings raised above ground on masonry pillars, and most with wrap-around verandahs, the hospital had an initial capacity of five hundred beds; later construction and the rearranging of staff quarters more than doubled this number.[100] The original nursing staff had been French nuns, Sisters of St Vincent de Paul. Most of them were replaced in the early summer of 1904 by a handful of trained nurses from the United States, all of them with military or Red Cross experience abroad. Macdonald was part of the expansion of their numbers to twenty-two in the fall of 1904 (a number that grew to more than one hundred by 1911.)[101] Her arrival in late September coincided with the general Americanization of the hospital: electric lights to replace candles, the screening of windows and porches, new beds and bedding, a modern laundry, a cold storage plant, and a concerted campaign against the "Lizards, Beetles and Bats and a thousand other things [that] parade all through our rooms."[102]

Among these "other things" were two genera of mosquitoes – the stegomyia and anopheles – which wreaked havoc with people's health, and were as big a challenge as the terrrain in the construction of the canal. One of them bit Macdonald in 1905. By then, the connection between certain mosquitoes and certain diseases had been established, if only recently. U.S. army doctor Colonel William Gorgas had spotted the link between the stegomyia mosquito and yellow fever when he was in Cuba during the Spanish-American War. He brought that knowledge with him, along with the relatively simple solution of eliminating the mosquito's breeding grounds in open containers of fresh water, when he was appointed chief sanitary officer for the Canal Zone in April 1904. It nonetheless took months of political wrangling and an outbreak of yellow fever in the late spring and early summer of 1905, with white employees of the Canal Commission leaving in droves, before Washington released the necessary resources for piped water and "incessant sanitary inspection."[103] It is unlikely that the imperturbable Macdonald was among the frightened, although she did take her annual leave in late July 1905.

Yellow fever ward, Ancon Hospital

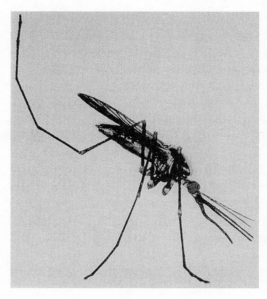

Anopheles mosquito
poised to transmit malaria

By the end of 1905 yellow fever was virtually eradicated, thanks to the sanitary measures. Malaria, however, was another matter, and Dr Gorgas was less successful with it. The anopheles mosquito, which transmitted it, bred in swamps and marshy areas, and lived longer and flew farther than the stegomyia. Its eradication was therefore much more difficult. Indeed, the disease it spread was much more prevalent than yellow fever and, barring death in either case, was much more debilitating. It was an anopheles mosquito that bit Margaret Macdonald. In spite of the precautions that she and all other canal employees were taking at the time – three grains of quinine a day, available as easily as salt and pepper at meals – she succumbed to malaria.[104] Her week-long illness in mid-April 1905 suggests a mild form of the disease,[105] unless she was able to conceal for a while the headache and chills and only give in when nausea, high fever, and exhaustion felled her. Nonetheless, she appears to have had recurring bouts in 1906 and 1907.[106]

How this affected her nursing is unknown. She would certainly have had the medical care promised in her contract, and once on her feet again she was probably assigned lighter duties by the head nurse, Eugénie Hibbard. In the medical wards of Ancon Hospital, for all the drama of yellow fever, the patients were mostly suffering from malaria, consumption, pneumonia, dysentery, and enteritis. There was even one instance of bubonic plague in July 1905.[107] In the surgical wards the nurses watched over patients recovering from amputations or other repairs as a result of accidents along the construction line. A photo of Macdonald at Ancon that predates her illness shows her and another nurse having tea on a verandah, both wearing high-necked long-sleeved white blouses and long dark skirts. The "Mr Luck" of the caption may be the photographer. Certainly, before malaria struck, luck was with her all the way.[108]

True to form and despite the malaria, Margaret had a fine time in Panama. She quickly became friends with the other "girls," and given the sex ratio in the largely male enterprise, they were all in great demand. Dinners and balls and masquerades filled the social life of the American elite to such an extent that Margaret planned to acquire two new evening gowns when she next came north.[109] She would have been a guest at the frequent dinners that Colonel Gorgas and his wife Marie hosted from their quarters at Ancon Hospital: seven-course Spanish affairs late into the night.[110] And she and another nurse called on the wife of an army general, as she described to her sister: "The rooms are very, very large, perfectly square, balcony all round, polished floors – their house faces on the water & the balconies on a moonlit night are an ideal place for making love. She offers

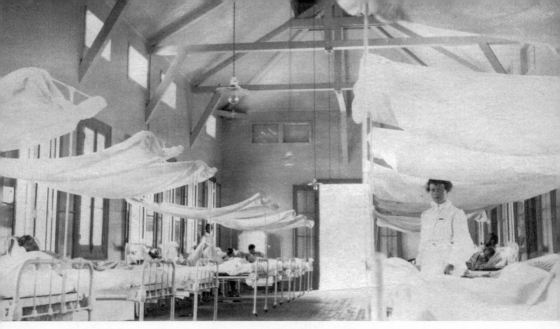

Nurse Macdonald at Ancon Hospital, 1905

me the use of hers any time I care for it. Nice? She has a beautiful piano and while we were in along came a little American chap we know with two Spanish girls. He played and we all danced – Mrs Jefferies is game for anything at any time. It was great."[111] She asked her sister to send her bathing suit for swimming expeditions: "When with the girls alone I float about in Pyjamas but when the boys are along I have to borrow a suit which is rather awkward especially as it never fits."[112] She went horseback riding by moonlight along the hard-packed beach, her South African lessons in sidesaddle coming in handy. With two other nurses she went over to Taboga island, a three-hour boat trip away, for a few days' "practically camping" and feigned surprise when their "respective male admirers" appeared on the scene.[113]

Romance was definitely in the air, and Margaret was as susceptible as anyone, so much so that her sisters at home speculated about a future brother-in-law.[114] Might this have been Jim, who sent on the notification of her extended leave in September 1905, complaining that she therefore owed him a two-cent stamp? He was worried that she might be thinking of quitting: "You know your weakness in that direction,"[115] Or perhaps it was Donald – from Egerton, just west of Bailey's Brook – a geologist who worked in Panama.[116] Whoever it was, Margaret laughed off the possibility: "He knows me too well to ever do me the honor of asking me to marry him."[117] In all likelihood she, along with other employees in Panama, was protected from any serious romantic entanglements by the vigilance of the

Canal Commission. It carefully orchestrated most of the social life in the Canal Zone as a "substitute for the salutary restraints of home, family and public opinion from which its employees are freed."[118] The commission could count on the nurses to be part of the restraint. For all the fun they were having, Margaret and her colleagues were expected to be well behaved. Apparently, they did not even need "rules and regulations" to govern their off-duty activities because "the chief nurse refuses to have women here who are not likely to maintain the dignity of the profession."[119]

Social expectations of this sort probably sustained Macdonald during the second blow to her equanimity that she experienced in Panama. Like malaria, the death of her father had a recurring effect on her life. Perhaps she knew before returning to Ancon in late October that something was amiss. Her almost eighty-year-old father was much less sprightly than usual, and he died two days after her thirty-third birthday in February 1906, as the result of a broken hip. She would have received the news by telegram and grieved in solitude. Like her family at home, she had the support of her faith and, in Panama, of a larger Catholic community than she had known in South Africa. Still, D.D.'s death was a big loss; and because of his wealth and prominence, it was a public loss in a family known for its intense privacy. For the rest of her life Margaret kept the press clipping that attested to his standing as well as his remarkable progeny: one physician son in British Columbia, another son studying law at Dalhousie, and two daughters as nuns in Montreal. But the only daughter of six actually named in the obituary notice was Margaret, nursing in Panama.[120]

To her, D.D. left the largest single sum of money – $4,250, which was almost five times her annual salary in 1906 – with the condition that she not receive it until three years after his death and even then that it come in three equal yearly instalments. Indirectly, he also provided a future home for her should she need one. To his wife Mary he left the house at Bailey's Brook, its contents, and all the property except that connected with the general store, along with an annual allowance "for the purpose of maintaining the household and house for my children under age, and my unmarried sons and daughters." D.D. intended the "homestead property" to remain in the family, and so it did for the next seventy years. Margaret came home permanently in 1922, and she and her sister Vie presumably obeyed another clause of their father's will that as unmarried daughters residing in the household they contribute "a reasonable proportion" of domestic costs from their own income.[121] She continued to do so until her death in 1948. She and Vie were the only two daughters who chose to be buried near their father.[122]

Mary Ann ("Vie") Macdonald, 1906

In early 1906, the death of her father may have caused Macdonald to rethink her presence in Panama. She could certainly have gone on working at Ancon Hospital with the still-expanding nursing force there. Her regular salary increases suggest that her work was more than satisfactory. But in mid-April, six weeks after her father's funeral, she took eighteen days' paid leave, added to it eight weeks of unpaid leave, and came north. The paid leave, half the annual amount, was presumably all she was entitled to since her return to Ancon the previous autumn. The additional unpaid leave would have been necessary in part because the journey alone – home and back by ship and train – would have absorbed most of her regular leave. Still, she clearly felt the obligation and perhaps the need to be near her family after such a major loss – indeed, her mother may have asked her to come. Years later, this kind of daughterly duty was one of only two reasons (the other being marriage) that she would allow nurses to break their wartime contracts. After two months at home in the spring of 1906 she must have started to wonder about breaking her own.

She may perhaps have had another bout of malaria at that time, with the worried family suggesting that she not go back. Or was the gentle spring and early summer weather of Bailey's Brook just too tempting a contrast to the heat and humidity of Panama? On the other hand, while at home she may have started imagining the possibility of future work with the Canadian military. Her family, with its lively interest in public affairs, would certainly have known of major changes underway, particularly those at Halifax between November 1905 and February 1906, when Canadian troops began taking over the manning of the garrison from the British. Part of that garrison was a hundred-bed military hospital, and it would require Canadian medical corps staffing. Although there seem not to have been British nurses at the hospital, someone might just be thinking of having Canadian ones there now. If that should happen, Macdonald needed to be nearby. In any case and whatever the circumstances, sometime in May or June she decided not to return to Panama. Displaying the very "weakness" that her friend Jim had teased her about, she simply quit. The last entry on her Panama employment card reads bluntly: "July 1 '06 – Dropped from rolls – failure to report from leave."[123] In the quasimilitary atmosphere of the canal construction, Macdonald had deserted her post.

But it did mean that she was in Canada in the fall of 1906 when the decision was indeed made by the Canadian military to appoint first one and then another nursing sister to the garrison hospital at Halifax. Macdonald may have let her interest be known to Lieutenant Colonel Guy Carleton Jones, who at the time was principal medical officer in the Maritime region and was about to become Director General Medical Services (DGMS) in Ottawa and thus head of the Permanent Army Medical Corps (PAMC). Certainly, she had kept in touch with Georgina Pope since their time together in South Africa; there had even been the possibility of Pope joining her in Panama.[124] Both women were still on the reserve list of the Army Nursing Service, a list that was enlarged in intent, if not in actual people, from the ten of 1901 to twenty-five in 1904.[125] Pope still headed that list, and as of late 1902 her name had RRC (Royal Red Cross) attached to it, the highest nursing honour of the British Empire. If a permanent job was going for nurses in the Canadian military and Pope wanted it, she was bound to get it. This happened in September 1906, and two months later Macdonald was appointed as well. "Nursing Sister Miss Margaret Macdonald is detailed for duty as assistant nurse at the Station Hospital, Halifax, with pay and allowances of a lieutenant, from the 2nd inst." read the militia order announcing her appointment.[126]

At age thirty-three Macdonald finally had a full-time job in Canada. And it was the kind she liked best: working with and nursing men within a military hierarchy that gave her security, status, and power. She dusted off her khaki uniform of South African days and launched into her three-fold responsibility of caring for sick soldiers, supervising and instructing male ward orderlies, and, more gradually, participating in month-long training sessions for civilian nurses who wished to join the reserve Army Nursing Service. Within a year she had donned the new brass-buttoned, dark blue dress uniform with its skyblue workday dress, complete with white apron and shoulder-length veil. The design of the uniform is attributed to Georgina Pope. As senior nurse, named matron in 1908, she would have been the one to recommend it to senior military officers.[127] But it is hard to imagine that fashion-conscious Margaret, who like Pope knew from experience the pros and cons of the South African uniform, did not also have a say. They both looked decidedly more handsome in the new uniforms.

So attired, Macdonald nursed the sick. Into her wards came the sick and injured of the Canadian permanent force in Halifax and also, though much less frequently, members of the militia on annual short-term exercises. On occasion, too, she nursed the wives and children of the few married officers.[128] The major ailment afflicting the soldiers in 1906 and early 1907 was gonorrhea, and these cases were probably left to the male orderlies, as they later were in the First World War.[129] But Macdonald would certainly have nursed the influenza patients, who were the most numerous in 1908. Other ailments that brought soldiers under her care included alcoholism, bronchitis, contusions, diphtheria, stomach troubles, tonsilitis, sprains, rheumatism, and wounds of various sorts. Surgical nursing took much less of her time; only fifteen operations were performed in the year 1907–8.

Altogether, some eight hundred patients went through the medical and surgical wards that year,[130] and Macdonald had a regular routine for dealing with them. Her first morning hour on the ward was very busy; she read the night report, investigated any irregularities, checked on the special cases, and took temperatures, and noted the patients' nourishment and the general state of the wards. She did the more serious surgical dressings, leaving the minor ones to the orderlies "after a few lessons." She ensured that the prescription bottles were ready for the dispensary, and she had all the necessary forms – treatment forms, diet sheets, visitors' passes – prepared and ready for the medical officer to sign. All this before ten o'clock, when he appeared to do his rounds. Macdonald accompanied him in order to convey information, pass on requests or complaints, and receive instructions. She then ensured that the instructions were carried out, gave the patients their medicine, and inspected their noonday meal before having her own. In the afternoon, she hustled less, "according to work or sickness in the hospital," tended the very ill at five o'clock, and came off duty herself in time for dinner.[131] Occasionally she had night duty, but normally that was left to the orderlies. Through all this activity, she had some say, albeit minor, in the gradual improvements to her workplace. By 1909 Halifax's garrison hospital, just below the citadel at Gottingen and Cogswell streets, was "a very completely equipped and up-to-date hospital" that compared "very favourably with any civil hospital."[132]

Macdonald's second responsibility, of supervising and instructing orderlies, meant that she watched them as closely as her patients. It was crucial that she do so, for as one of only two nurses at Halifax, she had to rely on orderlies to complete the work in the wards. On occasion, soldiers were assigned to orderly duty because of their aptitude, but more often it was because of their military ineptitude. If they had any objection to the recent introduction of female nurses as superior officers, they kept quiet about it. Under the nurses' direction their tasks were generally of the lowest order in a hospital ward: cleaning and scrubbing, bathing patients, handing out meal trays, and taking away bedpans. But they also had to learn from the nurses the rudiments of proper nursing: temperatures, dressings, medicines, diets. And they were expected to undertake these tasks with the same care and attention as a trained nurse. Woe betide them if they didn't. Macdonald had the authority to punish them and report them to superior officers, and she had no trouble in exercising this authority over men who came from a lower social background than she, had far less formal education, and no nursing training at all.[133] On one occasion, while on night duty, Macdonald spotted two orderlies sound asleep while they were under orders to watch and report any change in a gravely ill postoperative patient. She did admit silently that the pair, stationed one each side of the bed, had at least had the presence of mind to fall asleep over the bed with their heads touching so that the patient did not risk falling out. But she fumed at them. How could they be so irresponsible? But when she thought about it, just as she had done in South Africa she began to sympathize with the orderlies' situation. These two had been on

Marge in mufti, 1910

duty seventeen hours and had another thirteen to go. In all that time, they had had scanty food and no recreation. Was that quite right? Macdonald pondered the situation, designed some solutions, and presented them in the name of "efficiency and effectiveness" to a conference of medical officers. Orderlies, she argued, needed shorter hours of work and more recreation. They should be subject to examinations and incentives; a system of promotion should be in place to recognize ability and merit among them.[134] Whatever Macdonald's audience thought of the orderlies, they would surely have recognized in this nursing sister an administrator and a superior officer in the making.

Even more closely connected to her future work was Macdonald's third responsibility as a nursing member of the PAMC. Along with Pope and her male colleagues, she gave courses of instruction in military training to nurses who were members of the Army Nursing Service. These women had jobs as civilian nurses but were drawn to the military by family tradition or by interest or duty. One test of their intent was their willingness to take a month away from their profession and their home for the required training, which initially was given only in Halifax. As well as being graduates of a standard nurses' training school, they had to be of high moral character and dignified deportment, and aged between twenty-one and thirty-eight.[135] These qualifications presumably enabled them to absorb the lessons in "routine and ethics of Army Nursing" that were given annually (and, later, semi-annually) at a military hospital.[136] Both Macdonald and Pope would have drawn on their South African experience to initiate the newcomers, through lectures and supervised ward work, in the myriad rules and regulations, along with the requirements of patients and caregivers in a military hospital. Their medical colleagues added lectures on such matters as the legal framework of the militia, the organization of medical services in the field, the work of the medical officer, camp sanitation, and hygiene.[137] At the end of the course, an oral and written examination tested the students' learning.[138] If they passed, they became fully qualified members of the nursing reserve and could be called on for temporary duty, usually during the summer training of the male members of the militia, but sometimes to bolster nursing numbers in a military hospital, and occasionally to respond to crises.[139] When there were openings for nurses in the permanent force, they were to be filled from this reserve service. The numbers grew more rapidly than those of the permanent force. By the beginning of 1914 there were about fifty nurses in the reserve, not all of whom had taken the training course, and there were five in the PAMC. In fact, the training course at Halifax had only a handful of students each year: five in 1909, nine in 1910, four in 1911, six in 1912.[140] In April 1914 Macdonald taught her last course before the war to six students at the military hospital in Kingston. A picture from that occasion shows her in chummy companionship with them, albeit in the leading position. She was increasingly bothered by the low numbers – as she was by the nurses' exclusion from the summer camps where the medical men of the militia were trained. But before she spoke openly on such matters in 1913, she decided to arm herself with a study trip to England to see how things were being done there.

Nursing Sister Macdonald (left) with her army pupils, Kingston, 1914

Ever since her ten-day visit to London on her way to South Africa in 1902, Macdonald had hoped to be back there some day. She had thoroughly enjoyed the social engagements and public recognition bestowed on the eight Canadian nurses, but this time she wanted to be on her own and she wanted to work. Thanks to her position in the PAMC, she was able to arrange just such an opportunity. The Canadian military offered its officers the possibility of travel abroad to study "the military systems of other portions of the Empire."[141] It is unlikely that the program, dating from 1906, was intended for nursing sisters, but Macdonald, with her rank of lieutenant, made a claim for it sometime in 1910. By then she was working in Quebec City, the sole nursing sister at the military hospital – one woman among the four hundred men of the garrison.[142] Her status placed her among the elite of the city, and she would have been invited to functions for or hosted by the governor general, Earl Grey, when he was in residence in the city. There she may well have made connections with the members of the Grey family and their entourage who showed up later as wartime friends and acquaintances. Some of them may even have said, "Come see us in England."

Whatever the circumstances, she convinced skeptical army officials of the value of a first-hand look at British procedures for organizing and mobilizing military nurses.[143] She proposed a six-month stay, attached to the office of Ethel Becher, matron-in-chief of Queen Alexandra's Imperial Military Nursing Service (QAIMNS). Becher's second-in-command and principal matron was Maud McCarthy. Both women, whom Macdonald had known in Pretoria in 1900, worked at the War Office in London as part of the office of the Director General, Army Medical Service (DGAMS). This was serious business. And if the timing for her travel could be so arranged, Macdonald might just be in London in time for the coronation of George V in June 1911.[144] Wouldn't that be grand? Meanwhile, her army pay would continue and no doubt would include some expenses for the study tour. For any extras – well, there was always that paternal legacy to draw upon, the third and final instalment of which came to her in March 1911.

Three months later, Macdonald was in London. Thanks to the Canadian high commissioner, Lord Strathcona, she had a grandstand seat on the coronation route and all manner of invitations to garden parties and receptions as part of the Festival of the Empire.[145] As the one Canadian military nurse in attendance, always in uniform – the distinctive new blue one, much nicer than the QAIMNS's grey – Macdonald would have stood out in any crowd, despite her 5 ft. 3 in. height. She was sometimes accompanied by her cousin Mary Chisholm, the motherless daughter of her uncle Joseph, the mayor of Halifax. Eighteen-year-old Mary was in England for a year of schooling, and she and Margaret happily palled around together.[146] At least one of them sent their birth dates to an astrologer for a free test reading. Whether or not Macdonald was interested in astrology is unknown, but she did keep the response with its description of her as cautious, idealistic, observant, knowledge-seeking, and fond of travel – and its offer of lower rates for a "complete life reading" if she would mention the astrologer favourably to her friends.[147]

While she was in Britain, she may have taken her first trip to Scotland and to the Moidart and Strath Glass regions of her ancestry, and it is possible that her mother may have come from Canada to join her.[148] Macdonald's lengthy stay in London would certainly have exposed her to suffrage demonstrations, which were in full force at the time. She may even have noticed the military overtones of the more militant suffragettes. If so, she did not acknowledge any kinship with them, for she came home to declare publicly her intolerance of them.[149] It was probably the tactics and the violent reaction to them that troubled her more than the actual cause. In fact, she would have had much more in common with the suffragists, women (and some men) who were trying to achieve the vote for women by constitutional means. At the same time, she may well have thought that world events overshadowed any demands for women's rights. While she was in London, she became acutely conscious of international tensions over colonial claims by European powers and of the warlike alliances among those powers. She was well aware of the debate firing the Canadian federal election campaign in the summer of 1911 over the role that Canada should play in the naval buildup between Britain and Germany. Being in London made it that much more real. She was at the heart of the empire, and everything about it fascinated her.

Her work was very much part of it. Before visiting all the military hospitals in London and vicinity, Macdonald took her bearings in the medical-military establishment of the city. She reported to the War Office and renewed in person her acquaintance with Maud McCarthy, Ethel Becher, and the director general himself, William Launcelot Gubbins, who had been principal medical officer in Pretoria when she was there. From the three of them she would have gleaned first-hand knowledge of the myriad reforms that had taken place within the British army medical service since the South African War.[150] And as she observed the relationship between McCarthy and Becher, Macdonald may well have spotted similarities to her own connection with Georgina Pope. There was Becher heading the QAIMNS but with the administratively more astute McCarthy nibbling at her heels. Unlike their Canadian counterparts who were stationed at military hospitals, this pair worked at military headquarters with the senior staff of the army medical service. They had some three hundred nurses under their control, albeit scattered in numerous military hospitals where matrons exercised the real supervision.[151] By contrast, the Canadians had at most two nurses under their wings by 1911. The observant Macdonald would have caught any undercurrents between her two British hosts as she did between them and their colonial visitor.[152] She would also have assessed the relationship between the QAIMNS, formed in 1902, the newer Territorial Force Nursing Service organized in 1908, and the recent Voluntary Aid Detachments dating from 1909.

The QAIMNS functioned as a permanent force of military nurses, serving both in Britain and in parts of the empire; it also had a reserve wing for future recruits. The Territorials were designed solely as a reserve force to serve in Britain in times of national emergency. Members of both were professionally trained nurses. From the beginning, the Territorials had a more sophisticated and more successful approach to attracting and promoting its members than the QAIMNS did for its reserve nurses.[153] Whatever rivalry this situation suggested was overshadowed by the development of Voluntary Aid Detachments. These were local groups of untrained volunteers, recruited by the Red Cross and given a few weeks' rudimentary first aid training by the St John Ambulance; they then were to lend a hand in any major medical emergency.[154] Along with her hosts, Macdonald would have understood the dual implication of the VAD system: on the one hand the admirable preparation of large numbers of women (and men too) to help out "in case," and on the other hand the simultaneous threat to the status of professionally trained nurses in the military. None of this in fact played out for another three or four years, and by then the need was so great in Britain and in British military hospitals in France that all hands were welcome. But the visiting Canadian took the wariness home with her: Macdonald determined that the Canadian army's nursing reserve had to be bolstered, and untrained volunteers had to be kept at bay.

Before returning to Canada, she visited all the hospitals staffed by the QAIMNS. Maud McCarthy had previously been matron of two of them and she made arrangements for the visits.[155] In the much more complex military hospitals of Britain, Macdonald noted how army rules – similar in Britain and Canada – were carried out. She observed the hierarchies and interactions among a far more numerous staff than the Canadian military would ever have: medical officers, matrons, nursing sisters, staff nurses, and orderlies. Much of the complexity was still being worked out as the British army absorbed the painful lessons of the South African War. Among these was the need for a greater number of trained nurses. In Britain, military nurses and doctors were in parallel structures of command, the QAIMNS nurses (known as QAS) working for the army but not as an integral part of it. This, combined with the sheer number of British nurses and the Nightingale tradition of having a woman in command, justified a separate female authority structure for the nurses. The only link with the medical structure was the nurses' required obedience to doctors' medical instructions.

Canadian military nurses had this same obligation, of course, but because they were so few and were an integral part of the army, nothing justified a separate authority structure headed by a woman. Only with the large numbers and complex administration of First World War medical services did something like it emerge for Canada's nurses – although never separate from the army – and with Macdonald at the head of it. The situation in Britain in 1911 may indeed have whetted her appetite for administration, and it would have confirmed her sense that she had to work with and through men to advance the cause of military nursing. In this she had one advantage over her British counterparts, which must have struck her forcefully while touring the hospitals. She was an officer in what by then was called the Canadian Army Medical Corps; McCarthy, Becher, and all the others did not have equivalent status.

All of this and more she probably shared with sympathetic shipmates on the return voyage to Canada late in December 1911. She was one of eleven adult "saloon" passengers travelling first class on the *Grampian* out of Liverpool, bound for Halifax. Among the others was John S. Ewart, a prominent Ottawa lawyer and leading exponent of Canadian nationalism. Despite his sixty-two years and Macdonald's thirty-eight (which the ship's purser recorded as thirty-two), Ewart and she had many interests in common.[156] A conversation between the two would have ranged from her imperial experience in South Africa to his arguing Canadian court cases before the Judicial Committee of the Privy Council in London; or from his defence of the Catholic minority in the Manitoba Schools Question in the 1890s to her Catholic family's proximity to Laurier Liberals. She would certainly have quizzed him about the defeat of the Liberals in the federal election she had missed in September. What did he think – Was it the naval question or reciprocity that had undermined the Liberals? Had Henri Bourassa really acted as a spoiler? And what about the raging issue in Britain of votes for women? More than two hundred women had been arrested as a result of the demonstration in Parliament Square on 21 November.[157] In between any such conversations and the Christmas entertainment on board, Macdonald must have planned and perhaps written the report of her study tour. Sometime after her arrival in Canada where, according to the passenger lists, she was headed for Quebec City, she would have submitted it to the Canadian DGMS, Colonel Guy Carleton Jones, and from him it might even have gone as far as the new Conservative minister of the militia, Sam Hughes. But no trace of it exists.

In its place there is only the talk she delivered to the Association of Officers of the Medical Services early in 1913. With its broad and slightly misleading title, "Army Nursing," the speech probably reflects some of her recent English experience. Certainly, as the first such presentation by a woman in the association's six-year history, it reveals her increasing standing in the medical-military community. She urged her listeners to recognize the military nurse as a specialist and spoke of the need to train a larger number of nurses in this specialty. With more nurses trained and ready – albeit in reserve – Canada would be prepared for any military necessity.

Macdonald may have had in mind certain aspects of the British Terri-

Training camp, Petawawa, summer 1914.
Macdonald is the second nurse from the left.

torial Force Nursing Service, but its restriction to home service would not
have appealed to her. What she suggested, in order to increase the numbers of reserve army nurses quickly to about three hundred, was to alter
the existing practice of having nurses go to Halifax for a month's training.
Take the training to them in various cities across the country, she argued.
Spread the lessons out over a longer period so that nurses could take them
while still working at their regular jobs. Open the summer militia training
camps to nurses. Involve the lady superintendents of civilian hospitals.
And interest the country's nursing leaders. Only in these ways, she said,
could anywhere near the needed number be trained. Without some such
action, when the time came, Canada would be caught short. Not perhaps
in numbers – Macdonald acknowledged that all sorts of nurses would
rush to offer their services in time of war – but in quality. She knew from
experience that such women would be militarily untrained and, at worst,
unreliable. Was she thinking of Camp Wikoff in the Spanish-American
War? Or some of the English nurses she had encountered in South Africa?
Or perhaps what she had learned in England in 1911? What she did not

Prewar fun, Petawawa, 1914. Macdonald is the
nurse on the right.

even mention in her speech – probably deliberately – was the likelihood of
war attracting untrained women in a Canadian version of Voluntary Aid
Detachments.[158]

Macdonald's forthrightness charmed her audience, as did her personality. She combined deference and rigour. She played down any personal
credit for the reforms she was suggesting, let alone any ambition associated with them. Instead, she appealed to notions of progress and efficiency,
the good of the medical service as a whole, and the needs of the nation.
She likened the specialized military nurse to the new-style medical officer,
who was now a health and sanitary expert as well as a doctor. And she dis-
played her breadth of military knowledge with references to the war that

was raging in the Balkans; the one flaw in Bulgarian military strategy, she pronounced, was the lack of a plan for nursing the sick and wounded. She ended her speech with a fine rhetorical flourish by proclaiming that the expanded nursing reserve that she was advocating would be "ready for every duty, equipped for every work and equal to every emergency."[159] No wonder the men in the audience were impressed! They thanked her "for her most instructive and entertaining paper" and noted the intense interest of the most important member of the audience, Colonel Guy Carleton Jones. As the head of the Canadian Army Medical Corps, he intended to look into her suggestions carefully, he said.[160]

Jones was true to his word. He had spotted a kindred reform spirit in Macdonald. Ever since his appointment as DGMS late in 1906, a few weeks after Macdonald joined the PAMC, he had been noting her intelligence and abilities. She was a planner and he recognized it. Jones's public appreciation of nursing sisters dated from at least 1907 when he had acknowledged the important role they would play if Canada went to war or rallied to help defend the empire.[161] He was proud of the "increasing and highly technical duties" of his entire medical corps, which included the nurses.[162] By 1910 he was arguing for the presence of nursing sisters at all nine military hospitals in Canada (not just those at Halifax and Quebec) "in order that efficient nursing would be assured."[163] It was he who had given permission for Macdonald's study leave in England, and he was most receptive to the presentation she gave in 1913. Not surprisingly, therefore, within a year she was at the Kingston military hospital teaching nurse candidates for the army reserve; and a few months later she was doing the same at Petawawa (as was a colleague at Niagara) during the summer militia training camps.[164] The numbers of reserve military nurse trainees began climbing.[165]

In August 1914 Jones summoned Macdonald to Ottawa and asked her, over the head of Georgina Pope, to mobilize Canada's nursing sisters. For someone with a yen for wars, she was about to have her fill.

THREE

Matron-in-Chief

The First World War marked a major change in Margaret Macdonald's military career. She stopped nursing and began working principally for and with women. From being one of five nursing sisters in Canada's Permanent Army Medical Corps in 1914 and often the sole nurse at military hospitals in Quebec City and Kingston in the prewar years, she became the matron-in-chief of a cadre of nurses that by 1918 numbered close to three thousand.[1] Along with the new title – a first for Canada – went the military rank of major, the first such designation for a woman in the British Empire. From her base in London during the war years, Macdonald relished the firsts, as well as the challenges, as she organized the staffing and well-being of nurses in Canadian military hospitals in England, France, and the Mediterranean. Thanks to the war she and her nurses jumped the queue into history, if only briefly.

Little of this was foreseeable to Macdonald in August 1914. All she knew was that Canada would be involved and nurses would want to be part of the action. Because of the semi-autonomous status of Canada at the time, the country was constitutionally bound by the British declaration of war on 4 August, though the nature and extent of its participation could be determined by the Canadian government. In fact, there was a rush of popular enthusiasm for the war, fed by family attachments, tradition, the press, and the pulpit, to say nothing of the precedent of the South African War. Because of her experiences, Macdonald had a more informed notion of what war entailed, but she shared the general excitement about what was expected to be a brief European skirmish that would surely be over by Christmas. She knew that nurses across the country would apply in droves. Their profession was the only route for women to go to war, and Macdonald understood the fascination – a fascination that never flagged during the war. Canada never had to appeal for nursing recruits, much less conscript them as it did with young men in 1917. Consequently, Macdonald was able to keep her nursing corps staffed solely by trained nurses.

But she balked when appointed to military headquarters in Ottawa. Presumably, she was not expecting such a summons, for she could not be found for a few days; a camping trip had taken her beyond the reach of urgent telegrams from Ottawa. But Colonel Jones was determined to have her at the head of the nursing service.[2] When she did get to Ottawa, she protested her lack of administrative experience and reminded Jones of Georgina Pope's seniority in Canada's tiny military nursing ranks. Jones reminded *her* of a soldier's duty to obey.[3] He may also have thought, as he stated elsewhere, that seniority did not necessarily mean suitability.[4] In fact, Macdonald's deference may simply have been that of the dutiful daughter who demurs rather than displaying any personal ambition. Even at forty-one, she was mindful of the norms of decorum, especially for women in such a male world as the military. But once reassured, she settled in quickly and lost little time in exercising her newly acquired authority.

Her first task was to sort through the mountain of nursing applications. The original intent was to have nurses assigned to only two of the five hospital units that were to accompany the Canadian Expeditionary Force (CEF): fifty nurses with each of the two general hospitals but none with the two stationary hospitals or the clearing hospital. Macdonald had therefore to select one hundred nurses from the nearly one thousand who had applied by the end of August 1914. She was determined to have only "first grade nurses" and was glad of a "vouched-for list" from the Canadian National Association of Trained Nurses, though few of the more than two hundred names on the list were actually selected.[5] The reason may have been lack of military experience, for the first chosen were all from the Permanent Army Medical Corps or the reserve Army Nursing Service. The route to both these units was through the various military districts across Canada; all applicants were told to follow regular military recruitment procedure and apply first in the military district in which they resided.[6]

Macdonald's eventual list contained names from almost every district, suggesting her awareness of the political need for broad geographical representation among her nurses.[7] They were also to be British subjects (as Canadians were at the time), graduates of a recognized training school, single, in good health, and aged between twenty-one and thirty-eight.[8] Given that few nurses could even enter nursing training in Canada before the age of twenty-one, most of the applicants were considerably older. Macdonald herself was overage, a fact that the authorities chose to ignore – or camouflage (her formal attestation paper for the CEF has her born in 1879 rather than 1873, giving her an "apparent age" of "35 years and 8 months").[9]

In selecting the one hundred nurses, she first chose from the five in the permanent force, three of whom went overseas in 1914; next were nurses from the reserve, those who had at least taken the brief course in military nursing even if they did not have some actual experience. Three of Macdonald's colleagues from South Africa were among the chosen: Marcella Richardson from the permanent force, and Margaret Smith and Amy Scott from the reserve. A fourth South African veteran, Elizabeth Russell, joined later. Altogether, however, the experienced nurses selected made up barely half the required number, so Macdonald relied on her judgment in deciding which of the others were suitable. She interviewed candidates, scrutinized their credentials, and based her choice on family background and personal knowledge to ensure the character and deportment she considered essential. Canadian nursing colleagues working in the United States, such as Ethel Ridley, made the grade. So did acquaintances and even relatives from Pictou County: Margaret (Pearl) Fraser and Harriet Graham from New Glasgow, Myrtle Grattan from Pictou, and Macdonald's orphaned cousin from home, Janet McGregor Macdonald. Daughters of professional soldiers, such as Juliette Pelletier, also received the coveted telegram of acceptance. Missing from the initial list was Georgina Pope. She was even older than Macdonald, and it would have been hard to camouflage her fifty-two years. But she did go overseas in 1917, so there must have been reasons other than age, and possibly related to Macdonald's own appointment, for leaving her behind in 1914.[10] Similar hints of delicate manoeuvring on Macdonald's part appear in her sidelining to non-nursing positions the few women without nursing training who were imposed upon her by the minister of the militia.[11] Despite such obstacles, by the middle of September she had her hundred nursing sisters.

While at military headquarters in Ottawa, Macdonald had numerous other practical matters to attend to. Uniforms had to be made quickly for one hundred women, whose sizes and shapes were unknown until they responded to the mobilization order of 16 September. Each nurse was to have a full-dress uniform and four working dresses. The nurses needed to know precisely what they could take with them, so Macdonald had to devise lists of clothing and gear. She also had to adjust army regulations designed for men: the contents of a camp kit, the amount of personal luggage, banking arrangements, provision for leave; and she had to combine army rules and nursing practice into enforceable "instructions," particularly for the neophytes. For all of this, Macdonald drew on British precedent, much of which she had learned in England in 1911, and on the minimal planning the Canadian military had been able to do in the prewar years. She enjoyed the entire process and was quite prepared to stay in Ottawa doing the same type of thing throughout the war as the DGMS had originally intended for her. But she must have been thrilled when Colonel Jones changed his mind and added her name to those selected for overseas service.[12]

She therefore moved to Valcartier military camp near Quebec City in preparation for the nurses' departure with the first contingent of Canadian soldiers. In the midst of the bustle – and considerable confusion – of the military camp as more than thirty-thousand soldiers gathered there in late September, Macdonald's task was relatively simple. Now officially appointed matron, she had to arrange for the arrival of her nurses as of 23 September and for their housing somewhere in the city in anticipation of an as yet unknown sailing date; she had to ensure their equipment, and she had to organize all the last-minute formalities for them: medical examinations, vaccinations for smallpox, inoculations against typhoid, and forms of all sorts to be completed in triplicate.[13] Unintentionally, she also exposed her nurses to their first test of endurance. Their accommodation in Quebec City was awful, and for some of the nurses it turned out to be the worst of all their war experiences.[14] The old immigration hospital with its vast draughty wards, two- and three-tiered wire bunks without bedding was the best that could be found for one hundred women in a town abuzz with military preparations. The nurses made do for a week, using newspapers as mattresses and their cloaks for cover, and they seem to have passed Macdonald's test by taking it all in good-humoured stride.[15] Then, to the cheers of the more than one thousand soldiers already on the ship, they boarded the *Franconia*, bound for England. Macdonald was in charge with the assistance of Ethel Ridley.[16] Tentative plans for overseas postings designated Macdonald as matron of No. 1 Canadian General Hospital and Ridley as matron of No. 2, the nurses being divided between the two. The precise location of either hospital had not yet been determined.

Aboard the *Franconia*, Macdonald could watch her nurses much more closely. The trip took twice as long as a normal transatlantic passage because the ship, which left Quebec on 1 October, joined thirty-three other troopships at Gaspé and crossed the ocean in convoy, escorted by British cruisers and a battleship. The two-week voyage, with its precautions, rumours, and the very real danger of submarines, emphasized the exceptional turn of events and the immensity of the whole undertaking. In such a setting, Macdonald had ample time to observe the behaviour of her charges and assess their characters. She would make use of this knowledge in future postings for these nurses. In the meantime, she kept them more seriously occupied than she had been on the *Laurentian*, back in 1900, when heading for South Africa. She organized formal lectures on army nursing, noting its difference from civilian practice, and the discipline and obligations incumbent on women tending soldiers. She prevailed upon the officers on board to teach her newcomers the basics of military procedure, army hospital organization, and the collection of wounded from the battlefield. In short, she tailored the prewar training courses given in Halifax and Kingston to the needs of nurses on active duty in the Canadian Army Medical Corps (CAMC). She also insisted on formal drill and organized gymnasium sessions for the nurses. As recreation, they were expected to participate in the "music, song and dance" that were part of any ocean voyage.[17] If anything untoward occurred, as one gossipy officer from another ship intimated, Macdonald left no record of it.[18] Throughout the war, her own personal combination of playfulness, propriety, and duty became policy for the Canadian nurses.

The voyage thus allowed Macdonald to practise and ponder on the leadership of women. In the late nineteenth and early twentieth centuries there was a vast array of volunteer organizations headed by women. Each one was devoted to a particular social cause and each honed the political, organizational, and leadership skills of women. But Macdonald had left Canada for nursing training just when the National Council of Women was being created, and she returned only as its Catholic, and French-speaking affiliates were creating their own federation; so her models for the immediate task at hand – guiding one hundred nurses into war – were closer to her personal and professional experience. Her mother had certainly been an influence – juggling service to the family and community, offering hospitality to visitor and stranger alike, and nurturing ambition, initiative, and humour in her six daughters. Macdonald's schooling provided another kind of maternal example: the mothers superior at Stella Maris and Mount St Vincent were strict disciplinarians, expecting both the students and the teaching nuns to fit well into a hierarchy of obedience and seriousness. Combined with this, particularly at the Mount, was the tradition of independence from the bishop, of standing up to male authority. The same forcefulness appeared in the superintendent of Macdonald's nursing school in New York. Louise Darche had had to mould young women from all over North America into a coherent unit, proud of their professionalism, sensitive to their patients, obedient to senior nurses, subordinate to doctors, and sufficiently independent to earn their own living as private-duty nurses.

Those who then found their way into military nursing encountered a fourth model of women leading women. While Macdonald was in South Africa, Georgina Pope was the example among the few Canadian nurses, just as Sidney Browne, Maud McCarthy, and Ethel Becher were among the more numerous British nurses. They all worked within an army structure based on discipline, obedience, and rules and regulations that facilitated their own authority. Years later, Macdonald attributed to Pope qualities that she herself came to display during the First World War: "Splendid organizing ability," a "charming personality and ready wit," generosity, efficiency, and, "when occasion demanded," sternness.[19] In fact, all her models were variations on a maternal figure; all the settings – whether family, convent, nursing school, or army – were similar in their authoritarian structure, a structure rendered companionable by the very people within them. Macdonald may not have perfected her own leadership style in two weeks at sea, but she had all the material from which to draw.

She and her hundred nursing sisters arrived in England in mid-October to all manner of greetings. As the ships from Canada pulled into Plymouth harbour, a great roar of welcome reverberated around the shore. Friendly faces, old and new, shone from dockside or came aboard. Among the old friends, Macdonald spotted John McCrae, already disembarked from the *Saxonia*, sporting "the uniform he had worn in South Africa in 1900" and grinning up at the nurses on the *Franconia* with his "always humourous" eyes.[20] Now Major McCrae, second-in-command and surgeon to the 1st Brigade, Canadian Field Artillery, he and Macdonald had probably run into each other at Valcartier, for they were in camp at the same time.[21] In early August he had told his brother, "It will be a terrible war, and somebody's finish when all is said and done,"[22] but for the moment, in the general excitement, such sombre thoughts were put aside as new faces crowded around the nurses. Among them was a titled man with an invitation from St Thomas' Hospital to house the nurses in London while they awaited military orders. Macdonald thought she caught a look of relief on

Colonel Jones's face: one less worry now that the hundred women were placed.[23] On the face of another newcomer, Macdonald gauged a friend for life: she and Nancy Astor, wife of the local member of parliament, took to each other and developed a fine friendship over the next few years. She and her nurses could not accept Astor's offer of lunch, tea, and strawberries and a tour in the surrounding countryside, but later they were able to enjoy Astor hospitality at the family estate at Cliveden, a short train ride west of London, where the Astors gave land and buildings for a Canadian Red Cross hospital staffed by the CAMC. On that first encounter in Plymouth, however, Astor contented herself with a gift of vast pans of Devonshire cream (which had been prepared for the aborted tea party) so that the nurses could enjoy it on the train journey to London. Some of them may have had as much enjoyment from seeing Colonel Jones accidentally step into one of the pans.[24]

During the first few days of their stay at St Thomas', Macdonald and her nurses were justified in thinking that they had come to a grand social event rather than a war. The hospital was superbly located in central London, just across the Thames River from the Houses of Parliament. Macdonald had been there before, but it was new to most of her awestruck nurses as they walked in the footsteps of Florence Nightingale, through corridors and wards designed by her, and through the Nightingale training school that had been the model for their own, whether in Canada or the United States. Before they could stop pinching themselves – "But for her we wouldn't be here" – they were caught up in a whirlwind of sightseeing, theatre parties, receptions, and teas. They received invitations to tour the grounds of Buckingham Palace, to visit Windsor Castle, to be guests of the Ladies' Empire Club.[25] With such head-turning activity, it is perhaps not surprising that their only military-related activity in the first few days in London seems to have been the acquisition of more suitable hats for their dress uniform.[26]

But soon they all began to chafe. They had come to work not to play. Since some of them had never been inside a military hospital, Macdonald had small groups of nurses dispatched to the British military hospital at Millbank in southwest London for two hours a day.[27] This still left a lot of time for London attractions, but at least they were getting a sense of their working environment – and also of what was in store, as they solemnly pondered the growing casualty lists in the daily press. While in London, they were also absorbing the soldiers' dawning lesson that much of army life consists of waiting. In the nurses' case, they were awaiting orders for the two general hospitals that had been so sketchily organized aboard the

Franconia. No. 1 Canadian General Hospital, without nurses, had gone to Salisbury Plain with the Canadian soldiers; No. 2 had no definite posting for months.

Macdonald used this time in London to renew her contacts with acquaintances in British military nursing circles. Some of them dated from South Africa, others from her study tour in England three years earlier. These women were now shifting into position as the general war organization took shape. Maud McCarthy, who had opened doors for Macdonald in 1911, had been slated as of March 1914 to succeed Ethel Becher in September as matron-in-chief of Queen Alexandra's Imperial Military Nursing Service. But with the outbreak of war it was decided not to make the change, and McCarthy was sent to France as principal matron, with the rank if not actual title of acting matron-in-chief, in charge of all nurses attached to the British Expeditionary Force (BEF).[28] Meanwhile, in England, Sidney Browne, another nursing leader whom Macdonald knew, had become matron-in-chief of the Territorial Force Nursing Service, the reserve force initially intended for service only in Britain.

As Macdonald observed all this, she must have wondered how and where the Canadian nurses would be fitted into these structures. Were they to remain as a Canadian unit serving Canadian soldiers in Canadian hospitals? Or would they be broken up to reinforce British nursing units, as some Canadian military officials were beginning to suspect was the plan for their soldiers? And who would command them? A British lieutenant general had been in charge of the soldiers since their arrival in England, and they were to be part of the BEF when they crossed to France. The medical corps, as a unit of the Canadian Expeditionary Force, would follow suit, leaving an unanswered question of the relationship in London between Colonel Jones, Director of Medical Services (DMS) and head of the Canadian medical corps, and Sir Alfred Keogh, the British Director General, Army Medical Services (DGAMS) at the War Office. During Macdonald's first weeks in London, as she assessed the situation in light of the press coverage of a war turning very grim indeed – and therefore the likelihood of more nurses being needed from Canada – she must have determined that an overall organizing role was needed. If the British nurses had in effect three matrons-in-chief, two in the same service, albeit with different titles, surely the Canadians deserved at least one. And she should be that one, as she recommended to Colonel Jones.

Macdonald's recollection of this recommendation and the actual timing of it differ. In an account she wrote in the early 1920s, she left the impression that it was only towards the end of November after her nurses had dispersed to various postings that she proposed her nomination as matron-in-chief. In fact, the proposal must have been made at the beginning of November, for the official announcement of her promotion, with its accompanying rank of major, is dated 4 November 1914.[29] So the postings of her nurses, all of which occur after that date, would have been some of her first decisions as matron-in-chief. As of 6 November, she assigned some nurses for temporary duty with two London military hospitals. The same day, she sent her assistant Ethel Ridley to Boulogne with thirty-four nurses to staff No. 2 Canadian Stationary Hospital, the first Canadian medical unit in France. The next day, twenty other Canadian nurses left London to work temporarily in British hospitals in France. On 8 November two nurses went to Salisbury to tend the first of many sick Canadian soldiers, and a day later No. 1 Canadian General Hospital actually opened at Bulford, just north of Salisbury, with the tiny staff of an acting matron and nine nurses. They were joined ten days later by the nurses from the two London hospitals. By 23 November, the remaining Canadian nurses were on duty at No. 1 Canadian Stationary Hospital in Hampstead, a northern suburb of London.[30] Throughout most of November, therefore, Macdonald was fully occupied as matron-in-chief. Only in recollection did she place at the end of the month the realization that "some one would have to share with the DMS direct responsibility for the Nursing Service."[31] Throughout the war she always exercised this responsibility in the name of the DMS, in proper army fashion, but in fact she had claimed it as her own.

This meant that during the war she was never on active service as the nursing head of a military hospital. Instead, she remained close to the centre of power in London, one of her favourite cities. At the very beginning, she was the only Canadian medical authority in London, since Jones was in camp with the soldiers on Salisbury Plain before he established his official headquarters in London. Presumably, if Macdonald had wanted to be in France, it would have been arranged. But who, then, would oversee the potentially growing number of Canadian nurses? Who would shape them into a distinctive and perhaps lasting part of the Canadian military? As one of the two first nurses in the Canadian army, Macdonald imagined many more to come. She was beginning to feel the attraction of shaping events, taking advantage of circumstance to enlarge the place of women in a man's world.

By November 1914, it was clear that she would have time to do so. The war that everyone had expected to be over by Christmas was settling down into a long winter's nightmare. Being in London allowed her some

Matron-in-Chief

control of events, even if she was not personally experiencing the night-mare. If she had been in France she would probably have had to relinquish her newly acquired status as matron-in-chief. The Canadian nurses there were part of the BEF, and although they were in Canadian hospitals staffed and financed by the CAMC, they came under the overall nursing authority of Maud McCarthy. At most, Macdonald could have been something like "principal matron, Canadians." But the tiny number of Canadian nurses in France in late 1914 hardly warranted this, and in fact no one thought of such a position until 1917. By staying in England, Macdonald maintained control over those Canadian nurses – frequently more than half the total – who were posted to the growing number of Canadian hospitals in Britain. Then, too, there was the question of military propriety: Should Macdonald, as a major in the Canadian Army Medical Corps, be subordinate to someone who was not even an officer in the British forces?[32] Whatever the reasons, Macdonald settled into an office job in London, and except for inspection tours of Canadian hospitals in France and the occasional leave, she stayed there for five years.

Office work was new to her. She was of course familiar with the daily or nightly reports required of nurses in charge of wards. And she had been acquainting herself with army procedures since 1906. She had studied British nursing administration in 1911 and had mobilized, equipped, and deployed nurses from offices in Ottawa, Valcartier, and London in the late summer and early fall of 1914. But now she had to establish a semiperma-nent base in London, staff it with competent people, develop an office rou-tine in congenial rapport with the male staff officers of the CAMC, and find her way through the intricate bureaucratic maze that led to the British War Office – all in order to oversee the work and well-being of her nurses and their reinforcements from Canada. It was no small task, but one that Macdonald seems to have mastered so completely by 1918 that her broth-er could write home, "Her Department is so well organized and running so smoothly that there is not so much work as one would think."[33]

Getting to that point, however, was easier said than done. Army struc-tures had her office reporting to the office of the DMS; it therefore fol-lowed the vicissitudes of the more senior post. Once Colonel Jones moved to London from Salisbury, the medical service was always located in cen-tral London, but it changed address three times to accommodate a grow-ing staff, so Macdonald experienced all the disruptions of moving from 36 Victoria Street to 86 the Strand and then to Pembroke House at 133 Oxford Street. The larger staff meant that her own four-to-six-person office became proportionally smaller over the years. But she always had a

"Macdonald settled into an office job in London"

good working relationship with the DMS – her "little office in the Strand" was right across the hall from his. Jones appears to have given her carte blanche in the direction of her nurses, though she kept him well informed. She returned the confidence by being "one of his 'right hand men'" at CAMC headquarters in London.[34]

This close connection came to an end, however, when Jones fell victim to the politically instigated Bruce Inquiry into the organization of Canada's medical services in the late summer and fall of 1916. Colonel Herbert Bruce, a surgeon from Toronto, was a friend of the irascible minister of the militia, Sam Hughes, who appointed him to investigate the workings of the CAMC without so much as a by-your-leave to Jones. Bruce's report found fault with just about everything, from costs to the treatment of patients, location of hospitals, and deployment of personnel. In spite of Jones's cogent reply to the report – penned hurriedly in the five days he was allowed – the outcome was the replacement of Jones by Bruce. During his two months on the job, Bruce managed to create "the worst kind of a muddle" and was dismissed at the end of 1916, his report having been severely criticized by a board of inquiry.[35] But the reinstatement of Jones lasted only six weeks, after which he was shuffled off to Canada, and Macdonald found herself by mid-February 1917 with yet another superior officer, Gilbert Lafayette Foster.

Only one paragraph of the Bruce Inquiry mentioned nurses, part of Bruce's criticism that CAMC personnel were "not being used to best advantage."[36] But had Bruce lasted as DMS, the post of matron-in-chief itself might well have disappeared into that of an "assistant director medical services, personnel and nursing."[37] Macdonald did not comment on that possibility, but so appalled was she at the treatment of Jones throughout the whole episode that she applied for a transfer to nursing in the field.[38] In fact, what she called "underhand intrigue" and "insupportable tyranny" had her toying with resigning altogether "from an organization capable of so gross an injustice as meted out to General Jones."[39] While harbouring these thoughts, she still had to work on a daily basis with changing directors and in the midst of swirling rumour and general confusion. Things settled down in February 1917 when Foster was appointed surgeon general and DMS to clear the air and the mess. Whether Macdonald enjoyed the same easy rapport with Foster that she had had with Jones is unclear. But her growing reputation for tact and diplomacy would certainly have been put to the test.

Macdonald's staff came and went during the war. She and a senior assistant and two stenographers appear to have been the core staff. Of these four, only Macdonald and one locally hired stenographer, Jessie Donovan, remained the entire time. The other stenographer, Torontonian Mary Gladys Coxall, interrupted her five years in Macdonald's office with a year in the Mediterranean in the employ of one of the Canadian hospitals there. The senior assistant, who had the rank of matron, acted in Macdonald's name when she was absent. Three different women held this position for varying periods during the war. The most long-lasting of them, and presumably the most capable and compatible, was Mary Olive Boulter, whose time with Macdonald, from May 1915 to January 1918, was ended by illness and was interrupted by leave to Canada in late 1916. Macdonald's appreciation of Boulter remained so strong that in her will she left her black diamond ring "to my friend of the first great war."[40]

As of the fall of 1916, five nursing sisters had varying terms of replacement duty in Macdonald's office, most of them sequentially but sometimes overlapping for a few months. One in particular impressed her – Mildred

Forbes, whom she was clearly preparing for more senior administrative work. Forbes's talents were exceptional, and from the time of her arrival in October 1916, Macdonald wanted to keep her until the end of the war. But she understood the younger woman's desire for more active nursing duty and therefore arranged a plum job for her in mid-1917 as acting matron of a casualty clearing station. Forbes's replacement, Irene Cains, did stay until after the end of the war. How Macdonald coped with all the comings and goings is unknown, but judging from the increasing number of Boulter, Forbes, and Cains signatures on the routine correspondence from her office, she trusted her subordinates and let them get on with the job.[41]

Ostensibly, the job was easy enough. Macdonald had to ensure a sufficient number of nursing sisters for Canada's military hospitals and attend to their welfare. As their numbers increased, she had to shape them into a disciplined corps of enterprising, hard-working, cheerful, and healthy nurses. But it had never been done before. Macdonald may have seen her task as gathering them all "into the ranks of the elect of war," but these grandiose sentiments, which she expressed after the war,[42] did not get daily decisions made or action taken. In fact, she began with a series of very mundane activities. In a small notebook that she kept at the beginning of the war, she recorded an assortment of details: telegrams sent and the cost thereof; the names of nurses leaving on "Saturday"; concerns for their kit and just where they would join the receiving unit; the names and locations of British hospitals and of her Australian, New Zealand, and South African counterparts; the names and locations of people asking about job possibilities or about transfers; and the characteristics – good and bad – of some of her nurses. She even recorded small out-of-pocket expenses such as the cost of a taxi or the transfer of luggage. This kind of amateur record keeping gave way to something more professional once she had an office and staff, and the notebook then served as a depository for press clippings from daily papers and nursing journals. Those entries also petered out by late 1916, which suggests that any idea she had of keeping a wartime scrapbook had to be set aside as her attention centred on the recruiting and organization of her "elect."[43]

Recruiting nurses for service in the CAMC was never a problem, although Macdonald did not always control the process. In London, she had to make a case to the DMS for the need for reinforcements, and he passed the request on to headquarters in Ottawa.[44] She then had to rely on male officers in the military districts across Canada to do the initial screening of candidates for the numbers approved. Candidates were never lacking (two thousand applied for seventy-five positions in January 1915 alone),[45] and few were above seeking some quick access to the elect. Katherine Wilson relied on a relative in the office of the minister of militia to let her know when another contingent of nurses might be sent. He complied and even added, quite improperly, "Do you wish to go?" Wilson telegraphed acceptance and went.[46] On her way she was met in Ottawa by a senior army nurse "friendly enough in a very official way," who gave her the instructions about uniform and kit that Macdonald had worked out just a few months earlier.[47] That senior nurse then arranged for the new recruits to get to Halifax by train and then across the Atlantic under the watchful eye of yet another matron. Only when Macdonald met them on their arrival in London did she get her first look at her new charges.[48] Did they appear as woebegone as another group of new recruits whom Macdonald met later and immediately shipped off "to have our dresses and coats shortened and our hats (so unbecoming) reblocked."[49]

Macdonald may have been out of town when the nursing recruits of the first university-based hospital arrived in London in mid-May 1915, for she seems not to have greeted the nurses of No. 3 Canadian General Hospital (McGill). In this case, the university had chosen its own nurses, following Macdonald's guidelines about age and training, but entrusting the selection to the civilian lady superintendents of the nursing schools of the Montreal General Hospital and Royal Victoria Hospital. Each chose thirty-five of its best graduates but then placed them immediately under the direction of a CAMC matron, Katherine MacLatchy, who just happened to be a niece of the Canadian prime minister, Robert Borden.[50] Eventually there were eight such units raised by Canadian universities, and all followed the McGill pattern. When the University of Toronto's overseas unit, No. 4 Canadian General Hospital, was established shortly after McGill's, it too chose graduates from its own nursing school. One Toronto nurse complained to her chief surgeon about being turned down because of her American training. The surgeon, Herbert Bruce, passed the complaint on to Sam Hughes and the nurse was accepted.[51] In London, Macdonald was probably unaware of this specific case, but from her own experience with Hughes, she would not have been surprised. Still, it was well into 1917 before the need for direct coordination between her office in London and military authorities in Ottawa was acknowledged with the appointment of one of Macdonald's overseas colleagues to the senior nursing post in Canada.

Meanwhile in England, Macdonald had to cope with local would-be recruits. A number of Canadian nurses had come to England on their own, hoping to join the CAMC. Even more had signed up from Canada with both the regular and reserve force of Queen Alexandra's Imperial

Military Nursing Service (QAIMNS) and expected to be able to transfer easily to the CAMC. Still other Canadians took the Red Cross or St John Ambulance route in the hope of getting overseas quickly and, once there, of convincing Macdonald to take them on. Canadian nurses were also serving with hospital units formed and staffed by Americans and on the British lines of communication in France more than two years before the United States joined the war. They too looked to Macdonald for work at the end of their contracts. If they did not already know, all these Canadian nurses soon learned that the pay was better and the contracts longer in the CAMC. So Macdonald was plagued with requests from nurses and their influential friends. One woman involved her member of parliament as well as the Canadian high commissioner in London. Another got Sir William Osler in on the act, hoping that his prominence as a Canadian physician with a professorship at Oxford and a consultancy to the CAMC would help her case.

All these applicants ran into Macdonald's insistence on propriety and formality (although she was not beyond a bit of favouritism herself). She stipulated that they must complete their existing contracts before she would even consider a transfer.[52] She then ensured that they were "socially and professionally eligible" by checking up on them with their matron.[53] She suspected that misinformed army personnel at the military district level in Canada may have led the women to believe that they could transfer at any time to the CAMC. Indeed, some of the Canadians with the QAIMNS seemed unaware that they were under contract to the War Office rather than to the CAMC.[54] The whole question of transfers was muddied even more when Herbert Bruce appeared on the scene in the fall of 1916. He thought there should be no appointments at all from these overseas sources, given the lengthy waiting lists in Canada. Macdonald enforced this temporary policy, even to using some of Bruce's words in her rationale: "Fresh nurses" from Canada should have preference over "those who may have become more or less tired out" from service overseas.[55] She wisely left out his additional word "stale," but her phrase nonetheless reverberated and Macdonald must have regretted it. One pert newcomer insisted that she was not the least "tired out" after a month with the QAIMNS. Could she not transfer forthwith to the CAMC?[56] As soon as Bruce was gone, Macdonald reverted to her earlier approach. As long as a nurse honoured her initial contract with another nursing service, Macdonald would consider appointment to the CAMC.

There was one type of "nurse" that Macdonald did not want. Women without professional nursing training were not welcome among her "elect." They existed all over Britain in the Voluntary Aid Detachments that had been established long before the war as part of the planning for emergencies. So acute was the British wartime need, however, that professional nurses could not meet it and VADs, as the individuals came to be known, found their way into military hospitals as helpers of all kinds. The more gifted among them actually took on some nursing duties. Macdonald did not want such people in the Canadian military hospitals and throughout the war resisted any attempts to introduce them. She was fortunate in always having a supply of professional nurses willing and anxious to come from Canada, but her resistance was more than a question of numbers. She knew of the British wartime industrial practice of "dilution," the breaking down of skilled work into simple repetitive actions that could be performed by anyone (even women) with minimal training; the analogy to nursing could easily be made. As someone forging a place for professional nurses in the military and thus part of a broader contemporary movement for the professionalization of nurses, Macdonald did not want any watering down of the CAMC nursing ranks. If any woman could nurse just because of her femaleness, what was the point of all that civilian and military training for professional nurses? If any woman could nurse, why bother with the status, rank, and pay of a Canadian military nurse? To these questions Macdonald added the crucial one of discipline. She could count on the self-discipline of her trained nurses; obedience to army regulations was easy for them. She did not have the same certainty about VADs and was not about to risk the reputation of her nursing service by putting them to the test.

So the only way Canadian VADs (part of an organization begun in 1914 and intended initially for service solely in Canada) could get overseas, as some did in the fall of 1916, was to work in British hospitals. Macdonald had effectively shut them out. She would not budge even when Colonel Bruce was at the helm and wanted the cheaper VADs to be taken on. She would not budge when VADs appeared with the Red Cross on the fringes of Canadian hospitals to assist in recreational work with patients (she had to remind one matron that such women were not to be assigned nursing duties). And she would not budge when VADs began appearing in the specialized role of masseuses; she insisted that her professional nurses be trained as masseuses and assigned to the new rehabilitation function.[57] During the entire war, Macdonald fiercely guarded the professional integrity of her nurses.

She also kept poachers at bay. Even in slack times, she would not have her nurses lured away into non-military nursing. No, she said, a nurse was not available to assist with the birth of a grandchild. The very thought of it would have every Canadian officer's wife in England expecting such service during her confinement. And no, the CAMC did not have a maternity ward in its hospitals. No again, a CAMC nurse could not spend a month at a country home as a masseuse even if – perhaps especially if – Canadian officers visited that home. And no yet again, nurses travelling to Canada were not free to take on nursemaid duties for families crossing the Atlantic. Politely but firmly, Macdonald refused to have her military nurses undertake the most common of nursing tasks. In her desire to uphold the specialized nature of military nursing, she was quite willing to break ranks with gendered expectations of and for women.[58]

While she shaped and protected the tight parameters of her expanding corps of nurses, Macdonald had simultaneously to see to their deployment. The major task of her office in London was thus to direct all the comings and goings of the nursing sisters. The numbers were never stable, for reinforcements were constantly arriving from Canada and they all had to be assigned where the need was greatest. Macdonald had the initiative and the delegated authority to place nurses in different hospitals. Most of her official correspondence, increasingly standardized over the war years, concerns these placements, which were recommended to the DMS or carried out in his name. A typical letter of posting would read: "I have the honour, by direction, to inform you that you have been posted ..." and would be signed by Macdonald "for Surgeon-General DMS Canadian Contingents."[59] In the early years of the war, she assigned nurses to Canadian hospitals in England, or occasionally to a British hospital, in order to assess their skill and stamina, and their adaptation to military routine, before posting some of them to France.[60] Later, as the number of Canadian hospitals in England grew – to sixteen active-treatment units by 1918, mostly but not all in the southeastern part of the country, with some of them specializing in certain kinds of war wounds – she was able to distribute nursing personnel according to the knowledge, interest, or benefit the nurse would derive from a particular experience.[61] She was also watchful for light-duty postings – nearly always in England – for nurses who had already seen active service on the Continent or in the Mediterranean and required some respite.

Postings to and within France were administratively more complex. Macdonald's nurses there were attached to three different types of Canadian hospitals, the number of which varied from one to seventeen over the war years. Mostly clustered around Boulogne in the northeastern Pas de Calais region of France, the hospitals were on the British lines of communication and, along with British hospitals in the same vicinity, cared for any ill or wounded allied soldiers who came down those lines from the fighting. The patients were never solely Canadians. Seventy nurses, sometimes as many as one hundred (a number that was officially established in 1917), staffed the general hospitals, which were fixed units situated thirty or forty miles from the front. The smaller stationary hospitals were intended, inspite of their name, to be more mobile, and each had about thirty nurses (raised to forty in 1917). The casualty clearing stations were even smaller units in closer proximity to the troops, two or three miles from the trenches; as their purpose changed from dispersing the wounded towards hospitals farther back to being miniature hospitals themselves, their nursing staff expanded from fewer than a dozen nurses to twenty-five in 1917.

All the Canadian nurses in France were part of the British Expeditionary Force, so their movements had to be sanctioned, and were sometimes initiated, by British authorities. Over the war years, this meant increasingly complex layers of bureaucracy for Macdonald, as requests to post or transfer nurses had to go up, down, and across British and Canadian administrative channels. Initially, the path was relatively simple, from her office to that of the DMS and from there to the DGAMS at the War Office. Later, when the Canadians finally appointed an adjutant general, he became the intermediary to the War Office. Over in France, requests for more nurses had to go up or down the British chain of command there before crossing the Channel to the War Office and being sent on to the Canadian DMS. If, for example, nursing numbers were to go above an existing total (the "establishment") of a given hospital – something that could happen during a "rush" of casualties – a request had to come initially from the officer commanding that unit and proceed up the British medical hierarchy in France, over to the War Office in London, and back down the British and Canadian hierarchies to reach Macdonald's desk.[62] The complexities were such that even as late as the summer of 1917 Macdonald was having to remind a seasoned matron in France of the "proper channels" that had to be followed for the movement of nurses.[63]

Along with Macdonald, two other matrons-in-chief were part of these channels. At the War Office in London, Ethel Becher, head of the QAIMNS, likely saw the Canadian nursing requests and approved them on behalf of the British DGAMS, while avoiding any implication that the Canadian matron-in-chief was subordinate to her. Becher also had to keep an eye out for Maud McCarthy, her counterpart in France, who, as nursing head of the British Expeditionary Force, controlled all the nurses in France, whether they were British or colonial. Except for the occasional borrowing by the British, however, the Canadian nursing sisters were always in Canadian hospitals that had a Canadian military doctor as the commanding officer. In theory, therefore, Macdonald ought to have been able to move her nurses as freely among those units as she could in England. She may have tried to do so in the first six months or so of Canadian hospital presence in France, for in July 1915 McCarthy had to tell her to send any changes affecting Canadian nursing staff to the DMS on the lines of communication, the office to which McCarthy herself was attached.[64] Whether this was a question of authority or efficiency is not entirely clear. By 1917, however, and perhaps earlier, authority was the issue, and Macdonald was having to request approval from McCarthy for a transfer of nurses between two Canadian hospitals in France.[65]

On occasion, McCarthy acted solely on her own, moving some Canadians from hospitals farther back to the Canadian casualty clearing stations on the Belgian border, because the situation at the front required extra nurses. She then merely informed Macdonald. When a permanent increase in nursing numbers at a given Canadian unit was necessary, however, McCarthy "applied" to Macdonald to effect it.[66] The two eventually devised a system, seemingly at McCarthy's request, whereby Macdonald provided her with a list of Canadian nurses suitable for the grim work at the clearing stations. McCarthy would then select from the list. At the same time, she requested authority from Macdonald to remove nurses who proved unsuitable. Even with the two in agreement, this mini-system itself had to obtain the approval of both British and Canadian authorities.[67]

In her final report at the end of the war, the ever-diplomatic McCarthy made no reference at all to transfers within France. Rather, she spoke only of the movement of Canadian nurses to and from France. For them she claimed to have received "instructions" from Canadian headquarters, London, and to have carried them out "with as little delay as possible."[68] Be that as it may, moving nurses to France involved even more steps than orders or advice from London. Once Macdonald had in place all the multiple authorities for any move, she issued travel warrants from her office to authorize and pay for the nurses' passage. The women then awaited orders from a British embarkation officer, who assigned them to a particular cross-Channel sailing, usually from Folkestone to Boulogne. In Boulogne, a member of the British nursing reserve assisted them, as necessary, with local accommodation and their onward journey. During the war Macdonald made the trip herself eleven times, so she knew the route and the people involved and always kept close track of her nurses. She sent a list ahead of them to their posting, and she expected quick confirmation of their arrival.

Once posted, whether in France or England, the nurses rarely stayed put. Macdonald watched for compatibility, initiative, and interest, and moved people about accordingly. She responded to nurses' pleas to be elsewhere, particularly their requests to go to France and especially to casualty clearing stations. "They all want to get to France,"[69] Macdonald knew, and she tried to rotate staff so that as many as possible might have a chance to go, sending the best of them "up the line," closer to the fighting. The requests from Canadian nurses in England for postings to France were so numerous that a format for them was finally devised. A single piece of paper went from the nurse to her matron stating, for example, "I have the honour to make application for service in France. I arrived in England in July 1916 and have not yet [September 1917] been overseas." The matron, in passing the request to the commanding officer of the hospital, added her words to the same piece of paper: "Passed to you, please. Recommended." He in turn sent the form to Macdonald: "Forwarded herewith, please. Recommended."[70] She thus had a growing list of requests to consider and made the changes when possible and if appropriate. Nurses therefore rarely knew they were moving until she "drop[ped] a bomb in the shape of a list of transfers, into the midst of a unit."[71] In the ensuing hubbub, nurses would note a request granted, a chum being sent to the same place, a prize posting implying approval, or a shift to a quieter area, suggesting that even the matron-in-chief had noticed one's fatigue.

Macdonald was well aware of the beneficial effects of change: "The Sisters work much more happily and satisfactorily."[72] They also did so when near friends or family, something Macdonald also tried to facilitate in the multiple moves of her nurses.[73] Although she justified many of the moves on the professional grounds that nurses should experience the range of army medical service,[74] she knew the value of friend and kin in keeping the nurses of a unit working well together. Many of her nurses had brothers in the Canadian Expeditionary Force, and she arranged postings so that siblings could have an easier opportunity to see each other.[75] When weariness or worse overtook her nurses, Macdonald was quick to move them elsewhere. She transferred a surgical nurse who had lost her nerve in France to a medical ward in England.[76] She had sick nurses moved from their working units and cared for, and if the situation warranted it they were brought back to England to convalesce. The less serious cases, those suffering stress after duty in a casualty clearing station, for example, were sent to one of the Canadian Forestry Corps hospitals "in quiet remote places" of

France, where the work was "not so strenuous."[77] As of mid-1916, she was able to assign some nurses "in need of a complete change" to transport duty on ships bound for Canada with invalided soldiers.[78] All these postings kept Canada's nursing sisters constantly on the move.

Sometimes, when their hospital was assigned a new location, the nurses moved as a unit. Macdonald had no say in these decisions, but she always had to be ready with temporary placements for the nurses during a protracted move. Some hospitals took considerable time just to be established, let alone located and equipped. Months could pass between the need for, or offer of, a hospital and its actual functioning. In the interim, Macdonald had to keep the nurses occupied. Even when established, the large general hospitals did not always stay in one place. Nos. 1 and 3 Canadian General Hospitals both moved twice in their first year of existence, and during the moves Macdonald posted the nurses elsewhere.[79] She had to do the same with the smaller Canadian stationary hospitals, which moved even more often. No. 1, for example, moved from England to Wimereux in France, then to Lemnos and then Salonika in the Mediterranean, and finally back to England, all in the space of two years, 1915–17. From a very long distance, therefore, Macdonald had to be sure of appropriate stopovers for the nurses in Cairo or Alexandria, sometimes with work in British hospitals there. She also had to arrange for reinforcements and replacements for the nurses of No. 1 Canadian Stationary as well as for those of four other Canadian hospitals sent to the Mediterranean – two of the five initially on Lemnos to care for the sick and wounded from Gallipoli, and then three of the five in Salonika as support for British military action there.[80] Meanwhile on the Western Front, Canada's four casualty clearing stations had always to be ready to move if the fighting come too close, as it did, for example, in the spring of 1918. At that point, Macdonald had to rely on Maud McCarthy to ensure the safety and redeployment of her nurses. Given the nature of the fighting on the Western Front, with soldiers burrowed into trenches and emerging only to battle and die over a few square miles of mud, moves by the Canadian casualty clearing stations were relatively rare. But the work at them was intense and harrowing, and Macdonald seldom left a nurse there more than six months.

Needless to say, this movement of nurses was not always smooth. When things went wrong, the complaints ended up on Macdonald's desk. One army personnel officer, for instance, seemed unable to keep track of the various moves of her nurses and wanted Macdonald to provide a single list with names of replacements matching those being recalled.[81] Another senior officer thought that, on occasion, she overstepped her authority and did not follow proper army procedure in the supplying of nurses.[82] Both of these complaints occurred during Bruce's brief tenure as DMS, so they were likely part of the general office turmoil during the autumn of 1916. Indeed, Macdonald may have been exercising a bit of personal leeway in the midst of that turmoil. She had certainly retorted forcefully to Bruce's own complaint, probably picked up from the local commanding officer, of "unnecessary frequent changes" in the nursing staff at two hospitals in England. Without quite saying so, she indicated that Bruce really did not know what he was talking about and that she knew her nurses better than the doctors in charge.[83] But once Bruce was gone at the end of December she did begin to send a flurry of very formal requests, via the newly created Canadian post of adjutant general, for permission to move her nurses around.

Meanwhile, recipients of nurses also voiced complaints. Doctors in charge of some hospitals resented the frequent comings and goings, not only of nurses but also of other medical staff, because of the disruption caused to their units.[84] One grumbled that he had no sooner acquired an experienced operating-room nurse than she was snatched away.[85] Some of the doctors fought back: if nurses were to be sent to France from their hospital, the commanding officer would make the choice, not Macdonald, and he would pick "those to go first who have given us the best service."[86] Familiar with this kind of resistance, Macdonald knew the hazards of leaving the choice to the head of a particular hospital: "I find that occasionally when an O.C. is asked for a Nurse he very often selects one who has not had a very good report in the hope, I suppose, that her place will be filled by a really capable Sister."[87] She also refused to let doctors complain unjustifiably. When one fretted about inefficiency because of all the moves, she checked the records and found that he had been the one to recommend most of the transfers.[88] Nor would she take the blame for two nurses who had gone astray on their way to a posting in France. One of them had been in France before, she pointed out, and knew perfectly well how to get around. Give them a reprimand, she told the commanding officer (rather than complaining to me, she implied).[89] But she did acknowledge making the occasional error, as when she admitted to the office of the Canadian adjutant general that five extra nurses were "inadvertently instructed to report" for embarkation to France.[90]

She had more control over complaints that the nurses made about their postings. With a combination of shared assumptions and military means, she kept their grumbles few and far between. She knew that travel and adventure had been among the nurses' motivations for enlisting and that they were not likely to fuss over where they were sent. When making the initial selection of nurses, she had chosen them for their stamina and humour, and she expected all of them to take any difficulties or disappointments in their stride. She could also count on army discipline to keep nurses quiet: like soldiers, they were to obey orders, not question them. When some unhappiness did surface, military nursing structures defused it long before it could reach Macdonald's ears. A sympathetic tent ma·e or hut mate (often someone from the same part of Canada or the same nursing school), an understanding sister-in-charge in a given ward, a motherly "home sister" in the nurses' mess, and finally the matron of the unit all played a part in keeping nurses' complaints to a minimum. Unless a problem recurred, Macdonald might never hear of it.

She nonetheless insisted that nurses report to her office when passing through London on their way to or from postings or leave. She observed them, listened to them, and thereby kept her own ear quite close to the ground. Through the war years she devised a pattern for the posting of nurses that combined army orders with the nurses' own wishes and even their consent. "By all means keep Miss Willoughby for the Clearing Casualty [sic] or any other emergency work," she told a matron in France as early as 1915. "I had quite forgotten that she preferred that," she added, and excused her oversight by the number of requests coming to her.[91] When the nurses at No. 1 Canadian Stationary Hospital in Salonika were due to be replaced in the fall of 1916, she let them stay there when, on checking, she found that they were not "desirous of returning to England."[92] Some others, at No. 16 Canadian General at Orpington, responded to Macdonald's query about their wishes by saying they were not at all interested in leaving England for home duty in military hospitals in Canada.[93] If this pattern of taking into consideration nurses' views about their postings was followed consistently, Macdonald was sure to minimize complaints.

The movement of nurses to and from two particular Canadian hospitals raised special concerns for all involved. Macdonald, along with the doctors, matrons, and nurses of No. 4 Canadian Stationary Hospital (subsequently No. 8 Canadian General) and No. 6 Canadian General, all had to cope with the question of language. Both hospitals originated in Quebec, No. 6 being associated with the medical school of the Montreal branch of Laval University, and both were to operate in French. Prominent French-Canadian physicians and surgeons, some with a military background, staffed the hospitals, along with medical students as orderlies and bilingual nurses from all over Canada. For political and practical reasons, both units were given to the French government as gifts from Canada, primarily to serve the sick and wounded of the French army. The personnel, nonetheless, remained part of the CAMC and therefore were under the same overall British authority as the other Canadian hospitals in France. To the usual complexities of moving nurses about in France, Macdonald now had to add fluency in French for these two hospitals. Depending on their changing size and needs, she thus had to provide some seventy to one hundred nurses who could function in French – but also in English for temporary postings elsewhere. It did not always work to everyone's satisfaction.

Before No. 4 Canadian Stationary was even established at St Cloud on the western outskirts of Paris in November 1915, Macdonald was receiving veiled complaints about the temporary posting of some of its nurses. Did she really have to send "eleven French Canadian Sisters?" fussed the doctor commanding No. 1 Canadian General at Etaples. "We could get on better with a much smaller list."[94] In England, a similar short-term posting of French Canadian nurses caused an even more blunt reaction: "Nurses are sent to this unit who can only speak French and are absolutely useless for any duty whatever."[95] When Macdonald and McCarthy each had a look at No. 4 in the late spring of 1916, they both found problems with the nursing arrangements and as a result changed the matron. They made no mention of linguistic difficulties.[96] But Macdonald knew it was always an issue. In the winter of 1917 she cautioned the matron (of the now renamed No. 8) about her desire for only French-speaking nurses: "There is no likelihood of sending you many who have a knowledge of French, but we shall try to meet your wishes, in this respect, as far as possible."[97] Four days later she dispatched ten nurses with Sister Domville in charge, whom she thought very highly of as a nurse and who had "also a knowledge of French, as well as have several others in the party."[98]

Meanwhile, language difficulties had surfaced at the other French Canadian general hospital, No. 6 (Laval). After a number of moves, by 1917 it was established at Troyes on the Seine River well east of Paris. According to Macdonald, only a "small proportion of that staff is French Canadian and the English speaking Sisters are not keen on remaining in the Unit."[99] When she replaced fifteen of them, she said she "quite understood that the English speaking Sisters, with no knowledge of French, experience difficulty in caring for French patients," yet among the replacements there was not one French Canadian name, and Macdonald did not comment on their language ability.[100] Perhaps they, like so many of the other Canadian nurses, were intended to be frequently on the move.

Macdonald herself seems to have been the most sedentary of all the Canadian nurses. Her office in London was the centrepost of a nursing carousel which she directed. In a late-war photograph, intended for posterity, she radiates calm and control. Seated rather majestically at her desk, she is working on a document. Around her are three assistants, one seated deferentially – she may be taking notes – while another awaits completion of the document in order to replace it with another. Behind them on the wall are maps of hospital locations in Europe and the Mediterranean. Is it the beginning or the end of the day? Macdonald looks tired, older than her forty-five years. On her desk are only two personal touches: three drooping branches of wild flowers in a vase and, facing her, a small framed photograph. What did she see when she looked up from her work? Her mother? Her sister Vie? One, or all three, of her brothers in the war? The four women are in uniform. Macdonald and two others wear the workday garb of the "bluebirds": impeccable white collars and cuffs over the sky-blue brass-buttoned and leather-belted uniforms, with its long skirt. The fourth woman is in the navy dress version of the same uniform. Missing from their attire is the veil that nursing sisters wore when both on and off duty in hospitals. All four would have worn the regulation dress hat when out of the office. Here, at work, the photographer has caught a no doubt intentional combination of authority, serenity, and business.

This combination seems to have been Macdonald's style. There is no trace of her ever being rattled. But she certainly was busy. Vast amounts of correspondence crossed her desk. Sometimes she wrote her own letters – to such an extent that she missed engagements and had to write an additional note of apology: "When I looked up from my writing here it was seven o'clock so I knew it was too late. Won't you give me another try out?"[101] More often, judging from the clipped nature and tone of the letters (even the few to friends), she seems to have been dictating. To one of her friends she acknowledged, "There is little to write about of interest to you, our work being more or less routine."[102] Yet whenever an exciting idea occurred to her, she could wax very eloquent indeed. She suggested, for example, that the Canadian Red Cross "offer a prize for any member of the CEF Nursing Service for the most original idea for anything in the way of hospital equipment or surgical supplies, or anything that might further tend to the comfort of the patients. A prize would be an encouragement for the development of originality and any hidden talent, and would give the nurses something to think about during the periods when the routine work is slack at the hospitals. To my mind there is enormous scope for a scheme of this sort."[103] At the same time, Macdonald was a stickler when it came

Macdonald's office in London, 1918

to rules and authority, particularly her own. She would not allow her nurses to go over her head and wanted one "severely admonished" for having done so.[104] Nor would she explain to the adjutant general the recall of a particular matron from France: "In the best interests of the service" was her way of telling him to mind his own business.[105]

Meanwhile, Macdonald and her office staff minded much of the business of the growing number of Canadian nurses. If only because it was a known address, her London office received all sorts of things related to the nurses: letters, parcels, lost luggage, unpaid bills, cases of apples, Christmas gifts, bundles of laundry, misplaced umbrellas, all of which required forwarding and often called for Macdonald's direct involvement. By early 1916 the cost of this postal function was becoming more than her budget could bear. She asked the paymaster to assist, but when he wanted to know the average monthly cost, she balked and proposed a set amount to be drawn upon. He agreed.[106] Meanwhile, she scrutinized her nurses' travel claims and queried anything that was out of line. "How come you arrived at Charing Cross but claim for baggage transferral at Victoria Station?" she quizzed one matron.[107] The required forms for such claims were complicated, and she had to instruct her nurses – and matrons too – on how to complete them; she would then argue with the claims officer about how much they should be charged for excess baggage.[108] Having found accommodation for them in London, she confirmed the rates and then checked the incoming bills for accuracy.[109] She also spent an inordinate amount of time sorting out the nurses' pay of two dollars a day, plus an additional sixty cents a day when in the field, as well as a dollar-a-day "messing allowance" to pay the costs of the nurses' dining and social centre (their "mess") in their hospital. Since she found that many had "but the vaguest and often an inaccurate idea as to when and how much they were last paid," she served as go-between among the nurses, the London branch of the Bank of Montreal, and the paymaster, who wanted everything to be much more orderly.[110] In all this minding of the nurses' business, Macdonald appears to have drawn the line at their undergarments. When a corset company, seeking her advertising assistance, offered a "special demonstration ... on living models," she had her assistant merely acknowledge the letter.[111] But they must have had a good laugh.

From her office, too, Macdonald provided information, referral, and problem-solving services. Where was a particular nurse? Where was a particular patient? Could an English woman visit hospitalized Canadian soldiers? Could the English wife of a wounded Canadian accompany him to Canada and perhaps exchange her nursing services for free passage? Were there job opportunities for nurses in Canada? Could Macdonald help two Canadian nurses with the QAIMNS in India receive the pay they were due? And always there were the seekers of jobs. Macdonald kept a list of applicants in the hope of matching some with the frequent requests for nurses for non-military duty. She must have been helpful, for mention of her reputation often accompanied a request. One supplicant quoted Montrealer Lady Julia Drummond of the Canadian Red Cross in London: "Do approach Matron Macdonald; I know her personally, she is very obliging."[112] This in turn could lead Macdonald into many a merry administrative chase. It took her nine months, for example, of rerouting correspondence from her office to various military and political echelons in Britain and Canada, to obtain a favourable response for the two Canadians in India. Well might they thank her for her "kind efforts on our behalf."[113]

Kind efforts of a political nature were another matter. In August 1917 during the campaign for the "soldiers' vote" (which included nurses) for two members of the Alberta legislature, she refused a request for a list of the names and locations of all the nurses from Alberta. Her excuse was that she did not have the staff for the full day's extra work required to furnish such a list. But it is possible that she did not approve of the male candidate who wanted the list, for another of the candidates was a CAMC nursing sister, dietician Roberta MacAdams, who was with No. 16 Canadian General Hospital at Orpington. "I am quite confident that Nursing Sister MacAdams will be duly elected. She quite deserves the confidence of the voters," Macdonald told a friend. How public she made this view is unknown, but MacAdams was in fact "duly elected."[114]

All of this activity in Macdonald's office generated mounds of paper. Most of it was routine and often in triplicate: orders for nurses to go here or there; arrivals of nurses at one posting or another. Interspersed among the orders were copies of Macdonald's responses to queries – threads of a personal touch through an army bureaucracy that invented and refined itself throughout the war. Presumably, Macdonald kept her working files close to her, though there would have been some central system for the different offices of the medical service. Did she have any say in their preservation? Two sets of files, both confidential and both of great importance to her work, no longer exist. One set, filed by individual matron, contained correspondence from them as well as the monthly reports required of each of them. These reports may have been as succinct and dry as the few that do appear appended to the official "war diary" of a given hospital unit.[115] Or they may have been considerably more revealing, for Macdonald knew each of her matrons personally and kept in close touch with them. The other set contained a file for every nurse; into it went any personal correspondence with or about her, including the obligatory confidential report that each matron made when a nurse left one unit for another. Given the mobility of the Canadian nursing sisters, there were many of these reports. In them the matron was to comment on "nursing and administrative capability, tact, zeal, judgment, personal conduct and general fitness."[116] The resulting file thus had far more personal information than the military file of each member of the Canadian Expeditionary Force, with its attestation paper, pay sheets, medical and transfer records.

But those two sets of confidential files – on the matrons and on the nurses – are gone. Somewhere between Macdonald's London office in 1919, the Canadian War Records Office, also in London, the Department of National Defence in Ottawa and its Historical Section, and the Archives of Canada where all First World War records eventually came to rest by the 1970s, they disappeared. The explanation could be as simple as bad storage. Or it could be as complex as someone's decision that the files were too personal, too private, too potentially intrusive into a nurse's postwar life to warrant keeping. In either case, the loss of the files took Macdonald's nurses out of history and back into the privacy of women's lives.

For a while, however, Macdonald placed these lives at centre stage, with herself as a long-distance director. Thanks probably to sloppy filing, a few illustrations have survived of her exercising considerable authority over the matrons and, through them, over the nurses. She sent one report back to a matron, pointing out an inconsistency between its noting that a given nurse was "kind to the patients" and earlier correspondence indicating just the opposite. "Kindly exercise more care with regard to official correspondence," she admonished her subordinate.[117] She had her assistant, Mary Boulter, chase after matrons for "fuller reports" and remind them "that they were useless if not perfectly frank."[118] Macdonald appears also to have had someone in her office combine the reports from different matrons on an individual nurse.[119] The nurses themselves were apparently supposed to know of any detrimental comment in their file and have an opportunity to respond; in one case, Macdonald had to censure a matron and order her to expunge remarks that could not be substantiated.[120] Another matron, senior enough to know better, had to be commanded by Macdonald to attend more speedily to official communications.[121] For a more junior matron, who was in an acting capacity in a convalescent home for nurses, Macdonald gave strict instructions: "You will exercise the necessary discipline over all the Sisters under your charge; they must conform to the rules of the house, and you must see that they do not disregard these in any manner that may prove prejudicial to their health."[122] As for nursing sisters selected for duty at casualty clearing stations, Macdonald was rigid with her matrons: "Surely you must realize that a c.c.s. is no place for a nurse who is not satisfactory in every way."[123] She would indicate her displeasure and turn down proposed lists with a rebuke such as, "In future will you be good enough to exercise a little more care in your selection of suitable nurses."[124]

Even when such firmness was not required, Macdonald tended to be directive. For the opening of a new Canadian hospital in England, she wrote to the matron: "I trust you will make the hospital look as attractive as possible, and have quantities of flowers everywhere. I suppose you will have an unlimited number of guests for tea."[125] And when a matron sought advice on the housing of her nurses, Macdonald made her views quite clear: "It would appear to me very desirable indeed to have all the Sisters now occupying billets, housed under one roof. A ten minutes walk would be very good exercise. The Chateau of which you speak sounds very attractive and I should strongly advise you to have the o.c. arrange to take it over." Only then did she add the purely administrative consideration: "The fact that the rental is less than what is now being paid for the billets is of course the strongest recommendation."[126]

When not directing her matrons from London, Macdonald was on the spot, inspecting their work first-hand. During her five years in England she made eleven tours of inspection to the Canadian hospitals in France and some seventy visits to those in England.[127] She never did get to look closely at the Canadian hospitals on Lemnos and in Salonika; the dangers of submarine warfare in the Mediterranean seem to have prevented such a trip.[128] But the other inspections had her away from her London office many times during the war, sometimes for two or three weeks. During her absence, Matron Boulter was the acting matron-in-chief, who on one occasion told an inquirer that Macdonald "may not be back for some time."[129] The pace was in fact hectic. In 1917, for example, she inspected all the Canadian medical units in France three times – in April, July, and November – and also made four visits to hospitals in England in May, eleven in August, one in September, four in November, and two in December.[130]

During her tours of inspection, Macdonald was on official duty, so the few reports that exist are very formal indeed. Her task was to report to the director of medical services on "nursing arrangements" in the Canadian hospitals. Consequently, there is no record of what she privately may have thought of some of the more gruesome tasks of the nurses who were tending the mutilated bodies of "the boys" and whether she missed doing active nursing herself. Most of what she saw was carefully prepared before she arrived, for the units put on their best face and best behaviour for her visits. She rarely saw a middle-of-the-night scramble when a convoy of wounded arrived. What she looked for first were the working and living conditions of the nurses. She wanted to know about their workload. Were they overworked, underworked? Did they have adequate time off? Were they in good health? What about sanitation? And, whether they were housed in tents, huts, or billets, were they living and eating decently?

Behind Macdonald's concerns lay two assumptions: that if the nurses were well, they would do their work well; and if they were not well, the fault could be traced to the administrative capabilities of the matron. Macdonald therefore looked carefully into the administrative arrangements, but not before observing how the nurses cared for and attended to the patients. She also watched for order and aesthetics. Cleanliness, tidiness, attractiveness were all part of the nursing ethos, and although she never said so they provided sick and wounded soldiers with a soothing contrast to their experiences in the trenches. All these matters she reported on to the DMS. Lest he find her attention too narrowly focused, she added a word about the purpose of the nurses' work: "All patients are being very efficiently nursed, well cared for and well fed." She even suggested what he should be thinking of her nurses: "The work done by the Matrons and Nursing Sisters cannot be too highly estimated, their duties always being carried out cheerfully, devotedly and willingly."[131] She rarely missed an opportunity to remind male army officers of the importance of women as nurses in the military.

On occasion, Macdonald concentrated on a single hospital. Her entire report from an inspection tour in July 1916 concerned No. 8 Canadian General Hospital at St Cloud, one of the two French Canadian units. This was her second visit in as many months, and she was checking up on things since the change of matron that she and McCarthy had arranged. She found the wards untidy, "not as neat and clean as required," but offered as an explanation the fact that a "large number of surgical dressings" were being done at the same time as the patients' dinners were being served "at the early hour of eleven." She did acknowledge that the "actual nursing of the patients seemed to be well carried on, and the work evenly distributed." To her satisfaction, too, she found the tents that housed the nurses "neat and orderly." But she was appalled by the sanitary arrangements. The bathing facilities, consisting of "one small enamel bath ... on a wooden floor in a bell tent ... [with] no waste pipe," were "quite inadequate," she noted: "When I saw it, it had a quantity of dirty water which was oozing out over the floor of the tent." Even worse was the "substitute for a latrine" – several commodes set up in a bell tent. "Disgusting and far from sanitary," was her verdict, and she was not at all surprised "that some of the sisters had been suffering from gastric and intestinal troubles." No sooner was she back in London than she sent Matron Yvonne Beaudry from No. 6 Canadian General Hospital (Laval) to coach the new matron. And she had her own superior officer send a rebuke to the former commander of the unit, who was now the senior medical officer in St Cloud, asking why nothing had been done since April when these matters had been brought to his attention. He had promised proper latrines and Macdonald had suggested shower baths. Where were they?[132]

A different kind of inspection had Macdonald visiting a British military hospital early in 1917. She had of course no authority over the nursing arrangements at the Royal Military Hospital in Devonport; rather, she was to investigate the growing British practice of using women to replace men in a number of hospital functions. The implied question was whether Canadians should follow suit in the hope of running their hospitals more economically and also freeing men for active military service. Macdonald would no doubt have been in favour of both, but not at the expense of her nurses. While reporting on the satisfactory experiment at Devonport of hiring women as cleaners and to fetch and carry trays (indeed, all the kitchen employees at the hospital were women), she carefully pointed out that although some male orderlies were being replaced by women, those engaged in actual nursing tasks were not. And as for the large number of VAD women doing nursing and general service work at the hospital, Macdonald remained adamant in her opposition, attaching it this time to the question of finances: "Exclusive of the ordinary allowances, V.A.D.'s are paid one guinea per week so that far from their being any economy in labour, it would appear that large sums are being paid to unskilled hands. Comparison shows that whilst C.A.M.C. Nurses are more adequately paid, yet, as all are fully qualified nurses they must obviously, with saving of time render much more competent and efficient service."[133] Protecting the professional status of her military nurses was always uppermost in Macdonald's mind.

Her report was of sufficient interest to be sent on by her superior to the quartermaster general and, because of its policy implications, it went from him to the deputy minister of the overseas military forces of Canada.[134] There the financial and manpower advantages of hiring more women rumbled about for months as Canada debated the question of compulsory military service. When hospitals were asked their views, and the DMS aired his own, not a word was said about nurses. "Substitution," if it happened at all, was to be limited to "Cooks, Clerks, Store-keepers, Domestics, for Laundry work etc."[135] Macdonald had won her point.

But she, too, could be a stickler for economy. In the summer of 1917 she suggested that the books of Nos. 6 and 8 general hospitals be audited. During an inspection tour in France she had spotted "irregularities" concerning the "messing and billetting of Nursing Staff." The price of coal at No. 8, for example, was "quite exorbitant." What fund was the matron using?[136] Macdonald's worries occasioned an immediate letter from the DMS to the officers commanding the two units asking for details: What were the arrangements? Who signed the leases and contracts? Who provided the equipment for billets? How was fuel purchased?[137] In order to provide the answers, the commanding officers quizzed their matrons. Matron DeCormier of No. 8 provided a full explanation and insisted that all was well. The books could be looked at any time, she said. Moreover, when the matron-in-chief had been there recently she had "expressed her entire satisfaction with the manner in which the billeting and rationing arrangements for the Nursing Sisters were conducted."[138] Clearly, something was amiss. Either Macdonald had not communicated her concerns directly to the matron at the time of her inspection or something had caused her to raise those concerns only after the visit. Matron DeCormier in turn may not have grasped the meaning of a raised eyebrow or an oblique question and had taken Macdonald's politeness for approval.

Politeness and protocol required Macdonald to call upon the British matron-in-chief in France, Maud McCarthy. She seems to have done so on at least nine of her eleven trips to France. According to McCarthy, the early visits in 1914 and 1915 to British headquarters, at Abbeville on the Somme south of Boulogne, had provided Macdonald with "a better insight into all Office routine and the official procedure to be adopted when transferring nurses, etc."[139] Those first visits would also have allowed the two women, acquaintances since South Africa and again in London in 1911, to sort out just how their nursing services were to work together. For Macdonald, the best strategy was one similar to the colonial relationship then in evidence between Canada and Great Britain: as much autonomy for the Canadians as was compatible with the imperial tie. She was certainly not having her nurses act as reserve or replacements for the British. Yet McCarthy, hard pressed for trained nurses for the much more numerous British hospitals in France, must have eyed with a certain longing the seemingly limitless supply of nurses available from Canada. Now and again, Macdonald's use of a particular word suggests a certain unease about the relationship. For instance, in the early days of the Somme battles in the summer of 1916, she spoke of the British "robbing" the Canadian hospitals in France to fill in their own nursing ranks.[140] She knew from her experience in South Africa, and that of her nurses in England and France, that Canadian and English nurses often "crossed swords." Some of the Canadians were more blunt: "The [English] nursing is punk, in fact it is not nursing at all," one wrote home, while another confided to her diary that the English nursing sisters were "not what we would call good nurses."[141] For their part, the English sometimes looked down on the colonials and, while envying their military rank, could find them forward and even insubordinate.[142]

Macdonald and McCarthy were well aware of these tensions. McCarthy's Australian background probably facilitated things, and the two carefully navigated the shoals when they met. On one occasion, when Macdonald could have been affronted by McCarthy's moving six CAMC nursing sisters to a British casualty clearing station, she chose to interpret the action as an example of McCarthy's sensitivity to the needs of the Canadian soldiers being treated there.[143] She could also be charmingly deferential, without behaving as a subordinate. "I hope you have not forgotten me!" she began a letter inviting McCarthy to accompany her on an inspection tour in 1915. "I know that you can make many suggestions of value to us."[144] A year later the two were exchanging chummy salutations: "With kind remembrances hoping you are very fit," McCarthy signed off one of her letters, to which Macdonald responded in kind, "anticipating a long chat."[145] But they could wrangle too. If Macdonald felt McCarthy was infringing on her nurses, she let her know: "What I resent is the circumstance that whilst you have Sisters from No. 7 Canadian General, the Matron of that unit writes me that she is understaffed."[146] McCarthy tried to make amends, and for a while the two carefully requested and granted one another's authority for any matters concerning Canadian nurses. Within a few months, all was smoothed over, with Macdonald "trusting" she would see McCarthy "before too many moons are gone" and sending her flowers when she was ill.[147] The two clearly understood the ways of military and feminine protocol.

At Macdonald's suggestion, McCarthy hosted a conference in November 1917 of all the matrons-in-chief with overseas responsibilities. Could we not meet, Macdonald had proposed, "to discuss the pros and cons of our various duties in so far as they relate to the overseas Units. It certainly would be most advantageous to us Colonials."[148] McCarthy provided the setting and the hospitality in her office at Abbeville, but the agenda appears to have been an amalgam of "colonial" concerns. By that time, American nurses were in Europe, so their chief nurse joined the Canadian, Australian, New Zealand, and South African matrons-in-chief to discuss a thirteen-item agenda. On the minds of the six women were topics such as accommodation, messing, and uniforms of the nursing staff, transfers, inspections, length of service at casualty clearing stations, moves, VADs, Red Cross workers, confidential reports, leave to the south of France and Paris, recreation, honours, and mentions in dispatches.[149] Either the matrons-in-chief were very expeditious – they met at three o'clock, certainly would have had tea, and ended the meeting in time for dinner – or they gave scant attention to certain topics.

Among the topics, two at least were contentious: dancing as a form of recreation, and confidential reports. Macdonald argued forcefully for the existing Canadian practice of nurses being allowed to dance with fellow officers; McCarthy, whose British nurses were not permitted to dance, fretted about discipline and inconsistent rules. The two stood their ground, and as a result the separate regulations remained, no doubt to McCarthy's chagrin.[150] Perhaps in return Macdonald conceded on the question of confidential reports. Past practice had them going from the Canadian matrons directly and solely to Macdonald. McCarthy began asking for them to come to her. What exactly was decided at the conference is unknown, but Macdonald did subsequently soothe an uneasy matron, used to past practice, with the guarded words: "I think it advisable for the present, to accede to the request."[151] As for the conference proceedings, McCarthy sent a "summary" to Ethel Becher, the British matron-in-chief at the War Office, and she sent "extracts" to the head matron in each of the three British military districts in France, but only "copies of the extracts" to the participants.[152] None of these documents has come to light, so what Macdonald thought of the conference and its outcome can only be gleaned from her letter of thanks to McCarthy: "We, Overseas Matrons, are enormously appreciative of your many courtesies and have to thank you for your kind interest in our point of view regarding Nursing affairs. I feel that the Conference was a great success as far as it went, and that whilst only touching on routine matters it gave opportunity for a more thorough grasp of the situation and a better understanding all around. Next year I hope we shall have another meeting and go into the broader aspect of Active Service Nursing."[153] Macdonald was writing on behalf of her New Zealand and Australian counterparts, and one can detect some ongoing rumbling in colonial ranks. Within a year, however, the war was over and no further meeting took place.

Late in 1917, Macdonald did succeed in placing an intermediary between herself and McCarthy. In one of her inspection reports earlier in the year she had recommended the naming of a "principal matron, Canadians," to serve in France; but it took six months of persuasion on her part and balking on McCarthy's before the post was officially created. Macdonald's formal rationale was that her own work prevented her from going to France more than four times a year. In fact, when she first made the suggestion in May, she had not been there for nine months. She also wanted someone to take a more personal interest in the Canadian hospitals than the British matron-in-chief could do. All sorts of problems could thus be avoided: uneven distribution of work among hospitals; scrambling for personnel in emergencies; airing grievances and imposing discipline; even the correspondence overload in her own office.[154] She had in mind for the post her own assistant, Mary Boulter. Such an assignment would be both a promotion and a treat for Boulter, without there being any risk of her becoming too independent.

Macdonald carefully persuaded her Canadian superiors before mentioning the idea to McCarthy, and she had them make the suggestion formally. McCarthy objected in an equally stylized fashion. The "medical authorities in France," she recalled, "did not consider this appointment necessary at the time." Her own visits to the Canadian units sufficed; the matrons of those units could always refer to her for assistance. But the Army Council decided otherwise and informed McCarthy, just four days before the conference of matrons-in-chief, that an inspecting matron for the Canadian hospitals in France in the person of Mary Boulter was to be attached to her office. McCarthy quickly rejoined that a car would be needed for such a function and that Boulter should not come until it was provided. Clearly annoyed by having a Canadian imposed upon her to do work she considered her own, McCarthy then used the excuse that since Boulter had become ill and was to be replaced by Ethel Ridley, there should be a further delay into the New Year.[155] Ridley, Macdonald's former assistant from the *Franconia*, who had been the first Canadian matron to serve in France in 1914, thus did not take up her new post until the end of January 1918. In the meantime, the whole question must have coloured the relationship between Macdonald and McCarthy during the conference at Abbeville.

With Ridley in France as "principal matron, Canadians," Macdonald went less often and had fewer contacts with McCarthy. This may have been deliberate, but it risked an even closer administrative tie between the Canadian and British nurses in France. Although Ridley was Macdonald's delegate in France, she was in fact on McCarthy's staff and thus was engaged in much closer cooperation with her. So Macdonald took umbrage when Ridley appeared to be speaking for McCarthy in wanting Canadian nurses to work in British units on an emergency basis. A request would have to be made through official channels, Macdonald snapped to McCarthy, who, because of the German advance in the spring of 1918, needed to act quickly and had probably assumed that Ridley's presence in her office was to enable her to do just that. When McCarthy failed to mollify Macdonald with politeness, she simply went over both their heads and got what she wanted. Macdonald then made it sound all very correct by informing Ridley that the official request had been properly made and concurred in by the DMS. But, she added, only those nurses who could be spared from their own units were to go to the British.[156]

Meanwhile, Ridley was dependent on McCarthy for transportation to her various sites of inspection. The car that had been McCarthy's delaying tactic in the appointment of Ridley never did materialize, and by the spring she may have found the situation convenient, for it bound Ridley to her. Macdonald did not complain about the lack of a car until the following summer, when she came on an inspection tour with Principal Matron Ridley and the two virtually had to hitchhike to get to their various destinations. "Undignified" and "embarassing," Macdonald remarked, ostensibly about Ridley's position but implicitly about her own.[157] In the meantime, she had been receiving monthly inspection reports from Ridley, which in all likelihood were seen by McCarthy before they reached Macdonald. The various official stamps that marked the sending of these reports suggest an all-British route with the Canadian matron-in-chief at the very end.[158]

Macdonald will not have taken kindly to the implication. She kept Ridley on a fairly tight rein by indicating that she had better knowledge of her matrons and assistants than Ridley did. All manner of instruction and advice rained down on Ridley from London: Let Sister Pense "carry on for a time until Miss Wilson can form some idea as to her capabilities"; urge Matron Campbell "to have two capable Assistants"; "Matron MacIsaac is not very experienced and I fear would never be able to manage a large unit"; "When I go over I want to look into the matter of having Miss Willoughby's present Assistant promoted, also Miss Campbell's."[159] In reply, Ridley ever so gently reminded Macdonald that she was closer to the action; she would move a certain operating-room nurse whom Macdonald wanted sent to a casualty clearing station only when the situation warranted it.[160] But when Ridley requested Macdonald's approval to send a matron to a casualty clearing station instead of having her return to England with her unit, Macdonald replied firmly: "It is considered desirable to give her a less arduous post for a time."[161] In short, Macdonald was the boss, she knew best, and she would decide.

Macdonald's insistence on her authority may have been the result of the length of the war and its increasing administrative complexity. Since early 1917, she had had a new superior officer. General Foster, whom she had first encountered when she was posted in Halifax, appears to have been more efficient and more interested in administrative order than his predecessor Guy Carleton Jones. Or perhaps his tenure had simply coincided with the massive reorganization occasioned by the creation of the Ministry of Overseas Military Forces of Canada in London in late 1916. In any case, with Foster at the helm of the medical service, all manner of formal army documents were produced, including the first official "Establishment" for the CAMC nursing service – set numbers of nurses for hospital units and overall administration – a document that Macdonald must have worked on closely and at length. Foster also arranged for a "director of medical services, Canadians," to be present in France late in 1917 at the same time as Macdonald's principal matron was finally named.

It is not clear where the idea of a similar appointment at military headquarters in Ottawa originated. There was certainly a need to coordinate the nursing reinforcements required overseas with the staffing of the military hospitals in Canada, which were increasing in number to meet the needs of wounded soldiers invalided home. On the medical side, Jones had been assigned to just such a coordinating task in Ottawa when Foster took over the London office of the DMS in mid-February, and a few months later a similar nursing position was created. For some reason, the initial appointee, Irene Cains, was replaced by Edith Rayside. Cains was junior to Rayside and had much less experience, none of it as a matron. Yet she was to go in that capacity to Ottawa. Had she gone, it would have been clear that she was subordinate to Macdonald. But something interfered with her appointment, and Cains, who was assigned to Macdonald's office "for instructional purposes" before heading to Canada, in fact stayed in London for two years. In her place Edith Rayside – a contemporary of Macdonald's who had come to Europe early in 1915 and had been matron at two Canadian hospitals, in France and England – was named to the post with the title of matron-in-chief, albeit "temporary."[162] Only the latter word indicated any difference between her position and that of Macdonald. So by the fall of 1917, the Canadian nursing service, which had only one matron before the war – Georgina Pope – now had two matrons-in-chief. The possible implications were not lost on one of Macdonald's pals: "I'm awfully glad you have got Miss Rayside as your Second in Command; but I hope that doesn't mean a change to *your* plans? I suppose it is only for the war ?"[163] Was it Macdonald's or Rayside's idea to formalize the organization of the expanding army nursing service in Canada, with a matron-in-chief and assistant in Ottawa, principal matrons in all the military districts, and the usual matron and nursing sisters in each of the hospitals?[164] Was one or the other planning to be at the head of such an organization in the years after the war? Whatever their plans may have been, they seem not to have interfered with the relationship between Macdonald and Rayside, which remained a happy one well into the 1920s. Nonetheless, the appointment of Rayside to Canada and of Ridley to France could be seen as a diffusion of Macdonald's power. Equally plausibly, they could be seen as an enlargement of it.

Be that as it may, Macdonald appears to have exercised her wartime power with grace and diligence. After the war she modestly claimed that "an organization that expands gradually is easy of control. One grows along with it and finds that one thousand are quite as readily administered as one hundred; two thousand as two hundred and so on."[165] But the reality was that she worked hard at her job, and she was known for her intellect, organizing and executive ability, determination, tact, diplomacy, and good judgment. She had of course brought such qualities with her in 1914, but the war gave her ample scope to exercise them. And there is no doubt that she enjoyed doing so. Had she been a man, all of those qualities, including her sense of self and of office, would have taken her up the ranks of the military to positions of increasing power and prestige. But matron-in-chief, with its army rank of major, was the highest imaginable for a woman at the time, and Macdonald held it throughout the war.[166] Perhaps for this reason, she treasured the parting comment of a British aristocrat as she left for home in November 1919: "My word I should feel proud if I had done a *quarter* of what you have done ... I have never heard anything but praise of the way you ran the C.A.M.C. Nursing Service."[167] Macdonald had many an occasion during the war to garner such praise from similar people, but she was always very modest about her achievements. Indeed, she later attributed them and her ability to exercise authority to the support, loyalty, and generosity of the Canadian nurses.[168] She was, above all, an officer and a lady.

FOUR

An Officer and a Lady

For five years Margaret Macdonald graced the London scene in the name of Canada's military nurses. Her army rank and her nursing profession gave her a public persona which she enjoyed and used to good effect in the overseeing of her nurses. As a woman she stood out among the thousands of male military officers who flocked to London for work or play. And as a military officer herself, she stood out among the thousands of society ladies who were doing volunteer work in the city, to say nothing of the even more numerous female clerks who "manned" the war's growing bureaucracy. Macdonald's skilful combination of the traditions and expectations of the officer and the lady allowed her to be both mother and father to her nurses, seeing to their well-being and placing high demands upon them. The accolades that came her way and the pride she expressed in her nurses indicate that she had incorporated the two roles well. No wonder she loved her job!

She also loved being in London. This was her third and longest stay in the city, and she savoured every minute of it. The occasional grumble about the weather – "rainy days, which seem to go on ad infinitum" and the "abominable" cold indoors – could not dampen her enthusiasm.[1] Nor could the air raids that punctuated London life. She knew that her soldier brothers and their comrades were enduring infinitely worse, and like them she "grew to look upon danger in a detached sort of way; quite realizing it but feeling evil would befall the other fellow rather than one's self."[2] She also grew accustomed to the juxtaposition of casualty lists and theatre announcements in the daily press. The initial jarring of her sensibilities – how could one go to the theatre, much less enjoy it, in light of those horrifying lists? – gave way to one of London's great lessons for her: "A nation must wage War cheerfully."[3] By temperament Macdonald was well suited to such a task. Her job, of course, gave structure and a semblance of normalcy to her days, and the purpose of it made her feel she was at the very centre of things. Should there be a flagging moment, she knew it would be alleviated by a cup of tea at four o'clock, "the only time in the day when one feels more or less at peace with the world in general."[4] To know that her nurses were doing exactly the same thing in their mess tent or hut somewhere in England, France, or the Mediterranean added to her contentment.

It helped that she was comfortable in London. Her income was more than enough to cover expenses. She received the regular pay of a major in the Canadian Expeditionary Force, three dollars a day. In addition, as a single "officer or nursing sister" of the permanent force, she was entitled to a monthly allowance of $27.33 "in lieu" of "lodging, light and fuel." With this allowance, she made her own housing arrangements, sometimes in a hotel – she was at the Petrograd in late 1916 before it was turned into a hospital – sometimes at the Ladies' Empire Club, and, as of the spring of 1917, in the sublet apartment of an aristocratic connection. What the housing all had in common, including the apartment with a restaurant below, was the provision of meals. Like her nurses, Macdonald never did fend for herself. It was one of the great advantages of army life, particularly for a woman. On top of pay and lodging, she received a "messing allowance" of a dollar a day. In normal circumstances, this money would be her contribution to the nurses' mess. Given that she had no such mess in London, the allowance was presumably intended for her food. When actually "in the field" – across the Channel in France on her inspection tours – she received an additional three dollars a day field allowance. And then there was another fifty cents a day "sub[sistence?]."

Over the war years she therefore received between $230 and $259 a month, with travel and uniform allowances on top of that. She was well paid – so well, indeed, that she could assign $150 of each month's salary to a bank in New Glasgow.[5] Was some of it intended for her widowed mother or her single sister Vie, the only two family members living at home in Bailey's Brook? If not, Macdonald was able to put aside some

$9,000 during those five years, a considerable nest egg at the time. Meanwhile, in London she must have been able to live comfortably on the rest, even with rising wartime prices. She had her breakfast sent in to the apartment, she lunched and dined in good restaurants, went frequently to the theatre, and saw in at least one New Year with a "glass of ale."[6] It was a good life.

So was the ever-widening social circle she moved in. A few of her London contacts dated from her first brief visit in 1902, and more professional ones had been made with her study tour in 1911. Now the war added two different and sometimes overlapping groups of people. Many prominent Canadian women came to London during the war – the wives, mothers, and daughters of army officers, politicians, businessmen, and government and Red Cross officials. They all took up some form of voluntary work while in London, and they all showed up at any reception by or for Canadians. On the guest list for such occasions, Macdonald would likely have been in third place, after Lady Perley, the wife of the high commissioner, and Lady Drummond, who was in charge of the information bureau of the Canadian Red Cross. Major Margaret Macdonald was the highest-ranking woman military officer in the British Empire and the head of a group of professional women doing "the most important service women can render their country when at war."[7] That same recognition placed Macdonald on English guest lists too, if not quite so prominently. After all, she was not an aristocrat, she came from an unknown family across the sea, and was a working woman to boot. But she was known to Lady Sybil Grey and Nancy Astor, both of whom had entrées everywhere. So Macdonald moved gradually into London's high society, attending receptions, dinners, and dances hosted by socialites who prided themselves on their own voluntary war work.

For Macdonald, the social whirl was fun. If she thought her more gregarious sister Cell would have been in her element, she did admit that the elegant settings, classy people, and attention were "not entirely wasted on me either."[8] Like Canadian women travellers to England before her, she was somewhat in awe of English high society yet tickled to find herself quite at home in it.[9] She shared its values of authority, hierarchy, duty, and service, as well as the particularly female norms of deference, grace, responsibility, and dignity. To the mix she added her Scottish and colonial work ethic, and the unusual professional function of a single woman in charge of female work in the military. Her work made her an outsider, her uniform an oddity, but everything else was entirely fitting. The London scene took her in and confirmed her status and accomplishments.

Sometimes her reputation preceded her. One London hostess invited Macdonald to a gathering "to meet Lord Kitchener because she is the only woman in London not afraid of him."[10] But she was probably invited back because of her merry laughter.

During these social encounters Macdonald was also hard at work, for she was on show – for Canada, for military nurses, for women in war service – and everyone knew it. She needed their approval, the good words they could put in highly placed ears. She was also demonstrating to the leisured classes the value of women working. And she was watching out for her nurses: invitations, offers of housing, and other benefits could all come their way if Macdonald charmed the right people. Like her hostesses and the other guests, she was exercising a female social power of recognition and influence. One can just imagine the buzz around her:

She was in South Africa, you know, that's where she met Kitchener. And she's an army officer, fancy that! The colonials have one on us, don't they? Jolly good of them to come and give us a hand. Shows we did the right thing with the Empire. Isn't her uniform attractive? Frankly, I'd get a bit bored wearing it all the time, but it's ever so much nicer than the awful grey the QAs wear. But she's so tiny! Fancy a military figure as small as that. Still, I wouldn't want to cross her. Her eyes – what extraordinary blue eyes – seem kindly enough, but there's a no-nonsense air about her. Necessary, I suppose, in a job like hers. But I wouldn't allow my daughter to be a nurse; it's all I can do to keep her from rushing off as a VAD. It's all the rage with the young things, isn't it? I hear Miss Macdonald doesn't allow them in her hospitals. I wonder why. Let's ask her, look, she's coming our way. Ah, Miss Macdonald, how good to see you again. We do so admire the work you and your nurses are doing. When do you think the war will end? Now, I know a nice young woman …

And so it went. Lady Sybil Grey leapt into war work late in 1915 as the managing patron of the Anglo-Russian Hospital in Petrograd and took one of Macdonald's nurses with her.[11] The Duchess of Warwick asked Macdonald for a nursing job for the daughter of one of her tenants. The Dean of Westminster sent tickets to a Royal Maundy ceremony before Easter 1916. Mary Harcourt invited Macdonald to "our little garden fête" and later sent on her "most valuable suggestions" to William Whitelaw Reid.[12] Lady Warrington had Macdonald for a weekend visit to her country home.[13] The Graham-Murrays turned over their house in Chelsea to be a rest home for Canadian nurses, and the MP Colonel Gretton and his wife did the same with their palatial abode in Ennismore Gardens. Meanwhile the Victoria League opened its club to Canadian nurses.[14] Nancy Astor, on her way to being Lady Astor, virtually adopted Macdonald and would have had her come to Cliveden two nights a week had "Maria" not claimed the pressure of work.[15] The Royal Family itself had the pleasure of her company on at least three occasions.[16] Macdonald was tickled pink by it all: she had clearly made friends and influenced people.

She went on doing so on the frequent occasions when she did go to Cliveden. An hour or so west of London by train, the vast Cliveden estate had been a wedding present in 1906 to Nancy Astor, an American divorcée, and her new husband Waldorf from his father, a member of the House of Lords. When papa died in 1919, his hereditary title passed to Waldorf, who had to relinquish his elected position in the House of Commons in order to take on the peerage. Nancy then ran successfully in the by-election in Plymouth to replace him.[17] So politics was the order of the day at the weekend house parties, and Macdonald, brought up on political discussions, was right at home. Sometimes she arrived after having inspected the nurses serving at the Duchess of Connaught's Canadian Red Cross Hospital at Taplow on the Cliveden grounds; or she might have come directly from her London office for an overnight break. Her "cheerful countenance"[18] graced luncheons and elegant dinners for eight or twelve people, and she was a lively presence during walks on the estate and at entertainments around the huge fireplace in the great hall. Here she met and chatted with members of the Cunard shipping family, with aristocrats from the Devonshire and Grey lineage, with Lords Curzon and Lyttelton, ministers of the crown such as John Hodge, and the banker and public servant Robert Brand. And on one occasion, she met the prewar suffragette leader, now a war supporter par excellence, Emmeline Pankhurst.[19] Macdonald took a particular shine to Philip Kerr (subsequently Lord Lothian), private secretary to the British prime minister and a fellow guest on a number of occasions. She later recalled his "charming simplicity and immense mind" and marvelled that all this gaiety, comfort, and elegance had "happened to me"; but at the time she took it all in her stride.[20]

Meanwhile, in London, there were still other functions that had her in the public eye. In mid-November 1914 she had probably attended the funeral in St Paul's Cathedral of Lord Roberts, the British commander-in-chief who had praised her bravery in South Africa.[21] Similarly, she would have been part of the public mourning for the British nurse Edith Cavell, who was executed by the Germans in Belgium in October 1915.[22] She was present at the unveiling of a memorial to Florence Nightingale at St Paul's in February 1916;[23] she was the guest of honour and speaker at a swank dinner at the Criterion to mark the third anniversary of the *Franconia* contingent of Canadian nurses;[24] and she took part in the organization of a memorial service in April 1918, again at St Paul's, for the nurses who had died so far in the war.[25] She herself was fêted in October 1918, along with the other heads of military nursing services, at a grand luncheon at the Trocadero that was put on by women in government, the arts, and the professions.[26] When any of these occasions demanded it, she spoke out forthrightly. At a dinner of medical women at the Lyceum Club in the summer of 1917, Macdonald tore a strip off one of her own medical colleagues for his support for VADs. She was certainly "not afraid of her own opinions," as an awestruck reporter for the nursing press remarked.[27]

Along with the social gatherings and public affairs that sanctioned Macdonald's status as an officer and a lady came the major recognition of the Royal Red Cross for her professional work. The award, dating back to an initiative of Queen Victoria in 1883, was the highest military honour a woman could receive. Macdonald was the sole recipient in the New Year's honours list of 1916, and as she informed her mother, "This morning (I always glance over the morning paper whilst my bath is running) I got one of the surprises of my life to see my own name on the honour list." "The best feature," she exclaimed, "is that I shall have to go to Buckingham Palace to receive the decoration from the hands of his Majesty." Imagine the thrill in Bailey's Brook! Still, the family there would not have recognized her had she not added, "I feel sad to think that I get this honour whilst so many of the nurses deserve it equally. But then the nurses will feel glad that their head has received recognition."[28]

This reaction was typical of Macdonald, though it may have covered some less charitable thoughts. Hers was not the first RRC to go to a Canadian, and she may have been slightly piqued. In June 1915, Matron Edith Campbell, then at the Canadian Red Cross Hospital at Cliveden, though apparently singled out for her earlier work in France, had received the award. A week later, Macdonald had written to her close colleague Ethel Ridley, then matron of No. 2 Canadian Stationary Hospital at Le Tréport, north of Dieppe, regretting that Ridley had not been recognized. She said she was sure it was just a question of time and significantly added, "I have lost interest greatly in this matter."[29] Was this because she had not been consulted – the names going via British channels only – or that she herself had not been nominated? By 1917, when numerous RRCs had been bestowed upon Canadians, she and another close colleague, Matron Edith Rayside, then at Shorncliffe, could have a bit of a giggle: "The comments on some who received them are very amusing."[30] But Macdonald took her own award very seriously. She kept the medal in the desk drawer of her London office, and she carefully sent home for safekeeping the many letters of congratulations she received in the winter of 1916. So whatever her private thoughts, she clearly enjoyed others' high opinion of her. One wrote, "I don't believe there has been any honor conferred on any individual Canadian, throughout this campaign, so universally recognized as becoming the recipient with so much meritorious grace ... It is the most popular N.Y. honor in the whole of the Canadian Army." Another remarked, "I do not know what is engraved upon it, but it occurs to me that a very suitable inscription would be 'For Value.'"[31]

Although Macdonald was not home for five years, she did have family nearby. All three of her brothers were overseas, and like other nurses with soldier brothers she was always anxious about them. On each of their military records her name was added to their mother's as next of kin. She would thus be the first to know of any misfortune. Brother Ronald, a medical doctor seven years her junior, a professor of public health at McGill, had come to Europe with the university's hospital unit, No. 3 Canadian General Hosptial. Because of his specialty, he spent most of the war in England with a support section of the army, training others in proper sanitation. In the spring of 1918 he was attached to No. 9 Canadian Stationary Hosptial at Etaples and was its commanding officer as of late August, but even then he was in London frequently.[32] Brother Bill, formerly a lawyer in Halifax and thirteen years younger than Macdonald, had joined the Nova Scotia siege artillery as a lieutenant in the summer of 1916 and came overseas early in 1917. He was at Aldershot and Shorncliffe in England before going to France with the 3rd Canadian Siege Battery in November, where he remained until after the end of the war.[33]

The "kid," Donald, sixteen years younger than Margaret, was also a lawyer and a lieutenant with the Canadian Field Artillery. He had joined up in March 1915 and sailed for Europe in August. After further training in England, he served in France in areas so dangerous that he was reported killed in action in the fall of 1916. Macdonald probably received the report by phone; it was her mother who received the dreaded beige telegram that darkened so many Canadian homes during the war. His death was reported in the Montreal *Gazette*, where he was identified as the brother of the matron-in-chief and the McGill professor. Letters of sympathy thus came to Macdonald long after his military record laconically stated, on 7 October 1916, that he was "now reptd. at duty & well." Bouts of bronchopneumonia had Donald hospitalized for five weeks in London in the late winter of 1917, after which he had extensive sick leave

Ronald St John Macdonald, CAMC

before he was declared "fit for general service" in June. He seems to have been in France again, but after the war returned to Canada quite unwell.[34]

While the Macdonald siblings were overseas, they kept close track of one another. The brothers dropped in to "Marge's" office when in London, took in a show and had dinner with her, went to communion together, and reported all their encounters when writing home.[35] Although perhaps not together, they did all go to Scotland at some point to have a look at Moidart, the remote western Highland district of their ancestors. It may have been during or after such visits that they decided to suggest the name for the family home in Bailey's Brook. It is possible that Macdonald met with one or other of her brothers when she was in France on her inspection tours. Donald, for example, knew she was coming in July 1916, but, he said, "I hardly think she can get up near enough for me to see her."[36] She certainly used her network of friends to keep herself

William C. ("Bill") and Donald D. ("the Kid") Macdonald, CFA

informed about her brothers. Two nurses from Pictou County passed on to her their feigned jealousy when her brother Ronald came calling for a Montreal nurse in their unit without asking for them.[37] In turn, the brothers watched their older sister with pride: "Margaret is fine and in good cheer," Ronald wrote their mother in 1918. "She certainly loves London and has a splendid time ... She meets so many nice people – They all speak so highly of the good work she has done and think she is wonderful – which is quite correct – All the nurses swear by her, as well they might, for she is so good to them."[38] By war's end, she shared her assistant's relief that, "you and I are taking our brothers home," though she admitted, "Not until I know they have set foot on Canadian soil will I be assured in mind."[39]

Macdonald relieved her ever-present anxiety about her brothers by concentrating on her numerous friendships. She seems to have had a gift for friendship, both male and female. Surgeon General Jones, the DMS, was a friend, as was Jack McCrae. The friendship with the latter was sufficiently public for the matron of McCrae's unit to refer to him as "your friend Jack."[40] Macdonald wrote chatty letters to Colonel Roberts of No. 4 Canadian General Hospital in Salonika; and she received very warm notes from one Buzz Benson, a "lonely Canadian officer" on the Western Front. He wanted to hear from "My dear Mac," as he called her, about "the more intimate details of your life such as how you are and who sends you flowers and the shows you see and the things you eat."[41] In England her women friends were even chummier. She was "Clotilde" to one, "Mac" to another, and "Lady Bailey Brook" to a third.[42] She spent a camping holiday in the summer of 1917 with one friend, travelled to Ireland in August 1919 with another and went horseback riding with Nancy on the Astor estate.[43]

An illustration of the intimacy she shared with her women friends (and which poor Buzz Benson wanted in on) is the case of "B.G." or "Gil." Belfrage Gilbertson was a secretary to Lord Grey and had been in Canada when he was governor general, and she and Mac may have met then. As single professional women, they were very close during the war. They spent a day together in search of sunshine on the English south coast, and Gil wanted Mac to come up to Howick – the Grey family estate in Northumberland – to revel in the sights and smells of an English garden in summer. Gil was a keen hiker and on one occasion thought she might just drop in on Mac's caravanning holiday if Mac would reveal the route. The two swapped wartime anecdotes, Gil agreeing with Mac's assessment that the war, by July 1917, was going into overtime. Perhaps Mac would have

"Maria" on horseback,
with Nancy Astor, 1916

to "settle down for good in bleak old England." They discussed living arrangements – Gil knew the man from whom Mac sublet her London apartment – and revealed that, had she not had relatives, she would have felt her way "tactfully to a garret in *your* abode!!" And they must have talked about marriage, for Gil confessed that she "would have to love a man to distraction before [she] consented to live under the same roof."[44]

Whatever had Mac said to provoke that kind of remark? That she had an eye for the men was known to her friends. One of them added a perky postscript to a letter asking for her help in locating a missing soldier: "Don't fall in love with the photo."[45] Another entertained her during a brief respite on the Isle of Wight with a discussion of beaux.[46] And one matron clearly felt that Macdonald would agree – or at least not object to – a comment about the handsomeness of the DMS.[47] For all her attraction to men, however, Macdonald seems to have reserved her heart-to-heart talks for her women friends; she was close to her New Zealand counter-part Mabel Thurston[48] and her office colleague, Mary Boulter. Another friend was the superior of St Joseph's Convent in Devizes, north of Salisbury Plain, where Macdonald went as a lady boarder on a few occasions. The two women took to each other with great affection. "I hope you give the sisters enough to eat on Christmas day," Macdonald instructed Sister

Mary Dominic who replied in kind: "They know to whom they can make their complaints when I don't satisfy their wants."[49] Sister Dominic prayed for Margaret and her brothers, and she may have been the source of a charming description of saints, a text Macdonald treasured all her life: "Why were the Saints Saints? Because they were cheerful when it was difficult to be cheerful, patient when it was difficult to be patient; and because they pushed on when they wanted to stand still, and kept silent when they wanted to talk, and were agreeable when they wanted to be disagreeable. That was all. It was quite simple and always will be."[50] Friendships such as these bolstered Macdonald as she worked for women within the male confines of the army.

It wasn't always easy. After the war Macdonald used a family metaphor, with the army as parent, to describe nurses' relationship to the military. But the analogy obscured more than it revealed. Granted, the army provided for its members – food, clothing, recreation, transportation, health care – but it did so in the context of a single-sex system. Fitting women into this system required considerable effort. Even though the nurses were officers, the favoured treatment that went with the rank had been designed for men, and there was the lingering suspicion that an army wasn't really quite the place for women. One Canadian father tried to dissuade his daughter from joining the CAMC by telling her that "only trollops follow the army."[51] Macdonald knew that such views were not far below the surface. Hence her emphasis on the officer and lady status of her nurses, the key to distancing them from any semblance of impropriety in working so closely with the broken bodies of male strangers. The same status guaranteed the nurses relatively decent accommodation. But although it was similar to their fellow officers' in being segregated from that of the "other ranks," the purpose of the separation for the nurses was as much sexual as hierarchical. Macdonald's nurses in France thus had tented or hutted accommodation in their own "lines," well away from both their fellow officers and the enlisted men. In those lines, they enjoyed a structured female community of friendship and support centring around their own mess for dining and socializing. Highly ritualized activities such as teas and dances governed any encounters between the sexes, and then only among officers and always under the watchful eye of the matron. With her kindly eye and stern confidence, Macdonald exercised the same supervision from her greater distance in London.

Nurses in transit posed another question. The army worried about cost while Macdonald worried about control. She usually won. Whether her victories were due to her powers of persuasion or her trump card of propriety is unknown, but the two together seem to have been unbeatable. Her nurses were always on the move – arriving from Canada, awaiting postings, or moving from one hospital to another – and during those moves they had to be appropriately housed. If they could not be temporarily attached to a hospital with accommodation, they had to be placed in hotels or billets and never alone. And always there was the concern about discipline. The sooner they could be back under full military supervision in their own quarters in camp, the better.[52]

In London, Macdonald had a standing agreement with two hotels, the Kingsley and the Thackeray, where her nurses could be housed and fed for six, seven, eight, and then nine shillings a day as prices climbed during the war. The army fussed for years over these arrangements, never shirking its responsibility to house the nurses but querying the details: Couldn't the nurses pay their own bills and submit an individual expense claim rather than having a collective bill submitted by the hotels through Macdonald's office? Couldn't they have the usual officer's travel allowance and simply cope with their own accommodation and their own bills? Did they really have to stay so long? Macdonald – and sometimes the DMS himself – set the army straight on every count with a blunt no and always with a reminder of the disciplinary advantages of having the nurses kept together. If the army would like to provide a depot in the London area for nurses in transit – something Macdonald had advocated since at least 1915 – she would readily acquiesce in their going there. But in the meantime her nurses would stay at the hotels. Sufficiently cowed, the army agreed. It was mid-1917 before Canadian hospitals in Britain were numerous enough to provide temporary accommodation, and it took just as long for the various officials involved to agree that nursing reinforcements from Canada could go there while awaiting their postings.[53] But even that left many nurses on the move, and when in London they stayed in the hotels. They were, after all, ladies.

Macdonald was just as adamant about proper domestic surroundings for her nurses. She interpreted the army's willingness to feed its personnel as meaning that it would provide sufficient food in an appropriate setting. So when she heard that nurses at Moore Barracks Hospital at Shorncliffe were standing in a crowded office having a sandwich and a cup of tea for lunch, she intervened angrily. "Insufficient nourishment and a most unnecessary discomfort," she chided the matron. Either the officers' mess must be divided so that the nursing sisters could have their own private dining space or they must be sent by ambulance to the local hotel for a "proper and dignified lunch."[54] By this she meant a three-course sit-down meal at an elegantly laid table – the kind of meal that the Kingsley or Thackeray Hotel would be providing the nurses detained in London. If Macdonald's understanding surpassed army intentions (and even actual conditions later in the war), she was not daunted.

Macdonald's creation of the post of "home sister," ostensibly a means of excluding untrained women from nursing functions, was another way of ensuring the nurses' well-being. As housekeeper for the nurses of a given hospital unit, the home sister oversaw their living quarters, shopped for their mess and kept the accounts, supervised the servants (whether army batmen or locally hired cleaners and laundresses), and cared for any nurses who were out of sorts. Macdonald thereby guaranteed a maternal presence in all aspects of the nurses' lives except their work. When army officials queried the necessity for home sisters, they were easily silenced with a list of functions that any man would recognize as those of a house-wife. But a housewife for women? Yes, indeed, Macdonald was implicitly saying as she carefully constructed home support for the professional work of her nurses.[55]

Professional work required professional attire, and Macdonald was a stickler for proper dress. She and Georgina Pope had been the first women to don the new blue uniform back in 1907, and she insisted that her wartime nurses wear it as proudly. The uniform was, after all, a badge for Canada and for military nursing. The navy-blue dress uniform in particu-lar, with its brass buttons and the lieutenant stars on the shoulders, was the clearest indication of the officer status of the nurses. The more practi-cal working uniform emphasized a different kind of distance – the white apron over the cornflower-blue housedress suggesting a mother, the white collar and cuffs a schoolgirl, and the white flowing veil a nun. Soldiers called the nurses simply "Sister" and thought of them as angels. With so much symbolism stitched into the nurses' uniform, it is not surprising that Macdonald wanted it to be impeccable. No question, therefore, of person-al additions to the uniform – no spats over their boots, no veils over their faces, no silk, and no jewellery.[56] Nor was there to be any fancy evening attire: nurses would attend theatre performances and gala soirées in dress uniform or not go at all.[57]

Macdonald did relent over the comfort of the working uniform and allowed shorter skirts in the mud of Salisbury Plain, softer and slightly lower collars instead of the stiff, almost clerical neckbands, and even a more becoming dress hat that actually stayed on the nurse's head.[58] But once any changes were introduced, they had to be adopted by all. "We must have uniformity at any cost," she told one of her matrons.[59] The cost was borne by the army. Each nurse received an allowance of $150 for her uniform, after which she maintained it herself.[60] Macdonald's own uniform was under as much scrutiny as that of her nurses. One daring friend sent photos to the matron-in-chief with the comment, "The next time you pose for a snap see there are no buttons off first."[61] After a moment's mortification, Macdonald would have burst out laughing.

This quality was also required of her nurses. A cheery disposition may in fact have been an unwritten qualification for the job. In later years Macdonald made a point of recalling some of the war's more comic moments, and during the war she probably facilitated the publication of *Humour in Tragedy* by one of her nurses.[62] As sustenance for good cheer, she always advocated a balance of work and play and therefore watched out for both overwork and underwork. The first led to exhaustion and the second to boredom, and in either case shoddy performance and dissatisfaction were the result. Her nurses therefore were to be given two hours off in the course of an eight-hour working day and a half-day off during their seven-day working week. Macdonald took it as a sign of poor administration by a matron if this did not happen.[63] Moreover, the relaxation time was to be enjoyable: sightseeing, swimming, bicycle riding, shopping, a game of tennis, a ramble over the hillside to collect wild flowers, a donkey ride, lunch at a café – all modern, healthy, and energetic activities, but ladylike nonetheless. As these activities reach across the years in the few published personal accounts of Canadian nurses, they all echo with the sound of laughter. Even as an antidote to the horrors of war, the laughter reveals that the nurses were having a good time. And this was exactly what Macdonald wanted.

One off-duty activity did raise a few eyebrows. Dancing was one of Macdonald's own great pleasures, and she was not about to deny it to her nurses even when the British matron-in-chief said so. Maud McCarthy did just that in 1917. Because of certain "irregularities," she wanted to impose the British army ban on dancing in military quarters on all her charges in France, including the Canadians. She sent an order to that effect, which Macdonald simply ignored.[64] McCarthy then tried a softer approach: "I am anxious to learn your views on the question of dancing in the Sisters' quarters in France."[65] A mollified Macdonald replied:

For long you have been aware that dancing goes on in the Canadian Units and I have been equally aware that it is not permitted in Imperial Hospitals. We both recognize the importance of uniform rules for all and neither of us would wish to disturb the friendly relations that exist between the two Services.

That in off duty time all Nurses in the Field require diversion and amusement is an outstanding fact and without doubt, dancing is one of the favourite pastimes of the Canadians. The see[m]liness of it under existing conditions is a debatable point with the French but not so with the majority of English people, I judge. Observation proves that given pleasant and congenial surroundings, greater efficiency, regards work is assured.

The circumstance that the society of women has a healthy and wholesome influence among men is more evident now than ever before; it almost seems that dancing is part and parcel of a soldier's tonic and curative treatment over here. I am convinced that as long as it is recognized as legitimate in their quarters, Nurses will assuredly not break rules to seek entertainment elsewhere. Recreation in France being exceedingly limited, would seem to warrant a little more latitude in this regard.[66]

Macdonald and McCarthy pursued the debate a few weeks later with the other matrons-in-chief at their conference at Abbeville. They must have agreed to disagree, for the Canadians went on dancing. Two years later, McCarthy commented somewhat stiffly that Macdonald "considered dancing a necessary and very legitimate exercise and that nurses who were surrounded with an atmosphere of depression needed the recreation both mentally and physically."[67]

Nonetheless, such recreation had to remain proper. Macdonald needed no reminder of that. In the good name of her nurses, she hunted down the least hint of impropriety. Even an anonymous note decrying dancing and drinking between officers and sisters in uniform in the hotels of Folkestone warranted scrutiny. Macdonald quizzed the matrons of three Canadian hospitals in the area, and they in turn grilled their nurses. Nothing more lascivious turned up than a nursing sister having wine while dining with her officer husband; two others doing the same with the brother of one of them; and one taking a glass over a meal with a nursing colleague. Of the matrons who responded to Macdonald, one took umbrage and informed her, "the Nursing Sisters on my present Staff, would not stoop to any such behaviour." With so many people watching them, there was little room for these ladies to stray.[68]

Leave did, of course, provide other opportunities. As part of army support for the work of nurses, they were granted a ten-day to two-week leave about every six months, conditions permitting. When on leave, they could go where they wanted, though in fact their options were fairly limited. Most Canadian nurses took their leave in Britain. They went to London to take in a theatre and sample the night life, or they stayed with

English or Scottish relatives throughout the country, or visited places of family origin. A friend or relative was nearly always in tow. And because of special travel rates for officers and public respect for the "bluebirds," to say nothing of the bother of baggage and the storage of civilian dress, the nurses tended to stay in uniform. This in turn kept them in line. Unless their destination was Paris. There, one matron feared that the conspicuous uniform was more likely to attract attention than respect, and in "gay Paree" attention was the last thing one wanted, she said. Would Macdonald therefore consent to the nurses visiting the city in mufti (civilian dress)?[69]

In fact, Macdonald had to argue with McCarthy over letting the Canadians go to Paris at all. The British did not allow leave in Paris, and McCarthy, as always, wanted the same rules to apply. She was unmoved by Macdonald's argument that French Canadian nurses had more ties in France than in England, and she imposed a general prohibition in May 1916. McCarthy's rationale was that she was worried about "these enormous numbers of women of all classes and kinds of whom the majority do not understand the language, and who have come out to assist us in a great cause and whose record so far has been magnificent."[70] Macdonald acquiesced, for she understood the worry, even though her own Canadian nurses were in fact fewer in number, much more socially homogenous, and were army officers; she could count on their personal and military sense of self-discipline. Nonetheless, in passing McCarthy's ruling on to the Canadian units, she was in effect acknowledging the question of morality that seemed always to be just beneath the surface.[71] Women on the loose seemed to conjure up notions of loose women.

Even when the restriction was lifted a year later, McCarthy remained uneasy. Maybe the nurses could have leave in France, in Paris, she fussed, but only if they stayed in specially designated hotels "with a suitable lady in charge."[72] Macdonald was momentarily taken with the idea but balked when McCarthy tattled on Canadian nurses for staying in hotels in Nice and Rouen. She had no objection to their staying in a hotel, Macdonald retorted. Indeed, her "Ladies" might object if they did not have the same privileges as other "Officers" to go where they liked and stay where they liked when on leave. She warned McCarthy that they "might quite legitimately dispute any endeavour to control their movements when on leave."[73] Macdonald's capitalized emphasis on the status of her nurses implied that she trusted them to know how to behave.

The other form of leave the army provided its nurses was much less problematic. Sick leave was part of an intricate system of caring for the

health of army personnel. The nurses themselves and their doctor colleagues in the CAMC were of course the key figures in this system, but they
too could fall ill. When they did, Macdonald had everything in place for
their care – from the home sister in the nurses' mess, who could offer some
maternal sympathy, all the way to Sir William Osler, who was available
for consultations in London. Depending on the nature of the ailment,
nurses could be isolated in camp or sent to an army hospital specially designated for them. Then, when well enough, they went on to a convalescent
home selected and sometimes even furnished by Macdonald herself. She
planned for these contingencies, consulted with physicians, foresaw the
need for sanatoria, and badgered the Red Cross into financing and admi-
nistering rest homes. Always she kept a close eye on the physical well-
being of her nurses, watching for any sign of "seediness" that might
presage something more serious. Even from a distance, she took her nurses' pulse and wanted them returned from places such as Salonika if the
climate was not agreeing with them.[74]

Macdonald's attention to the health of her nurses led to altercations
with the Red Cross over the upkeep of the rest homes. It was easy enough
to find appropriate accommodation: wealthy English families were eager
to offer their houses as havens for the Canadian nurses. Indeed, so numerous were the offers that Macdonald had to turn down some benefactors.
She personally inspected the places she thought acceptable, and she
planned the equipment and drew up a budget. Then she turned her considerable charm on the Canadian Red Cross commissioner in London,
Colonel Charles A. Hodgetts, to have him pay for the maintenance of the
homes. Hodgetts resisted. He preferred to put Red Cross energy and
money into actual hospitals, such as the one at Cliveden, perhaps on the
assumption that Canadian donors would give more readily for wounded
soldiers than for tired nurses. He may also have thought that his responsibility extended only as far as Red Cross nurses, a totally different organization from the Canadian army nurses. In any case, he and Macdonald
haggled for months in the spring of 1915 over Red Cross support for a
rest home for the CAMC nurses in Cheyne Place, in London's Chelsea district. They argued over the principle, the cost, the furnishings, the regulations. She wanted a lovely home for her weary nurses, equipped in a style
befitting ladies, with glass, linen, and plate for the dining room, white
counterpanes from Harrods for the beds. He thought grey army blankets
and second-hand quilts would do. She intended to have a CAMC matron
oversee the home; he wanted to impose the rules. She finally put her foot
down and he acquiesced.[75] A second rest home for nurses established a

year later at Margate, on the English southeast coast, seems not to have created as much conflict. Perhaps Hodgetts did not relish tangling with Macdonald again. Indeed, on this occasion she sent him an effusive letter of appreciation. Her words have the tone of a peace offering, with phrases that were eminently quotable for fundraising purposes:

If you ever have any doubt as to the necessity for such a place I should recommend you to call there and see for yourself the happy, contented, sunbrowned and appreciative occupants and hear their expressions of praise and gratitude. "First time I've ever experienced a homey feeling in a strange place" – "better looked after than Members of any other Nursing Service" and so on, ad infinitum.

When the Nurses who are so faithfull and cheerfully carrying on their work – often under very trying conditions, when they in turn become patients it will undoubtedly be a source of comfort to their parents and other relations to feel that nothing is left undone in the matter of the necessary care and attention; to that given during convalescence we are indebted through you to the Canadian Red Cross Society.[76]

That Hodgetts was not entirely pacified is suggested by his annoyance in the late summer of 1917 when, because of enemy air raids, the nurses were moved out of the Margate rest home without his knowledge.[77] Nonetheless, in 1918 he carefully requested Macdonald's comments on the proposed house rules for a third rest home that was to be supported by the Red Cross in an elegant London house in Ennismore Gardens. Just as carefully, she corrected all the rules he wanted to impose. Not allowing meals to be served in rooms, she said, eliminated "the chief raison d'être of a *Rest* Home"; requiring nurses to make their own beds should be "dependent upon nature of malady"; not permitting guests because of government rationing was much too severe (the sisters could themselves provide the "tea and cakes"); and the visiting hours were far too limited.[78] Once again, it seems, Hodgetts assented.

On one question related to the rest homes, however, Macdonald could budge Hodgetts only so far. She thought Ennismore Gardens, in particular, an ideal place for launching some of her nurses into matrimony, and she wanted them staying there in the time leading up to the ceremony. Like a good mother of the bride, she expected her daughters to be married from the family home, with all the comfort and flurry appropriate to the occasion. She herself hosted at least one reception at the rest home in Cheyne Place, and probably more, given the accusation that came her

Nurses' rest home, Ennismore Gardens

way of running a "matrimonial agency."[79] The source of the accusation is unknown, but Hodgetts himself is a likely candidate.

He huffed over her request that two or three nurses, without friends or relatives in London, be permitted to stay at Ennismore Gardens for a week before their weddings. Macdonald assured him that the nurses would not return there after the ceremony. Hodgetts grumbled that this was not the purpose of the rest home but said he would permit it in this case. When she then tried to extend the time to two weeks for one of the nurses, he puffed even more angrily. This really would undermine the "institution," he claimed; the nurse in question should go to a hotel. He probably would have blown the house down – had he owned it – when Macdonald reacted with special pleading. The elderly mother of this nursing sister had been knitting socks for the Red Cross since 1914, she entreated. Would he not make an exception? Hodgetts refused, fearing perhaps that all the female relatives of sock-knitters would descend on the rest home. One can imagine him muttering to himself, "Doesn't that matron-in-chief have anything better to do than run a matrimonial agency?" Her chirpy assurance that Cupid was now on leave for the rest of the month could not budge him.[80]

In fact, Cupid fluttered around the Canadian nurses quite regularly, and Macdonald kept herself well informed of his activities. Her cousin Janet wrote from a casualty clearing station about all the romantic goings-on, including "a real English guy" who had a crush on her: "Thank heavens we are moving as I should hate to fall in love. They all seem to get it so badly up here – What do you think?"[81] Whatever Macdonald's reply, her interest in such matters seems to have been well known to her friends. The assistant Red Cross commissioner in Boulogne, with whom she was clearly on much friendlier terms than with Hodgetts, joked with her about his falling in love with three of the sisters at the nearby No. 3 Canadain General Hospital. He knew only their first names, "but seeing how serious it was I felt I ought to report the matter at once," he told Macdonald.[82] It did seem that the longer the nurses were abroad, the more of Cupid's arrows hit their mark.

By 1917 a policy was in order. Until then, no one had paid too much attention to the matter. Some nurses who were already engaged to doctors in 1914 had joined the CAMC at the same time as their fiancés. This was the case of Juliette Pelletier and Stuart Ramsey, who did not marry until after the war. Some were already married and had slipped by the requirement to be single. Some married in secret while overseas, fearful, probably, that they would lose their jobs. Others followed the norms of the time and resigned prior to marriage. Still others were engaged one, two, even three times, only to be bereft time and again as the battlefield claimed their fiancés. Then there were those women who wanted to marry openly *and* stay in the nursing service. At this point Macdonald stepped in. She checked with Maud McCarthy and found, surprisingly, that it was possible for the Queen Alexandra's nurses to do both. The constant shortage of British trained nurses probably explained the exception to social norms. But Macdonald did not have that problem, so she weighed the pros and cons.[83]

She seems to have had a soft spot at least for the idea of marriage. Back in her nursing school days, she had revealed her own expectation of marriage in a jocular fashion when playing with a hospital form intended for ambulance patients: she had circled the category "Married" and added "Willing to B."[84] During the war, a fellow nursing student, who was now a matron with the CAMC, reminded Macdonald of that time: "Do you remember that Dicksie promised us each a black opal when we were married?"[85] And there had been those admirers in Panama. As matron-in-chief, Macdonald was quite willing to add marriage to the list of reasons for moving nurses about. She even brought one back from Salonika at the request of an intermediary, adding as an afterthought that she hoped the young woman in question was willing.[86] She, who was a stickler for abiding by contracts, thought nothing of nurses breaking theirs if the purpose was marriage. She knew that nurses nearly always bettered themselves financially through marriage. As single women, most of them were dependent on their own earnings, which although more than adequate in wartime were not so otherwise. When one Canadian nurse snagged a British colonel, that was a coup indeed.[87]

To the social and financial advantages, Macdonald added a moral one. Marriage entailed "higher responsibilities"; it was a "calling," nobler even than the "divinely appointed" mission of nursing. This being the case, nurses should give up their profession for "reasons of state," by which presumably she meant the production and raising of children, especially sons to replace the ones lost to the war.[88] All this invocation of religion, politics, gender, and social expectations may merely have been the required language of the time, voiced by a woman who had found in the army a much more interesting career than that of a housewife. Or possibly she was being genuine when she remarked after the war that she had always advocated marriage but simply had never had the opportunity to practise it herself.[89]

Certainly, the policy that she developed in 1917 was clear: nursing and marriage did not go together. In proper army style, she asked her superior, the DMS, for a ruling on the matter, but she provided all the rationale. Much of it was based on propriety. It was the custom of "ladies" to give up their profession on marrying. They should not be hanging on to jobs when so many nurses in Canada wanted to come overseas. Those who had married "clandestinely" had occasioned "undue and unkind criticism," which was bad for the nurse in question and bad for the entire nursing service. Moreover, Macdonald added, in an oblique reference to pregnancy, "it is usually only a question of some little time until circumstances necessitate her retirement." But there were practical reasons as well, ones that could be just as persuasive for army administrators. Husbands and wives would "naturally" like to take their leave together, and arranging that could be quite complex and disruptive to hospital routine. And if the husband was killed, the wife might be eligible for both a widow's and a nurse's pension.

It simply made more sense, morally and practically, that nurses automatically resign from the CAMC when they married.[90] Macdonald so recommended, and barely ten days later the army so ruled.[91] She could then turn down a request for an exception by quoting the policy – in effect, her own – and adding, "It is not in my power to disregard this ruling."[92] With such a ruling in place, statistics could be kept to confirm it: of the 199 resignations in the two years from July 1917, 136 were for reasons of marriage.[93] But the ruling posed an additional problem related to nursing reinforcements from Canada. The increasingly cost-conscious army was not at all keen to pay for uniform, upkeep, and transportation, only to have the newcomers marry and resign within a few months. They were therefore subject to an additional requirement. They could not resign in order to marry until they had served overseas for one year; and if they married without permission, they would lose their CAMC status, their right of return passage to Canada, and any claim to a post-service gratuity.[94]

And what of Macdonald herself? Was marriage ever more than a policy question for her? Did Cupid hover anywhere near her heart during the war? According to family lore, there was indeed a "love of her life" while she was in London, someone she would have married had he survived the war. If so, the romance was very well hidden by all concerned. Not a hint of it can be found in the documents of the time. And given the notoriety of the man in question, one would think that the many forays into his life would have unearthed some shard of evidence. But although friends at the time and writers ever since have tried in vain to marry off John McCrae to any number of women, it was never to Margaret Macdonald.

Yet that is precisely the family reminiscence – that the two "very special and dear friends" would marry after the war.[95] If they did indeed have such a plan, it was compatible with McCrae's statement to his mother that he was "'sot agin'[opposed to] lovemaking in wartime."[96] As for Macdonald, she would have understood both the language and the sentiment, at least for herself if not for her nurses. To both Jack and Margaret, the war, their work, and their duty took precedence. If she was an imperial daughter, he was an imperial son; if she an officer and a lady, he an officer and a gentleman. Of course, he may not have told his mother everything, although he told her a lot. The closest study of this correspondence and of McCrae's emotional state concludes that "there was no romantic attachment during those awful years."[97] But there is no doubt about their friendship. It went back to the *Laurentian* and South Africa in 1900 and continued through his greeting of her as the *Franconia* docked at Plymouth in 1914. He had left her a note at St Thomas's Hospital in London barely two weeks later, saying sorry to have missed her by two minutes. And he told her where he was – Devizes – the very place where she subsequently found convent lodging when she took a break from her work in London.[98] Although there is no trace of their doing so, the two would certainly have written to each other while he was in France, first with the Canadian Field Artillery and then, as of June 1915, with No. 3 Canadian General Hospital (McGill), where she probably saw him during one or other of her inspection tours. He would have called on her when on leave in London, and their paths may also have crossed through mutual friends: the Greys, the Oslers, the Adamis, Andrew Macphail. The Oslers, for example, invited them both, on different occasions it would seem, to their home in Oxford.

But does it add up to a romance? McCrae's leaves in London were few and far between; her inspection tours in France were whirlwind affairs. She had known his poetry since South African days so would have recognized the anonymous author of "In Flanders Fields" in *Punch* in December 1915, if indeed she had not received, as others did, a copy of the poem before its publication.[99] Did she notice the change in him after the second battle of Ypres in the spring of 1915, the battle that occasioned the poem? And did her friends at No. 3 report on his being uncharacteristically short-tempered with the nurses in late 1915?[100] When he died of pneumonia and meningitis in January 1918, what then? His close male colleagues wept. She must have done so too, for she would have been as shocked as everyone else by the sudden loss. Some forty nurses attended the funeral at Wimereux, but Macdonald was not among them, even though the service was delayed so that officials from London could be there.[101] Nor did she note the anniversary a year later in the one diary from those years. The only hint of intense private grief is a press photo of her dating from February 1918; she is almost unrecognizable, so drawn and old.[102]

Still existing among her effects is a photograph of McCrae's burial site – wooden crosses row on row, with a pencilled X on his grave. She must have stopped there, perhaps in July 1918 or May 1919 when she was in France, or again during her tour of the battle areas in 1923. So few of Macdonald's personal possessions have survived that one is tempted to read special meaning into the few that have. No letters from that time exist to reveal what if anything she told her family. But over the long years of Macdonald's retirement, she and her sister Vie would have shared all sorts of stories and secrets, and it is from Vie that the McCrae connection became known to her nieces after Macdonald's death. Into her copy of *In Flanders Fields*, a book which the editor Andrew Macphail gave her in

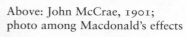

Above: John McCrae, 1901;
photo among Macdonald's effects

John McCrae, c 1916

1919, Macdonald (or someone else) has tucked, glued, and pinned bits of McCrae memorabilia: photos of a young McCrae in civilian dress, in uniform, and on the *Laurentian*; the note he left for her at St Thomas's; the cemetery photo from France; and an undated mimeographed poem by S.M. Bainbridge, "In memory of Lieut-Colonel John McCrae," as well as an enclosure, added in 1989 by one of Macdonald's nieces, that records the story in one sentence.[103] Are these the remnants of a romance or merely a filing system that looks like one?

Macdonald's few annotations of Andrew Macphail's "Essay in Character" in the book *In Flanders Fields* certainly reveal that she knew McCrae well. But she was not one to wear her heart on her sleeve, much less attach it to the margins of a book. And at the time her Catholicism and his Presbyterianism would have constituted a huge barrier, to say nothing of the fact that they had both been single for more than forty years. Would they have given that up easily? And what of Macdonald's professional ambitions for after the war, ambitions that her friend Gil, for one, knew about? They would have been incompatible with marriage. Even so, the possibility of a romance between John McCrae and Margaret Macdonald remains an enchanting one. Whether it is fact or "fairy dust," it really ought to be true.[104]

If the McCrae connection reveals anything, it is the importance of discretion to Macdonald. She certainly expected it of her nurses: they were to be well behaved at all times, prudent, judicious, thoughtful, attentive, loyal, respectful, and obedient. Woe betide those who weren't. Lack of discretion seems to have been at the origin of the few problems that surfaced among the nursing sisters during the war. One nurse fussed because her matron was a former classmate, so why should she take orders from her? Two others behaved frivolously, more like children than young ladies. Five more disobeyed house rules and were impertinent to their British matron. A few others were absent without leave. A twosome were such a nuisance that everyone heaved a sigh of relief on their departure. Another nurse was just unmanageable.[105]

The matrons involved appear to have coped and merely informed Macdonald after the fact. However, in one instance, the matron-in-chief revealed her own impatience and the high standards to which she held her nurses – and, no doubt, herself: "Really it is a bit trying that some of the Sisters allow personal interests to take precedence over hospital duties."[106] It was all the more trying when a nursing sister took her personal interests over Macdonald's head. To complain to the DMS about lack of recognition or promotion and then, through political connections, to involve Sir

Edward Kemp, the Canadian minister of overseas forces was not only contrary to army procedure but also, in Macdonald's mind, indiscreet to the point of disloyalty. On two occasions, Macdonald had had this nurse's file scrutinized by all concerned, and she had even excised one unsubstantiated negative report. But still the nurse grumbled about "a common R.C. woman like Miss Macdonald" using "personal spite" to deny her advancement.[107] More likely, the nurse was simply not living up to Macdonald's expectations; and as a result, no promotions or favours came her way. In another instance, Macdonald pounced on a glaring case of indiscretion. A nurse had complained to the press, albeit anonymously, about not having leave before embarking for Canada in 1919. Macdonald tracked her down and shipped her home even faster.[108]

She was just as adamant about any hint of group indiscretion. In the fall of 1917 it was reported that Canadian nurses travelling through Italy had distributed "blows and kicks with masculine vigour and great impartiality to Italian passengers trying to get into carriages occupied by these 'ladies.'"[109] It was bad enough to receive such a report directly, but this one had come from a British brigadier general via the War Office, along with a rebuke to Macdonald's superior and eventually to her. "An unseemly scene in Italy," clucked the British DGAMS to the Canadian DMS. "Watch for anything of this kind in the future."[110] The incident appeared to correspond with the return of three Canadian hospitals from Salonika, whose staff had travelled by ship to the south of Italy and thence by train to London. Macdonald and her male colleagues at CAMC headquarters investigated immediately.

She was still anxious to wipe the slate clean five months later, for no such behaviour could be found. On the contrary. What the doctors, matrons, a quartermaster, and the nurses all confirmed was the impeccably discreet conduct of the Canadians. A reassured Macdonald nonetheless dug deeper, for she needed to clear the "unmerited" and "unjust" "imputation that rests upon the Canadian Nursing Sisters."[111] As a result, she found that the incident had in fact occurred before the Canadians were even in Italy. She then wanted a retraction and had the DMS demand it of all the senior British officials involved. All she obtained, and only indirectly, was a semi-acknowledgment from the brigadier general about the origin of the story. Canadians? He didn't remember anything about Canadians. As he had heard it, the women involved had been Red Cross.[112] Accompanying the acknowledgment was the suggestion from the DGAMS that the matter now be dropped. With the graciousness of a lady and an officer, Macdonald did so.

Along with the reputation of her nurses, Macdonald had to protect their lives. This task was all the more difficult in that she could not count on the nurses' complicity, as she could (with very few exceptions) on their sense of propriety. One nurse wrote to her parents, "I do hope I will never do anything to cause you one minute's distress as far as conduct goes."[113] But risking their lives was another matter. Many nurses wanted nothing better than to be in the thick of the action, and as the war continued, their chances of doing so increased.

So Macdonald was caught between the army's gendered sense of protecting its womenfolk and the nurses' desire for dangerous postings. She watched for conditions that might imperil her nurses and at the same time organized their postings so that the best of them could court danger at a casualty clearing station. To her army superiors, she pointed out the hazards at one hospital in France where the nurses had to pass anti-aircraft guns at least twice a day on the way to and from their billets.[114] Worse still were the dugouts for nursing staff at two other hospitals: "In the event of a direct bomb hit, there would probably be no survivors."[115] But to her British counterpart she could voice her nurses' keen appetite for risk. "I am firmly convinced," she wrote to Maud McCarthy after an air raid on St Omer had killed four English nurses, "that every Nurse in the Field is not only prepared but willing to make the great sacrifice and to share equal risks with the men in the trenches."[116]

A few of Macdonald's nurses had already died of illness, and she had had to adjust her usual reassuring letters to relatives to ones of sympathy for their loss.[117] But killed or wounded in action was quite another thing. In May and June 1918, when Canadian hospitals in northern France and a Canadian hospital ship at sea became targets, twenty-six Canadian nursing sisters were casualities: three dead and five wounded at No. 1 Canadian General Hospital at Etaples on 19 May; another three dead and one wounded at No. 3 Canadian Stationary at Doullens in the night of 30–1 May; and fourteen dead in the torpedoing of the hospital ship *Llandovery Castle* on 27 June. For these women, the language reserved for soldiers was suddenly appropriate: sacrifice, bravery, fearlessness, heroism. Yet from London, according to a grieving but proud Macdonald, the nursing sisters were "more keen than ever to go to France."[118] If the likelihood of death was now to be part of the job description of an army nurse, the nurses were becoming combatants, just like the men.[119]

Nonetheless, the death of women was shocking. Indeed, attacks on hospitals and hospital ships were legally and morally beyond the pale of even the hideous practices of the Great War. Macdonald would have seen

Nurses among the ruins of No. 1 Canadian General Hospital, Etaples

the Red Cross poster that depicted a nurse as an immense Madonna cradling, Pieta-like, a tiny, immobilized wounded soldier. Were her Catholic sensibilities disturbed at the sight, or was she quite comfortable with the popular image of nurses as maternal, devoted, religious – the very symbols of civilization? A Canadian war poster certainly counted on this symbolism, as well as on the shock value of dead women, when it portrayed a drowned nurse from the *Llandovery Castle* as an illustration of German barbarity. "KULTUR VS. HUMANITY" the poster shouted as part of the ongoing effort to have Canadians purchase Victory Bonds to help finance the war. Although more than two hundred men – CAMC personnel and the ship's crew – also lost their lives on the *Llandovery Castle*, the emphasis in the official report and in the press was on the women.

Over and over the story was told of the fourteen nurses, together in one lifeboat, recognizing and silently meeting their fate as the small craft succumbed to the vortex of the sinking ship. Even had they surfaced, the German submarine was there, firing on survivors in the water. Macdonald knew them all – five had come over on the *Franconia* with her in 1914 – and had appointed each one to hospital-ship duty as a respite from their

Bombing of No. 3 Canadian Stationary Hospital, Doullens

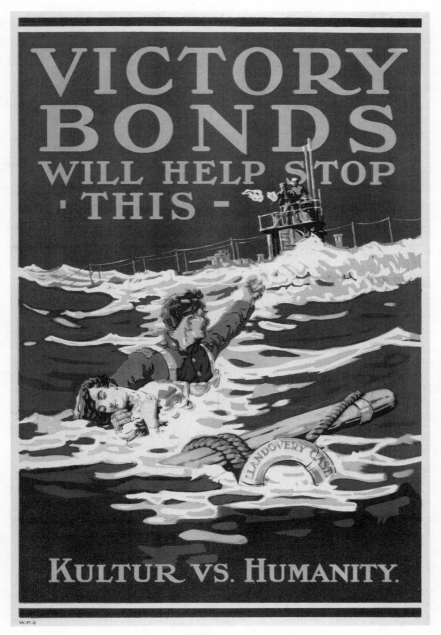

"The shock value of dead women"

earlier postings and to give them a chance to be home in Canada for a
week or so between sailings. Did the nurses' prominence in the official
report soothe her shock and sorrow? Certainly, their behaviour was
exactly as she would have expected. But she had not been able to protect
them. Publicly, she was amazed and proud when a nurse came to her
office the following morning to offer her services for ship duty.[120] Privately, her grief was so strong that it can still be felt, leaping from the page of
an archival document that lists the names of the fourteen drowned
women. Some clerk had designated them all "Nursing Sister," and Macdonald had corrected the list by writing "Matron" beside the name of her
friend from New Glasgow, Margaret Marjory (Pearl) Fraser. She had
done so with a force of emotion that has the cross on the "t" almost
breaking through the paper.[121]

With what a heavy heart she left for an inspection tour in France barely a week later. There she had her first look at the damage that had been
done in the air raids on the Canadian hospitals in late May. There she
could visit the nurses' graves. But no such site marked a final resting place
for the victims of the *Llandovery Castle*. She therefore made a point of
being back in London in time for a solemn requiem mass for the drowned
nurses (possibly delayed because of her absence) on 23 July. In the meantime, Canadian officials in London had sent the report on the sinking of
the hospital ship to prominent British politicians. She would have been
pleased with the foreign minister's reply: "I do not know whether it
demonstrates more clearly the inveterate brutality of the German Naval
Authorities or the glorious courage of the women of Canada. The latter
stands out as a splendid episode in a war crowded with examples of devoted bravery."[122] This was the message that the nurses' next of kin were
meant to absorb when they received a tiny printed version of the report,
complete with the names of the fourteen victims.[123]

And then it was all over. Had the war ended in late 1917, which Macdonald had begun to think possible after the Canadian success at Vimy in
early April, most of her nurses would have survived.[124] But the final year
took its toll, as did the epidemic of influenza in late 1918 and early 1919.
All told, Macdonald lost thirty-nine of her nurses, thirty-four in the last
year alone.[125] Compared with the appalling number of soldier deaths – well
over 9,000,000, including 60,000 Canadians – the nursing numbers were
minuscule. But they were tragic losses nonetheless. Macdonald made a
point of visiting the graves of her nursing dead in England before she
returned to Canada in 1919, and she asked Lady Sybil Grey to do the same
for her in France.[126] Macdonald never did get to the Mediterranean, where

two Canadian nurses were buried on Lemnos. Nor did she travel to Russia, where four CAMC nurses were working at the Anglo-Russian Hospital in Petrograd. All four survived, as did most of her nurses. But every one of them carried the memory of death with them, the death of brothers, cousins, fiancés, nursing friends, and so many of their patients. Women had been to war. It had been great and it had been ghastly. As one nurse recalled years later, there had been nothing in all her life to compare with it.[127]

At eleven o'clock on 11 November 1918, the Great War came to an end. So busy and so relieved was Macdonald that she didn't write home for three weeks. When she did, her urgent scrawl conveyed the onging exuberance:

Dearest Mother, Since this wondrous peace has come I have simply been breathing without writing. I should have liked to have sent a cable but I hate having it reach you second hand and again most cablegrams were held up two weeks etc. I can quite imagine the joy, and relief of the friends. Miss Cains first remark was "and you and I are taking our brothers home"! My reply was, "Not until I know they have set foot on Canadian soil will I be assured in mind"!

We got the news by 'phone and at 11 am the guns went off – such rejoicing – we rushed to the General's office & then thro' the other rooms, shaking hands & congratulating each other & everybody we met regardless of knowing them. In no time the streets were filled with clamouring, shouting crowds, carrying & wearing flags in every conceivable manner. Our stenographers went off, orderlies & almost everybody. Sister Odell we sent to reconn[o]itre – she seemed so long in getting back that I got restless & said I could'nt stand it another minute – that I must get out & *shout* too – bade Miss Cains get her hat & off we went across the street to call on Lady Drummond, Lady Perley & Mrs Rivers Bulkeley at the Red +. Then to buy some flags – I remember giving one to everybody I met as we went back & in to the office! No one could settle to work – so off we trotted down Regent St which was by this time a mob of people. – all shouting, waving, dancing and kissing indiscriminately. Bus'es and taxis were filled and running over – on the engines, sides, top, foot boards & everywhere – saw as many as twenty-five in one taxi – pandemonium was let loose. The shops closed. Every conceivable form of locomotion, crammed with shouting, gesticulating men, women and children appeared as if the sound of the guns was a magic wand. For three days & nights this went on. The usual thing was to see a crowd soberly form a ring into which several couples stepped to dance: it did'nt matter that all were strangers – they shared one thing in common – peace in their hearts. You might be jostled about by drunken soldiers & sailors – a frequent occurrence indeed but not once did I see

anyone resent it. I saw an immaculately groomed London *swell* – top hat &
spats – being taken by the arm by a flower seller in a shawl. He looked a bit
bewildered but not resentful and soberly walked on with her clinging to his
arm. Then I saw two sailors & a girl each walking abreast – a drunken Australian soldier walking towards them – stopped the party and quite leisurely
took the face of one girl between his hands, *slowly* kissed her and passed on.
There was no protest from anybody – like the crowd, I grinned broadly. Peace
reigned again & nothing else mattered for the time being. London crowds are
so remarkably good-natured – nothing ever upsets their good humour. When I
recall picnics at home – our men when they get the least bit intoxicated, immediately and out of a clear sky assume a fighting attitude and nothing satisfies
them but a fight.

To go back a bit, we went on to the Piccadilly Café – every table booked
for Lunch & Dinner for three days in advance. We had a cocktail & then to
the Carleton – a sign out "Every table booked." We then got a taxi to come to
a modest little Restaurant near here. We had a dinner party at the Carleton
that night & there was dancing after. It was a wonderful evening – at various
stages of the Dinner (there were innumerable parties, large & small) some one
of the guests at each table was inspired to get on the table – which was done
on all sides without protest from anyone. Then perhaps someone wd make a
speech – some[one] else wd sing or think his mission was to lead the orchestra
– then *every one* wd get up, form a procession & march around the room & in
and out amongst the tables. It did'nt matter that you ate fish at your own table
& the next courses anywhere around the room. But everybody had a good
time. I would'nt have missed it (the three days) for worlds.

Going home the crowds were so thick in various spots that one had to get
out off the beaten track & dodge thro' back streets etc. One saw fearfully
funny sights – but all were so thrilled with the thought that hostilities had
ceased that nothing else on God's fair earth mattered.

Peace night will probably be a memorable one but the spontaniety and first
enthusiasm can never equal the others. Many people went to Buckingham
Palace – the crowds clamored for the King from time to time and he frequently
had to come out on the balcony.

My best or most recent experience of interest was the Victory Ball. I had no
thought of going when suddenly one fine day an invitation appeared from the
Red + Com. Col. Blaylock – "wd. I dine at the Ritz at 8:30 and go on to the
Victory Ball." I replied that Cinderella wd be delighted & wd at once go out
and buy herself glass slippers. The party was Gen. & Mrs Foster, Mr & Mrs
Cambie (Bank of Commerce), Major Low, Miss Mona Prentice, Col. & Mrs
Blaylock & Dr Martin (Florentia will recall this man if you send her this let-

ter!). The Ritz was like fairyland – to begin with one walked thro' a line of lookers-on from the taxi to the door – (I recalled the numbers of times I have been amongst the eager onlookers!). The majority of the guests were in fancy dress. Our party the ladies in evening dress – Officers in uniform. It was a merry atmosphere from start to finish – the circumstance that the waiter broke a whole bottle of Creme de Menthe over my chair and saturated my scarf and gown did not dampen my spirits. I was wet & sticky thro' to the skin but fortunately my gown (a blue tulle) was not ruined – the only effect it seems to have had was (after drying) to stiffen the material. Well, at 10:30 we walked out thro' an admiring (?) crowd to a Limousine or two & were whirled off to Albert Hall. The crush of Cars there was stupendous but, as always in London, orderly. The scene from our box (adjoining the Royal Box – no Royalties present) was what you might imagine without ever realizing. It is impossible to describe my impressions – how could I picture to you the costumes. Everything you ever thought of in that line, passed before your eyes – from a window-cleaner to an Empress, Rintinin & Ninette, Pierrots of every shade & description, Nymphs, fawns, "Powder" puffs, little clothing & much clothing & every conceivable form of dress. Lady Drogheda (she had also dined at the Ritz) was very striking as "Air" – a [?] effect. Lady Di Manners as Britannia – Countess Hoey Stoker as a Chinese (which she is in reality). Duchess of Sutherland in a drapery sort of costume – the peerage and the stage went arm in arm & I elbowed them both. I had several dances – fox-trots. In the intervals one walked in the foyer or around the edge of the ball room floor and viewed the people. Lord Jellicoe, Lord Lonsdale the Duke of Sutherland & all such people one recognized readily. Coronets, stage-lights and Mrs Asquith – she was in Russian costume. It was all wonderful and recalled to my mind pictures that I had seen in the Sketch etc in my early youth. It lasted till 5 am.[128]

Later – immediately after Lunch, I betook myself Piccadilly-wards intending to go to the Lyceum Club to view Marshall Foch on his triumphal drive from the Station. I found a clear nook on the pavement & stayed there – preferring to see him at close range rather than from a balcony window. The streets were well lined, flags waving & all expectant. Presently there was a faint sound of cheering which grew louder & we were all on the qui vive – only to find it was a solitary cyclist – who was looking most uncomfortable at the joke played on him. Shortly after a guard came along, then in an open carriage, the Duke of Connaught & Marshall Foch. The latter is younger in appearance than I anticipated – looks about 60 – a spare, thin man reminds me a little of Dan D. McGillivery! – the next carriage had Clemenceau and the irrepressible, smiling Lloyd George the third carriage had Baron Sonnino, Signor Orlando and Bonar Law. Clemenceau is fat and quite old but looked so pleased over the ovation they were all getting. Lloyd George's smile alone could win him the election![129] The Italians are not generally trusted I find. Now, have I not seen nights of late? I wish I could transport the whole to B[ailey's] B[rook] for you all. Wouldn't Foch & the others look smart coming down Donald Duncan's hill?!

You will appreciate that there are times when I feel as if I were in a moving picture concern.[130]

For all the glamour and excitement of late November 1918, Macdonald had another year's work in London before she herself could walk down Donald Duncan's hill. She and her nurses were a small part of the massive, time-consuming plans for dismantling the war effort. Most of the hospitals continued to function for months after the end of the war. Two casualty clearing stations accompanied Canadian troops into Germany. Other units had still to care for the sick and wounded for whom 11 November meant only that they would not have to go back "up the line." And even when the wounded gradually moved on, their places were filled with influenza patients. Macdonald's nurses continued, therefore, to be hard at work. Some of them transferred to other units when a given hospital changed its purpose, as was the case with No.3 Canadian General at Boulogne, which in February 1919 became a centre for venereal cases.[131] Gradually, however, the hospitals closed down, packed up, and headed home. Even that was not an easy task, because everyone else was doing the same. Slowly the nurses regrouped in England, helped out in British hospitals, took leave, and awaited embarkation orders for the too few ships going too infrequently to Canada. In all this organization, Macdonald's was a tiny task, but she still had to watch out for her nurses, place them appropriately, ponder their future employment (as well as her own), plan their return to Canada, arrange battlefield and gravesite tours for them, and sort out all the paperwork that had accumulated in relation to them during the war.

What the nurses themselves had accumulated was a vast and varied experience. Could it be put to postwar use? They had nursed some men with the traditional diseases of tuberculosis, pneumonia, and influenza and others with the grotesque injuries of modern warfare. They had been in the operating theatre, and some had become anaesthetists. Others had assisted in x-ray and pathology laboratories. Still others worked in rehabilitation: massage, braille, prosthetics, plastic surgery. Some had acquired dietary expertise, and almost all had gained some inkling of social work as they listened to the patients' stories, and watched over their recovery. How would they put all this experience to use after the war? Would there be openings for all this talent? Well before the end of the war, a number of overseas military nurses had already been assigned to accompany the wounded home and then to work in the growing number of military hospitals in Canada. Some of the very experienced nurses had become matrons in those hospitals. But there already was a "home establishment" in Canada, some five hundred military nurses who never did get overseas, and they were assisted in their hospital work by large numbers of VADs. At their head since September 1917 was Edith Rayside, matron-in-chief for Canada. Now, with the end of the war, some two thousand overseas nurses would be returning to Canada, and at their head was another matron-in-chief, Margaret Macdonald. Civilian hospitals still had very few graduate nurses on staff, relying instead on student nurses, whose numbers had vastly increased during and because of the war. So it was unlikely that Canada's military nurses could be successfully integrated.

When Macdonald and some of her male colleagues in London asked military headquarters in Ottawa about postwar employment for nurses, they were politely rebuffed.[132] The Permanent Army Medical Corps was not taking on any new recruits. In fact, the number of nurses projected for the corps, although twice the prewar figure, was tiny: two matrons and eight nursing sisters.[133] As for the military hospitals in Canada, they did require an additional six hundred experienced nurses, but only temporarily. The newer Soldiers' Civil Re-establishment hospitals might well use another two hundred, but that was not the army's business, since those hospitals were under civilian administration.[134] So, too, was the proposed Dominion Ministry of Health, whose future work might possibly foster new opportunities for nurses. In the meantime, it was too bad if some of the best nurses headed for the United States; that had always been the case. As for those with a specialized skill, they could abandon any thought of being anaesthetists, for instance. That was quite out of the question.[135] In short, the army wasn't interested. No nurses need apply. Their contract with the Canadian Expeditionary Force did, after all, specify termination six months after the end of the war. So, with their passage home provided and a service gratuity in their pocket, the nurses, like the soldiers, were left to fend for themselves.

Macdonald must have received the reactions from Ottawa with increasing dismay. She would recognize, of course, that no one had "any prescriptive right to military employment."[136] But perhaps her own job was to be on the line. Unlike nearly all of her nurses, she was a permanent member of the CAMC and had been since 1906; but officially, during the war, she and all of Canada's other military personnel had been members of the temporary Canadian Expeditionary Force. Presumably, she would be automatically transferred back to the permanent force. But what then? Would she have the position or authority to implement those postwar plans that her friend Gil had thought might be jeopardized by the appointment of Rayside as matron-in-chief for Canada? These plans might have included an army nursing school – something like the one the Americans did in fact establish in 1920. Its head, Julia Stimson, had gone to Europe in June 1917, working with the American Red Cross and then as chief nurse for the American Army Nurse Corps, and Macdonald would certainly have met her.[137] Indeed, a rumour circulating in Ottawa in the spring of 1918 had the government establishing nursing schools in its military hospitals.[138] Did Macdonald know of that? Or was she ever tempted to stay in England? One of her friends thought that she should and even suggested a job for her. In the early fall of 1918 the Women's Royal Air Force required a new head: "Beaverbrook could wangle it for you & heaps others 'quite easy.'"[139]

In the meantime, Macdonald had to return her nurses to Canada in an orderly fashion. It took almost a year. She followed the same policy in this final disposition of her nurses as she had for all their wartime postings, taking their interests into consideration while meeting the needs of the medical corps as a whole. By early January 1919 she was sending home those nurses who had requested home service or who had family obligations in Canada. After them went "those whose Services are not wholly satisfactory from a health as well as a general efficiency point of view." Third in line were the nurses who had three or more years' service.[140] Because of the length of their service, they qualified for the maximum service gratuity – 183 days' pay and allowances. By sending them home, Macdonald could keep on duty in England other nurses who had not yet reached the maximum.[141] Even if she could not guarantee jobs for them on their return to Canada, she could at least ensure the army dowry. Similarly, in August 1919, when 465 nurses were still in England, Macdonald so organized their transatlantic passage that some would have transport duty – tending the lightly wounded and convalescents on regular ships – and others would do hospital-ship service, nursing the more severely impaired, and would thus gain a further seven to ten days towards their gratuity before they were "struck off strength" on arrival in Canada.[142] The system seems to have worked well. Certainly, Macdonald defended it vigourously in 1922 when Julia Stimson commented that nurses had been fed up, anxious to return home and shake off government control. That may have been true of Simpson's American nurses, retorted Macdonald, but not of the CAMC nurses. "So anxious were all to remain overseas," she said, that only the call of family or the hope of a job in a soldiers' hospital in Canada had any of *her* nurses rushing home.[143]

In fact, leaving the army seems to have been quite a wrench. "Divorce" was the word Macdonald used for it, a word with shocking connotations at the time. But it fitted the image of the family which she had so often used when describing the relationship among the nurses themselves and between the nurses and the army. In their mess, the nurses had experienced a happy community life; in the army, they had been well parented, all their needs supplied in return only for their work. Never again would they find better support and appreciation. As Macdonald remarked, "The regret with which embarkation orders were received betrayed an unwilling acceptance of the inevitable divorce from the army – surely the best proof that the partnership had proved an agreeable one."[144] Going home meant leaving home.

At Macdonald's insistence, the army offered a final gesture of parental favour by allowing nurses to travel to France before returning home. She would have liked some of them to go there on actual duty and proposed, a week after the end of the war, that some nurses who had served only in England be transferred to France. She also passed on the requests from bereaved nurses to go at their own expense to visit the gravesites of relatives and fiancés. Canadian authorities balked at the first suggestion – more than one hundred administrative transfers, now!? – and British authorities waffled over the second. How many nurses? What was their relation to the dead? Where were the graves? Macdonald's office began to resemble a tourist bureau as she gathered all this information. She also asked Maud McCarthy in France whether Canadian matrons in England might join nurses from Canadian hospitals in France on tours of the former front lines. But no sooner were things arranged and trips organized for both kinds of tourists – the bereaved and the curious – than logistics interfered. Cars broke down, graves could not be located.

Whenever Macdonald had better information or knew of more reliable transport, she tried again. Part of her own last inspection tour to the Continent, in May 1919, when she was in northern France and Belgium and went into Germany as far as Köln and Bonn, may have been to scout the terrain and the facilities for her nurses. In any case, groups of nurses did regularly cross the Channel to France, from at least late April until late July. All of them would have been awestruck by the terrain and the silence of the front. They had known of it only by its sounds: the thunder of the heavy guns – audible even in England – the names of battles won or lost, the moans of wounded men. Now the front was just a ruined landscape. Silent. Some of the nurses had two and even three brothers in the graveyards of France and Flanders. What despair they must have felt when an impassible road prevented their last link with their siblings before returning to Canada.[145]

Even when the nurses were on their way home, Macdonald kept an eye on them from London. She expected them both to behave and to be treated as officers and ladies until the last minute. When a group of nurses complained of shoddy treatment on embarkation at Liverpool, she was not sure which line had been crossed. As with any complaint, she investigated thoroughly. Had her nurses really had no food or sleeping accommodation on the train to Liverpool? Had they detrained in a stockyard and carried their own baggage a mile through filth only to be given second-class cabins on the *Celtic* while male officers occupied the upper decks? It seems that this had indeed been the case. Even though Macdonald was reassured that most of the nurses had taken it all in good part, she pursued the matter with the chief transport officer. Three of the complainants did the same on arrival in Canada, taking their grievance to the minister of the militia. This is probably when Macdonald thought they had gone far enough. One of her male colleagues sent a reply to Ottawa arguing that the nursing sisters had been unreasonable; it was only their hand baggage they had had to carry, and they really had no grounds for complaint.[146]

While investigating the grumblings of these nurses, Macdonald heard a complaint about some others that may have bothered her even more. She was not at all pleased to learn that four Canada-bound nurses, even if not travelling on duty and therefore not obliged to do any nursing, had refused to assist a woman passenger in labour. Their behaviour was neither properly feminine nor that of a good Samaritan. Worse still: "These Sisters have created an impression which may serve to neutralize, to a certain degree, the previous good record of the Army Nursing Service."[147] Ten months after the end of the war, the reputation of Macdonald's nurses was still on the line.

Macdonald had spent five years creating and sustaining that reputation, and she was immensely proud of the performance of her nurses, indeed of all military nurses during the war. As she told the newly formed British Association of Hospital Matrons in London in June 1919, "Their work in the great war had eclipsed anything the nursing world had ever seen. These noble women, by their work, carried on without aggression, without parade or self-consciousness, had attained for the profession at large a recognition that years of peace might not have brought." Macdonald charged her audience (none of whom would have missed her oblique reference to the unladylike activity of prewar suffragettes) with maintaining nurses' "place in the sun." For theirs was not just the extraordinary achievement of nurses, it was also that of women: "It seems almost incredible that such vast organizations, composed entirely of women, governed by women, should during a crisis extending over four and a half years present an unbroken line; this at a time when not only governments, but high individual reputations, became wrecked and one's confidence almost changed to despair. In the Nursing Service not a weak spot, not even the semblance of a breakdown, was found, and what is dearer than all, the breath of scandal never blew across its name."[148] She gave no credit to the army for providing the opportunity for women to shine so brightly; nor did she comment on its careful confinement of them. Rather, she praised women's own talents and their ever-present sense of themselves as ladies.

If Macdonald ever wearied of looking after her nurses during the war years, she kept it well hidden. Like them, she appears to have enjoyed remarkably good health, a sure sign of satisfying work. Like them too, and following her own advice, she worked and played in equal measure. Although her official military file records only one wartime leave of six days at the end of August 1918, she did in fact attach a holiday to one of her inspection tours in France in 1916. And Scotland beckoned her at some point. She also tried to keep Sundays for a jaunt out of London into the English countryside, even turning down invitations to tea to do so.[149] Presumably, her extensive social life in London itself made up for the lack of leave.

However, once the war was over, her health wavered. Like millions of others in the winter of 1919, Macdonald caught the flu – badly enough to require two weeks in hospital in February. At "her urgent request" she returned to duty, in spite of lingering bronchitis,[150] and within a few weeks had such a bad cold that she missed Easter mass – the first time ever. Her teeth bothered her as well that spring, and she had three extracted. Nonetheless, her zest rarely deserted her. She lunched at Frascati's and dined at the Carleton. She entertained the Australian and New Zealand matrons-in-chief at her club. She took in the Derby and was presented to the Queen at a garden party at Buckingham Palace. Two of her brothers came to town, and she saw them three days in a row. On several occasions she had tea or lunch with the BEF matron-in-chief, who was now Dame Maud McCarthy. She went to the theatre, even on a Wednesday afternoon, and danced in Trafalgar Square. And she tripped off to Ireland for a week in August. All these activities she noted briefly in her diary for 1919; there is no mention of work. Clearly, things were winding down. The office was emptying of both people and paper; she could go in at noon on a Monday in October 1919 and find the place deserted. On 11 November she recorded the "anniversary of armistice" but nothing about the silence of the entire city for two minutes at eleven that morning.

By then, her plans for departure were fixed. Her last diary entries, for the three days before leaving, were even more laconic than the others: 16 November, "Packed all day"; 17 November, "Shopped"; 18 November, "Busy day. Woodbury attended to luggage." Into her diary she tucked a horoscope for 26 February (her birthday) from a wartime London paper. Whether or not it is an accurate portrayal of her character and experience, something about it tickled her fancy and she kept it: "Neither want nor protracted illness here ... several love affairs and all of them culminate in long friendships ... jealousy and envy play little part in this life ... fitted to occupy a responsible position where [s]he will be at the head of affairs. Much confidence is placed in [her] judgment and it is well placed ... some tendency to worry and fret about trifling details, but big problems of life are always met bravely."[151] Having met bravely the big problem of war and the big loss of one of her long friendships, she boarded the *Megantic* in Liverpool on 19 November, bound for Halifax. With a bit of an English accent now on her tongue, the officer and lady was on her way home.

"The officer and lady was on her way home"

FIVE

Memory, Echoes, and Silence

Margaret Macdonald's "wondrous peace" was not kind to her. She came home to a place of forgetting and a place of memory,[1] and both left her on the margins of the military, the margins of nursing, and the margins of society. For someone who had so enjoyed being a first, exercising power, doing things and being recognized, she burrowed into an existence that was as private as the other had been public. Like a war widow she emerged for ceremonial recollections of a previous life – tributes as much to a way of being as to the specific dead. For a time she tried to write up her nurses' story for the history books, only to be stymied by gender and a commitment to silence. The speed with which she offered her services on the eve of the Second World War suggests that her yen for wars had in no way abated in the intervening years. But even with her portrait hanging in the office of the minister of national defence, the army had no further use for her. She was too old.

In late November 1919, however, things seemed slightly more promising if not entirely clear. Macdonald was one of the last veterans to return from the war. Most of her nurses, most of the soldiers too, had by then returned to civilian life, their farewell to the military being the final administrative act of demobilization. But she was not to be demobilized because of her permanent position with what was now named the Royal

Macdonald's portrait, now at the Canadian War Museum

Canadian Army Medical Corps. What exactly she would do was as yet unknown – to her and to army headquarters. Indeed, the men there must have been wondering what to do about the two matrons-in-chief they now had on their hands. They had become used to Edith Rayside since the fall of 1917, and she in turn was much more familiar than Macdonald with the army bureaucracy in Ottawa and with the array of military hospitals that had been established in Canada during the war. Macdonald had not been in Ottawa since 1914, and then only briefly, and the corps of nurses that she had been supervising no longer existed. What role would she play now?

Before an answer was found Macdonald had two months' leave following her arrival in Canada. From a Halifax still scarred by the explosion two years earlier, she headed straight to Bailey's Brook for the first Christmas in years in the family home. Her three brothers had returned ahead of her, Ronald back to his faculty position at the McGill medical school, Bill to Halifax to resume his legal career, and Donald still convalescing before establishing a legal practice in New Glasgow. All three bachelors likely came home that Christmas. Margaret's sisters would have crowded round – Cell and her family from over the meadow at Egnaig; Kate and her family in from Inverness on Cape Breton; Vie still keeping the home fires burning for her mother at Moydart – all of them except the two teaching nuns, Adele in Montreal and Florence in Waterbury, Connecticut. And while neighbours came calling to see how Maggie had fared with her big job in the Great War, she herself stepped right back into a pre-war rural world. The house had neither electricity nor phone. The contrast with London and the great country houses of England could not have been greater. Upstairs was her own small bedroom from which she could glimpse the buildings of the family store – not quite the major business it had been in D.D.'s time, but still functioning. Everything was in its place, the place to which she always returned over the years. It was small, it was familiar, it was home. For two months she relished it.

Beyond the family, greetings and requests for her presence poured in. Women in particular wanted to reclaim her. Her welcome was thus more prolonged than that of the soldiers, but it was also more one-sided. No crowds of men and women greeted her at stations, no front-page press coverage marked her return to Canada. On the other hand, neither did the public's interest turn so suddenly and sullenly away, as it did for the soldiers. Macdonald went on being a celebrity, among women, long after the end of the war. Women wanted to hear about her experiences, they wanted to see her, to know what she was wearing, to give her tea and flowers, and they wanted to reassure themselves that she was still a woman.

No sooner had she arrived in Bailey's Brook in late November 1919 than the Women's Council of East Pictou organized a pre-Christmas reception in New Glasgow for "Pictou County's most distinguished daughter."[2] The Graduate Nurses' Association of Nova Scotia followed suit in Halifax. Matrons and nurses at military hospitals in Toronto and Winnipeg fêted her. A group of her wartime nurses, organizing themselves in Edmonton in 1920 into an Overseas Nursing Sisters' Association, elected her honorary president, as did the national group when it was formed in 1929.[3] Meanwhile, the Graduate Nurses' Association of Ontario, holding its annual convention in Ottawa in the spring of 1920, wanted her as guest speaker. She unveiled a plaque at the Montreal General Hospital to the nurses lost on the *Llandovery Castle* and another in the legislative buildings in Toronto to the five dead from the Ontario hospital at Orpington. The Catholic Women's League held and elegant luncheon for her at the King Edward Hotel in Toronto in June with five hundred people in attendance, and the Hospital for Sick Children invited her to address the graduating nurses in November. A Manitoba chapter of the Imperial Order Daughters of the Empire, whose motto was "Britain expects every girl to do her duty," named itself "Nurse Macdonald" early in 1921 and requested her photo for prominent display.[4]

She attended the inaugural meeting of the Canadian Council on Child Welfare in Ottawa in May as the representative of the Catholic Women's League and was immediately charged with committee work.[5] In the early autumn she was the guest of honour among two hundred and fifty invited guests at the Women's Day luncheon at the Canadian National Exhibition, an event described as the "first public recognition since the war" of Canada's military nurses.[6] And she was the star alumna when Mount St Vincent Academy organized former students into an alumnae association in December. To the International Federation of Catholic Alumnae, she was then the obvious choice as first "governor" for Nova Scotia.[7] When a memorial tablet was placed in the Children's Hospital in Halifax in November 1922 for Nova Scotian nurses who had lost their lives in the war, Macdonald again did the honours, as she had done in May at the Nurses' Home of the Montreal General to mark the postwar passing of one of her administrative favourites, Mildred Forbes. She did the same at Aberdeen Hospital in New Glasgow, this time a tribute to her friend Margaret (Pearl) Fraser. In 1924 she was still being acknowledged publicly as a woman "who had won distinction in so many ways."[8]

Press coverage for these events was usually on the women's page or in the society columns. It often included an interview with Macdonald, excerpts from her speeches, and a comment on her appearance. A reporter for the *Toronto Star*, for example, felt the need to put female readers at ease: "The possessor of so many titles, honors and responsibilities is not, as one would naturally expect, a tall, austere, uniformed person, but a petite, alert little lady who at the luncheon today was wearing the daintiest [of] figured voile summer frocks, blue shoes which matched the frock, and a blue flower-trimmed hat which was the exact shade of its wearer's eyes."[9] Apparently, neither the reporter nor *Star* readers could fathom the notion of an officer and a lady. They needed to be reminded that in spite of her career in the military and her proximity to war, she was essentially feminine. They thereby gathered her safely back into acceptable female norms. Her homecoming, prolonged as it was, was part of Canada's return to normalcy.

Macdonald herself contributed to that image. And given her scrap-book preservation of the press comments, she may even have savoured it. She had, after all, chosen the clothing for her public appearances. She also chose her language carefully in the speeches she gave on these occa-sions. She, too, drew her own and her nurses' experiences back into the ken of her largely female audiences. Perhaps it was the only way for her, or them, to make any sense of it all. While still in Britain, she had admit-ted to the kaleidoscopic nature of her wartime impressions.[10] Now she had to make them understandable to a Canadian audience. She therefore insisted that service had been the prime motive of the nurses; support, loyalty, and cooperation had been their watchwords. "Doing the right thing at the right time in the right way" was their reward and their joy.[11] Women listeners would have nodded in recognition and approval. As for her own work, Macdonald presented it as not very different from that of women running households in Canada. Like them, she had ensured com-fortable surroundings in mess or rest home for her family of nurses and had advocated domesticity and facilitated marriage; like them, she and her nurses had taken things in their stride with both a seriousness of pur-pose and a cheery manner. Even her decision making Macdonald attrib-uted to "that indispensable quality possessed by nine-tenths of our Canadian women – initiative."[12]

The members of her audience thereby found themselves both flattered and on comfortable terrain. The rougher terrain of war she glossed over with humour, counting on her listeners' own experience of the ridiculous at moments of great seriousness. She even entitled an entire speech "Comedies in War Tragedy," most of the examples in it being domestic ones. She knew that her audience would recognize and be amused by the widow who was more anxious about payments due on the furniture than she was about the death of her husband; by the young woman bewailing the loss of a third fiancé in a row; by the novice nurse worrying about how to launder the white collars and cuffs of her uniform in the trenches.[13] Macdonald deliberately invited a chuckle in another speech with her com-ment that in 1914 "men were faced with two dangers – War and the inva-sion of Women."[14] By the end of the speech, she was back to flattering her audience by comparing their domestic and war work with that of the nurses overseas; they had all been doing the same thing. And then she offered them the final assurance: her nurses had not betrayed the "trust and confidence" of the women at home.[15] In other words, they had not made off with those women's husbands. All was well, all was normal.

In making her audiences comfortable, Macdonald distanced herself

and her nurses from the great adventure. Her speeches were a prolonged
farewell to a world she could not describe, so foreign was it to Canadian
women of the time. She and her nurses had earned power, status, and
privilege through their professional work. Now they had to let it go. Normalcy required it. But what, then, would happen to their story and the
memory of it? As early as the summer of 1920, barely six months after her
return, Macdonald expressed worries about the short duration of public
memory.[16] All around her, the war, the soldiers, the nurses seemed to be
disappearing from public view. In spite of a proliferation of public monuments, in spite of Armistice Day services with their direct or implied warn-
ings of "Lest we forget," that is precisely what people wanted to do. In
some small way, Macdonald's speeches, by normalizing her nurses' experience, contributed to the public forgetfulness. For all her brave claim at the
Canadian National Exhibition that "generations yet unborn will bless the
memory of these heroic women" and that "the lofty ideals, aspirations
and attainments of the Army Nurses ... have given us traditions that will
survive till time is at an end," it simply was not true.[17] Even the photograph of the occasion captured the very normalcy she was evoking in her
speeches and gave the lie to her words about memory. Pictured was a non-
descript, grandmotherly figure (Macdonald) holding a doll's crib (a miniature hospital bed). Everyone had photos like that: nothing special there.
The miniature bed in fact was serving as a container for the tributes to
Canada's nurses that came to Macdonald during the CNE ceremony.[18] A
cute idea on someone's part, but the photographic effect all these years
later is one of belittlement of Macdonald and her nurses, and of the soldiers too. At the time, Macdonald hoped that the memory of her nurses'
contribution would grow with the years and that the tributes would one
day "adorn the walls of a Women's Section of a Canadian War Museum."[19] This, too, did not happen. Indeed, two of the tributes surfaced in a
garage sale in 2004.[20]

Memory also had its part in Macdonald's messages to more specialized
audiences. She urged her nursing colleagues to recall the traditions of the
profession, many of which had been confirmed by wartime practice. For
Macdonald, the military nurses represented the standard of devotion to
"the service of humanity" which younger nurses should emulate. New
graduates were not to forget that the "mission of nursing is a divinely
appointed one." They were not to be seduced by the material offerings of
the postwar world.[21] Nor were they to be frightened off by hard work:
"Did you ever hear of hard work hurting anyone? It is the best training
a girl can have."[22] Macdonald worried about the effect on nursing of

Tribute to Macdonald and her nurses, Canadian National
Exhibition, 1921

increasingly scientific and technical training, particularly in the growing
field of public health. It was too intensive, too mechanistic, too reminiscent of "Boche kultur." Where was the "honoured sense of vocation"?
Where was the "spiritual side of nursing"? Without these, nurses were
"wandering far from the path of Florence Nightingale."[23] To stay on that
path they needed memory, an appreciation of the origins of nursing and of
its spiritual purpose.

While all this might make Macdonald sound slightly old-fashioned, a
different tone is equally evident in her postwar speeches. Without ever
saying so directly, she believed that she and her nurses had been part of
a vast wartime movement towards "sex equality." By that she meant
women's proven ability to take on "responsibilities formerly borne by

men."[24] The war had demanded and drawn upon the immense capacities of women; indeed, those capacities had been an "indispensable factor in the winning of the war."[25] As a result, according to Macdonald, there was greater tolerance of women, broader fields of endeavour for their talents, and greater cooperation between men and women. She predicted an end, in the very near future, to "sex disqualification"[26] (British shorthand for the barring of women from certain occupations). She and the New Zealand matron-in-chief, both of whom would likely have been highly placed army doctors had they been men, were gleeful about the changes. "It really does seem that women are coming into their own," the New Zealander responded to Macdonald's chirpy account of her homecoming.[27] The two of them had clearly spotted the signs of change in Britain during the war. They were in London during early demonstrations of women's "right to serve"; they knew about industrial changes that made some aspects of skilled work available to women; and they would have followed the intricacies of British electoral reform as of 1916, including that which finally accorded the vote to property-owning women over thirty as part of the Representation of the People Act in 1918. And Macdonald was still in London when the House of Commons accepted the Sex Disqualification (Removal) Bill in October 1919.[28] She was there, too, when her friend Lady Astor won a seat in the House in a by-election in mid-November.

From the debates over female suffrage, Macdonald adopted the arguments of British parliamentarians. Women had earned their place in the public realm. In her mind, as in theirs, equal citizenship for women came as a result of worthy civic behaviour; votes for women, the symbol of equal citizenship, were a reward rather than the natural right of an individual. What a conversation Macdonald must have had with Emmeline Pankhurst when the two were at Cliveden together at the beginning of December 1917! They would certainly have agreed on the war's priority and perhaps on votes for women, but not at all on the meaning and methods. Might they have discussed Macdonald's own partially acquired right to vote, which she was about to exercise in the Canadian federal election? Thanks to the Military Voters Act of 1917, she could vote as a member of Canada's overseas military forces. In fact, the Wartime Elections Act of the same year also qualified her in that she was a female relative of Canadian soldiers. She must have had a strong sense of betrayal of her family's Liberal loyalties as she voted for the Union government and its policy of conscription. By the time she was back in Canada in late 1919, virtually all Canadian women had the federal vote, and their first use of it would come in the federal election of 1921. Some of them might even take the plunge into public life themselves. If so, Macdonald had a recipe for them: they would require "a strong faith, patriotism and high ideals, a balanced judgment, the power to eliminate the ego, dignity, ardent enthusiasm and a touch of humour." As an afterthought, she added "a good digestion" to the recipe.[29] Might a personal dream have been behind her list? All the qualities she named – including the good digestion – were her own, and in 1921 she thought "even the Senate would soon be invaded."[30] In fact, it was ten years and many a court case before one woman was named to the Senate.[31] As for "sex equality," it too turned out to be another of war's illusions, Macdonald herself being part of the fallout. But at the time her optimistic views had the press presenting her as "a champion of women's rights in the sanest, broadest fashion."[32] She would have been pleased, but she would have replaced the word "rights" with "responsibilities."

This was the kind of woman – experienced, responsible, idealistic, and moderately feminist – who reported for duty at military headquarters in Ottawa in February 1920. During the two and a half years she spent there, she collected the accolades of women for herself and her nurses, but the men of the military were nonplussed by her presence. Oh, they kept track of her officially as she wended her way out of the Canadian Expeditionary Force to the Overseas Military Forces of Canada and thence to the Permanent Force as it was being reconstituted, and finally to the Royal Canadian Army Medical Corps, with authority to be employed at Militia Headquarters, Ottawa.[33] But until June, what she was to do there was never specified. She did accompany the other matron-in-chief, Edith Rayside, on inspection tours of military hospitals in Toronto and Winnipeg, acquainting herself with Canadian practices and renewing links with nurses who had been overseas.[34] She must have been planning a long stay in Ottawa, for she took an apartment on Gilmour Street and set it up cosily.[35] And she acquired two major honours that spring, signs of public esteem that her male colleagues could not have ignored. In May 1920, St Francis Xavier University gave her an honorary doctorate, making her only the second Canadian woman to receive such a distinction. "It's always nice to be among the first chosen," she preened privately.[36] In public she was always more modest, but she would not have hidden the Florence Nightingale Medal of the International Red Cross, another rare and prestigious honour she received that June.[37] It was obvious to the military that it had a prominent personage on its hands.

But the military was simultaneously engaged in shrinking the army and the medical corps to almost prewar size. Part of the shrinking was the demobilization in June of the matron-in-chief for Canada, Edith Rayside. That left only one matron-in-chief to worry about. But what was she to do? Her former London superior, General Foster, was himself caught in the same tangle of postwar rearrangements. After being Director General Medical Services in London, would he or would he not replace the DGMS in Ottawa? The eventual answer for him was no, but for Macdonald he had an idea. To his superiors, he suggested attaching her to the historical section of the newly named Ministry of National Defence with the task of writing an official history of the nursing service. He would have known of her recent talk in Ottawa on "Aspects of War Nursing" and also that she was about to give another in Toronto entitled "Echoes of the Great War." Why, she was well into the topic already. With her "first-hand knowledge of the subject," Foster considered her the ideal person to undertake such a history. Moreover, she could do it at the same time as being "available to assist the office of the D.G.M.S. whenever questions in connection with the Nursing Service arise."[38] No one expected these duties to be very oner-ous as the nursing service headed towards its post-war establishment of ten permanent members. To the army, and presumably to Macdonald, the proposal seemed appealing, for it was all agreed to in five days. For some reason, she kept her office with that of the DGMS, and personnel matters concerning her continued to pass through that channel. But as of 15 June 1920, she reported to the historical section. The only direction she seems to have received from the head of that section was to "take plenty of time," there was no hurry.[39] She appears to have taken his advice literally as she began a task for which she had no training and less temperament, a task that eventually proved to be impossible.

For two years Macdonald struggled with the new assignment. She combed the *War Story of the* CAMC written by her London colleague George Adami and marked, without comment, those passages that touched on nursing.[40] But Adami's account, published in 1918, only brought the story to 1915; he never completed a projected second volume. So Macdonald had to rely on the mountain of official files that had accumulated in Lon-don and were sent back to Canada after the war. Yet she seems to have con-sulted relatively few of them.[41] Instead, she relied on her own reports and recollections and those of her colleagues.

Among those colleagues was Jean Cameron-Smith, a friend of Mac-donald's since New York days and one whose "ready pen" she had acknowledged in 1917.[42] At that time, she had "especially employed" Cameron-Smith for almost a year – since April 1916 – to collect historical data; partly this was to give her something to do after a fall had rendered her incapable of active nursing and partly, perhaps, it was to match the medical service's own resident historical scribe, George Adami.[43] By November 1916, Cameron-Smith was calling on the British matron-in-chief in France "in an official capacity as historian of the Canadian Nursing Service."[44] What this designation meant for relations between her and Macdonald after the war, when Cameron-Smith was demobilized, is unknown. But if a note of reassurance from New Zealand is any indication, Macdonald had a few qualms both about Cameron-Smith and about her own ability to complete the history. "I haven't the slightest doubt as to the success of your war history," wrote Mabel Thurston, encouragingly. "I am looking forward to the pleasure of reading it one of these days – it is quite right it should be given to you."[45] Thurston never did have that pleasure but the material Macdonald gathered for the history did include a number of texts by Cameron-Smith. In fact, Macdonald may have had in mind a collaborative undertaking with matrons and nursing sisters writing accounts of hospitals and events that she only knew about second-hand from London.

She certainly wanted their input for colour and anecdote. In the fall of 1920 she solicited reminiscences from former matrons and nursing sisters:

In connection with the Canadian history of the Great War, it is proposed to include therein the story of the C.A.M.C. Nursing Service, with a full account of the conspicuously distinguished work of this corps. It is desired that the narrative of the Nursing Service should be not only an accurate record of achievement but something that may in future serve as a useful comparative reference. In order to assure the success of this undertaking and to guard against oversight of an important item bearing on the subject, it is hoped that members of the Nursing Service will extend their co-operation. All who were actually engaged in the care and observation of sick, wounded and convalescent soldiers had excellent opportunity for appreciating the infinite courage, pathos, and even drollery of these patients.

Will you further amplify your good offices by contributing a characteristic incident, a telling photograph or authentic circumstance of historical value that came under your personal observation?[46]

The recipients of this letter may well have been puzzled as to just what was being asked of them. Of the twenty-five hundred people to whom the letter was sent, eight responded. Two could contribute nothing, one because she was engaged in medical studies, and the other because she possessed "none of the arts of composition." Her experiences, she said, "droll and otherwise ... would lose colour and interest in the telling."[47] A third, less modest, was awaiting copyright on a story she had already written; she would send it along for criticism or use (and in fact Macdonald extracted five segments from this story for inclusion in the first three chapters of her history).[48] The fourth respondent took literally the only specific illustration Macdonald had provided in her letter and wrote to her about two soldiers.[49] The fifth, Lady Astor, who was neither nurse nor matron, couldn't think of a single "characteristic incident" from the four years of having a Canadian hospital on her estate at Cliveden but said she would try to find a photograph for "Maria."[50] Two responses included accounts that Macdonald considered "outstanding": one from Matron MacLatchy about No. 3 Canadian General and one from Matron Tremaine about No. 1 Canadian Casualty Clearing Station, though Macdonald suspected that the latter had been written by the commanding officer of that unit. As for the eighth respondent, Matron Leishman promised "an item of importance ... and was never heard from again."[51] Nor were the vast majority of Macdonald's wartime nurses.

She should have expected this. Her letter seemed to request the soldiers' stories rather than the nurses' and she had qualified it with the phrase "of historical value." What woman in the 1920s would have used that phrase to describe any experience of her own? All would have been flattered to know that the nurses were to be included in the "Canadian history of the Great War," but they would have been right to be sceptical of its realization. Besides, as nurses, they had been enjoined to silence since the very beginning of their nursing training. The ability to maintain silence was both an occupational qualification for a nurse and one of her professional skills. In tending patients, a nurse used her eyes, hands, and nose to detect a change of condition, but talking was a carefully constrained part of her activity. She even imposed silence on others for the benefit of the sick. And she certainly was not to talk about them when off duty.

The military augmented each one of these professional obligations, and the conditions of war added even more. To a wartime nurse, silence was both armour for herself and a tool of her trade. She even represented silence; in her presence, wounded soldiers knew they were temporarily protected from the thunder of guns and the explosion of shells. She was the one hovering in the silence between life and death. As for her written words, they were subject to the censor's eye for any possible breach of military security, just as her spoken words were considered a breach of military propriety if she talked too much. Macdonald knew all this. She had been careful in letting any of her nurses speak in public and had insisted on reviewing and approving any written text destined for a public audience.[52] In such a setting and in the midst of the unspeakable things they were witnessing, nurses began censoring themselves. As one remarked to Macdonald halfway through the war, "Thoughts fit for putting down on paper are pretty foreign to me at present."[53] In any case, much of what they had experienced was literally beyond words. Between the work they loved and its purpose of repairing and shipping men back to slaughter the gulf was just too deep. Like many of their soldier comrades, the nurses went silent after the war. The long public memory that Macdonald was happily predicting for them in her postwar speeches was drying up at its source.

She nonetheless trudged on with her history. Through 1921 and 1922 she gathered and organized material, in between her other activities: her public appearances; her supervision of the dwindling number of military nurses; her initiation of a section in the *Canadian Nurse* devoted to the nursing sisters; her Christmas and summer leave in Nova Scotia; and her happy welcome of Lady Astor, MP, on an official visit to Ottawa in May 1922. At least two newspapers knew of her undertaking, but the publicity seems not to have netted any additional information.[54] She therefore limited her range to the few close colleagues she could count on for texts, and she appears to have written more and more of the texts herself to fit an evolving table of contents. Hers, for example, were the pieces on the prewar nursing service, mobilization, the first general and stationary hospitals, No. 3 Canadian Stationary Hospital, the French Canadian unit, and the Anglo-Russian hospital.[55] Did she really expect to write something about every hospital? And how was she intending to integrate the material? Some of her own accounts begin bravely and well but degenerate into chronology as if she had run out of steam and was simply transposing from official war diaries or administrative reports.[56] Jean Cameron-Smith's contributions are much more polished but are so florid in comparison with Macdonald's that the whole would have lacked unity.

Still, Macdonald was making progress, as her pencilled additions to the table of contents attests.[57] By the spring of 1922 she could be far more specific about what she wanted, asking one former nurse, for instance, to provide a "short sketch of your experience on the s.s. *Ansonia*, when it was torpedoed on June 11th, 1917." Another was asked to "freshen" her memory of "the day you were stooping to fasten your shoe when a shell hissed over your head." A third she instructed to "sit yourself down and answer these questions" about the early days on Lemnos.[58] Of the three, only the last obliged, protesting all the way: "Anybody else in the unit could have done better, however gardening and writing do not go well together."[59]

In the meantime, one of Macdonald's London colleagues was in the process of upstaging her with a history of his own. Sir Andrew Macphail took on the official history of the medical services late in 1921 and completed it two years later. He had a much more facile pen than Macdonald as well as the career to back it up. Macphail was a doctor, professor of the history of medicine at McGill, and editor of the *University Magazine*; he had been with a Canadian field hospital at the front, and from mid-1917 to the end of the war was in London as assistant and adviser to General Foster, the DMS. So he and Macdonald had known each other for at least two years – he used to pop into her office for tea – and after his return to Canada he asked to be remembered to "the young ladies" of her staff.[60] What she made of his notorious anti-feminist sentiments can only be guessed.

Macphail must have known of her work on the nurses when he began his own work on the medical services late in 1921. Their two volumes were to be a pair in the planned multivolume official history of Canadian participation in the war which the historical section of National Defence was preparing. For his history, Macphail drew extensively on his personal experience as recorded in his diary. Unlike Macdonald, he appears not to have engaged in consultations with colleagues, though after he had completed his manuscript, senior military officials did go over it for any "needless asperity." Macdonald's did not even get that far. The summer after Macphail began his work on the project, she stopped hers. When his book was published in 1925 it contained the only public remnant of her effort, a six-page section on the nurses, unacknowledged as that of Margaret Macdonald.[61]

By then she was no longer in the army. In mid-June 1922, the men at military headquarters decided they no longer needed a matron-in-chief. In the name of "the most stringent economy in Militia matters ... [as] demanded not only by Parliament but by the public at large," the military members of the Militia Council determined that Macdonald and her post were redundant. They said nothing about the history; rather, they suggested she take the matron's job at Tuxedo Barracks hospital in Winnipeg and thereby "save the salary of one matron." If she was unwilling to do so, there was "no alternative but her retirement to pension."[62]

Did Macdonald see this coming? The decision was transmitted to the DGMS, and it is not clear when he informed her, or even if she was in Ottawa at the time it was made. She was certainly in Bailey's Brook as of mid-July for her annual one-month leave, and it was from there in early August that she replied to the decision with a sharpness that suggests its recent announcement: "As the proposal that I take over the duties at present administered by a Nursing Sister of the R.C.A.M.C. is made in the interests of economy, it would seem the measure would be best served by my accept-ance of the alternative suggested, viz. Retirement to Pension."[63] In other words, the army would save more money by giving her an annual pension of $1,260 than by continuing her annual pay (and allowances) of $3,000.[64] Macdonald's colleagues in Ottawa may have known that she was unlikely to push one of her nursing sisters out of a job or be willing herself to accept what amounted to demotion. So she agreed to retirement. But in doing so, she specified certain conditions. She wanted six months' leave of absence with full pay and allowances as of 18 August (the end of her annual leave) before the official retirement. She wanted her name on the Retired List, Reserve of Officers of the Canadian militia. And perhaps of most impor-tance to her, she wanted the right to "retain the designation of Matron-in-chief."[65] This, after all, had been her wartime identity and her wartime pride. The speedy acceptance of these conditions suggests that the men at headquarters were glad to see her go. She was even told that she "need not return to Ottawa for duty."[66]

Her demands, in fact, were minimal. The six months' paid leave was the precise amount she or any other army nurse was entitled to as dis-charge pay after three or more years overseas; and the other two were normal for retiring army officers in good standing. But there was also the fact that the timing of the leave, ending as it did in mid-February 1923, would bring her within a week of her fiftieth birthday. Her age, along with her years of service (sixteen with the PAMC, one and a half in South Africa, and five in the nursing reserve) no doubt had a bearing on her pension. In any case, it was all agreed and Macdonald never did return to military headquarters. She let it be known to her nursing public that she had requested "permission to retire, in order to take a long holiday."[67] Whether her retirement was by request, bargain, persuasion, or order, it meant the end of her history of the nursing service.

The project nonetheless continued to hold the attention of the histori-cal section at National Defence for another year. Colonel Duguid, who had been appointed director of the section in June 1921, a year after Mac-donald began work on the history, had had relatively little to do with her because she did not work out of his office. He was not even informed of her retirement. So when he went looking for signs of a completed manu-script or even preparatory files, he was troubled. What had she been doing all that time? And where were the documents? If she had them, he wanted them back. The more he fussed, the more she resisted, and a very murky situation, bordering on the unsavoury and probably reflecting her post-

retirement state of mind, developed between the two of them. He suspected she had kept material that rightly belonged to the government so that
she could one day complete her own story. Whether or not there was anything to suspect, she did have some material with her in Bailey's Brook;
she may have been working on the history there in June at the time of the
Militia Council's decision about her future. But if that was the case, what
to make of her apology to Duguid for not having notified him "before
leaving Ottawa that the step was preliminary to retirement from the Service"?[68] Whenever that "leaving Ottawa" occurred – sometime in June or
in mid-July for her annual leave – she would not have taken documents
with her if she knew she was retiring. She went on to surprise him with her
assumption "that the data supplied to Andrew Macphail completed my
connection with the history of the Nursing Section." She did admit to having "some few notes" among her still unpacked effects, notes that she
might "pad" out at some point. If she did so, she would send him a copy.[69]

Duguid wanted more than a vague promise. If she would send him the
"detailed draft of contents of chapters" that she was planning, he would
gladly look it over, give her advice, dig up information, have the manuscript typed in his office – do anything, in short, to move the project along.
He flattered and cajoled her and called upon her sense of duty.[70] She was
unmoved and simply did not reply. When he sent the same letter two
months later, she merely listed a series of family obligations that had
absorbed her time, adding: "I cannot say when the time may be opportune
for me to concentrate on the more or less sparse notes I have in hand."[71]
She clearly did not think she owed the army anything, and he just as clearly thought she did. He showed his annoyance by calling in the higher
authorities and suggesting legal action against her through the judge advocate general.[72]

Instead, the deputy minister of defence took it upon himself to request
from her the "notes, documents, memoranda, diaries, and other material
compiled, collected or prepared by you."[73] In response, she sent him a
package of "documents pertaining to the Nursing Service that rightly
belong to the Department" (which he passed on immediately to Duguid).
And she in turn let her pique show: "It seems a matter of regret that the
present concern over the interests of the Nursing Service was not made
manifest whilst I was at H.Q."[74] She was bitter, but Duguid was not
assuaged. He was sure that she had not handed over all she had. Where,
for example, was the circular letter she had sent nurses and matrons in the
fall of 1920? There was no sign of it in Ottawa. Moreover, some of the
documents she had sent looked like duplicates. Where were the originals?

At Duguid's urging, the deputy minister tried again, but Macdonald clammed up once more. She had sent all she had, she insisted. Anything else was on file at National Defence. After one more attempt in the summer of 1923 to pry information or documents out of her, the men in Ottawa gave up. They had to make do with what she had already sent and with her final word on the topic – eighteen chapter titles which she penned from memory while in England that summer.[75] No more was heard on the matter, but Duguid remained wary. In 1926 he suspected that she was working on something and huffily informed the Canadian Nurses' Association that whatever it was would not be official. Again in 1933, thinking she was up to something, he let it be known that she could only see documents in his office and only during working hours.[76] There was some foundation for his uneasiness, for she did have other material and must have justified it to herself as being of a personal nature or gathered before or after her two years as historian.[77] What is clear from the Duguid-Macdonald exchange is that she was not going to be harangued by him, much less accept any lessons in loyalty and duty.

Duguid's own sense of duty had him trying to complete the history of the nursing service. He asked one of his colleagues, Major Raymond Myers Gorssline, to make some sense of what remained of the project. Gorssline edited and condensed Macdonald's outline into sixteen concise chapter topics and began extracting "transcripts" to fit the topics, using the material Macdonald had sent and what he unearthed himself from official sources.[78] He then saw what she had seen – the need for the nurses' own contribution. Unlike her, he designed a specific set of questions about the nurses' actual work in order to put some flesh on the administrative bones of the history that was beginning to take shape. Before circulating the questionnaire, Duguid sent Gorssline's outline to a number of CAMC doctors and a few nurses with whom he was personally acquainted, and asked their opinion.[79] He received some blunt replies. Colonel Lorne Drum wanted to know why Macdonald was not doing this work. She was by far the best qualified person, he said, and should be prevailed upon to continue the task: "I can readily understand how a lady of her active disposition may have shrunk from the idea of months of possibly uncongenial work digging into the past, such as any historian must face; especially when such work could not but mean the emblazoning of services which had their mainspring so often in her own tireless energy and forethought, and owed their success largely to her own tact, judgment and common sense. To a lady of so retiring and modest a disposition as Miss Macdonald, and one to whom any limelight would be utterly distasteful, I can readily imagine that any work which would seem like self glorification would be repellant."[80]

However accurate a portrayal of Macdonald, this wasn't exactly what Duguid wanted to hear. Nor was he happy with former nursing sister Isabella Strathy's reaction to his grand purpose for the history. He wanted it to reveal "characteristics of devotion and fearlessness" and be read "by every Canadian girl before leaving high school." In response, she pleaded with him, "On behalf of the present day school girl may I make so bold as to say 'Have a heart.'"[81] As for the select group of matrons and nurses he may have approached with the questionnaire, Duguid was no more successful than Macdonald had been in having them speak up. So, like her, but in different circumstances, he crept away from the history. The remnants of it are in the national archives in Ottawa, as the Margaret Macdonald Papers. (Just whose victory their naming as such is not clear.)[82] As for Duguid himself, he was having a difficult enough time getting on with the overall history of Canada's participation in the war. Apart from Macphail's volume in 1925, nothing appeared until 1938 and then only one volume of a projected eight-volume series.

Duguid and Macdonald had both confronted the same impossible problem: how to tell a woman's story within the male narrative of war. Stories of men at war have been the stuff of history since recorded time; women in such stories have been inspiration, prizes, victims, or mourners. When an exception occurred, the story quickly absorbed the character into the norm. Joan of Arc, for example, played a male part temporarily at the head of an army, but she enters history in her female role as victim, a woman possessed. The military narrative requires action and battles, strategy and materiel, heroism and death for a cause. None of it fits women. When nurses were let into the narrative, barely twenty years before Macdonald was born, they were given a bit part, supporting actors to the main players, tending soldiers who were temporarily out of action. Beyond this, they were marginal to the story. Not only did they not engage in battles, but most of them did not die. After the First World War most of them returned home, in many cases without their brothers. They would have been sensitive to the ennobling of the dead as antidote to the unspoken, terrifying question of whether the war had been worth it.[83] But where did that leave them? The language of bravery and sacrifice was not quite appropriate; theirs was not the same experience as that of the soldiers, and it was the soldiers' experience, and notably their death, that was privileged in memory. In the face of this, how could they talk about work that was exhilarating, work that gave them a sense of importance and adventure, work that was so structured they could put all their energies into it? No one would understand – indeed, they could hardly believe it themselves – and moreover it would be shameful to admit to the thrill. Neither Macdonald nor Duguid could fathom the stumbling block to a history of the nursing service. They had run into the question of gender, and they had no idea what to do with it.

Nor would Macdonald have had any sense that gender played a part in her retirement from the army. After all, what could a military organization do with a senior staff woman in peacetime? Had she been willing to be demoted to a matron's position, the army would have found work for her, despite the dwindling number of military hospitals. But she was a skilled – and skilful – manager and leader, and no one in military circles could have imagined her managing or leading anything other than women. That she might have had something to say about military health care in general seems not to have occurred to anyone; that was the army doctors' business, and their numbers were being slashed too. And so, with the decline in nursing numbers, there wasn't much for Macdonald to manage or lead. Indeed, an army without women was one of the major signs that things had returned to normal after the shattering experience of the First World War.

Macdonald's demobilization, her "divorce" from the army, was thus simply delayed by a few years and given another name – "retirement." Like millions of other women in the Western world, she was to step out of the role that this war had temporarily provided and return whence she came. Unlike most of them, she at least had a pension. But even what she would do in retirement was part of normal expectations for a woman like her. As a middle-aged spinster, she would return to her family home in rural Nova Scotia and take up housekeeping duties with her single sister Vie, including the care of their aging mother. Macdonald shared these expectations. In fact, she had acted on them during the war when she had sanctioned the breaking of army contracts by nurses who were needed at home to care for ailing parents.[84] She herself had had virtually no domestic life since childhood and may have felt the pull. Indeed, if there was any substance to Macdonald's wartime romance with its prospect of marriage after the war, she would have foreseen a home of her own and the relinquishing of her profession. Gender expectations were all around her in 1922, and they required her to give up her "atypical life."[85]

If her retirement was a way of atoning for her unusual career, she certainly succeeded. She did not take on the "future enterprise" expected of her by former nursing sisters who had been overseas with her.[86] She never was "engaged in some other sphere of activity" that demanded "all her time," as one old friend from South Africa thought was the case.[87] No civilian hospital sought her services. No one summoned her out of retirement, as happened with her British colleague Maud McCarthy, to reorganize an entire nursing service.[88] No one courted her as a candidate for public office, although her former DMS in London, Guy Carleton Jones, privately suggested it to her.[89] She even withdrew from her connection with the *Canadian Nurse*, and she passed to someone else the rubric on the CAMC nursing service that she had started in 1920.[90] And although persuaded to remain a member, she was no longer active on the committee of the Canadian National Association of Trained Nurses that was planning a monument to Canada's nursing dead.[91] Instead of all this, she took up the life of a proper middle-class countrywoman.

She graced the family home, Moydart, which her sister Vie continued to run. She took for granted the presence of at least one live-in servant (the daughter of a local family or, in one case, a newcomer from England) who did all the domestic chores. Along with Vie, she watched over the hired help (mostly Freddie Burke, sometimes Dougal Macdonald, both from the vicinity), who kept the Macdonald farmland productive for thirty dollars a month. She did much of the gardening herself, proud of the English touch she brought to Moydart's extensive flower beds. She corresponded with friends and nursing colleagues in Britain and North America, keeping the rural postal delivery in Bailey's Brook busy with her mail alone. She designed a weekly "Brook Bulletin" with information about the farm and the neighbourhood for her brother Ronald in Montreal. And she entertained. Everyone who was anyone came calling: bishops, politicians, former nursing sisters. They would stay for tea or a meal and chat away the afternoon – world events, politics, gossip, reminiscence – and always there was much laughter in the homey Scottish-bedecked living and dining rooms of Moydart.

Then there was the family. Brothers, sisters, nieces, nephews, and cousins all came in a steady procession, particularly in the summer months, to be greeted by "Marge," by "Aunty Marnie." The most frequent of these visitors was her beloved brother Ronald, with his new young family, who came down from Montreal every summer after he purchased the nearby house Egnaig from his sister Marcella and her husband. Youngsters Mairi, Ronald junior (to whom Macdonald had sent her "best military salute" on his birth in 1928),[92] and Elizabeth scampered over to Moydart daily to see what their aunts were up to – a card game, croquet on the lawn, a caper with the little white dog Gyp, or perhaps a picnic in the meadow above the brook or on the beach at the old MacIntosh and

Chisholm shore, two miles distant, or a chicken supper to celebrate one or other of the children's birthdays. In rainy weather, they poked about "Greenland," that part of the second floor of Moydart, above the dining room, that stored, among other keepsakes, Aunty Marnie's mementos of the war. From their parents they knew she was someone special, and they soon grasped that she was both more formal and more informed than her ebullient sister Vie. Well dressed, well spoken and well read, she told them character-building stories and had answers to all their questions. She was the perfect chatelaine – gracious, spirited, decisive, and self-effacing. Except for the quantity of mail and visitors, no one would have known she had ever left Bailey's Brook.[93]

The outside world did, however, continue to beckon her, but only in the manner befitting a woman at home. She had time to devote to the Catholic Women's League, to the Federation of Catholic Alumnae, to the Nova Scotia Girl Guides, and to the Liberal Party via its women's associations at the county, provincial, and national level. These activities took her to Pictou, Halifax, Ottawa, Boston, and Philadelphia. After the death of her mother in 1927, she and Vie were free to go away during winter. They headed south to the sunshine – Macdonald describing herself as a "woman farmer" – or west to relatives in California and once as far as Spain. In the late 1930s they took to closing Moydart for the snowy season and spending the winter now with one married sister, now with another in Antigonish or New Glasgow. During at least four summers or early fall, Macdonald went to Europe, possibly accompanied by her mother in 1923 and certainly with her sister Vie in 1925 and her brother Donald in 1938. She travelled in style: cabin class on transatlantic ships, with room and meals at the Ladies' Empire Club in London, invitations from the Canadian high commissioner, guided coach and boat excursions through the Trossachs of central Scotland, and tours into France, Germany, Austria, Italy, perhaps as far as Egypt.

Her connections in England thrilled her sister Vie, who boldly asked Nancy Astor if she could try on her ladyship's million-dollar pearls. Astor was probably the one who arranged seats for them in Westminster Abbey for the funeral of Queen Alexandra in 1925. Travelling alone in 1934, Macdonald witnessed the crash of a RAF pilot, the son of the Lord Mayor of London, during a ceremonial flypast. "I saw this happen," she noted on her copy of the *Sunday Dispatch* that reported the accident and, in her ongoing admiration of things royal, added "saw the P of Wales too." A few days later she attended the funeral of the Duke of Marlborough in London. And when she and brother Donald returned from Europe via

England in 1938, she brought with her newspaper extracts of a controversial book about the abdication of Edward VIII. Whenever she and her sister travelled together on these forays into the world beyond Bailey's Brook, Macdonald was the more dignified, Vie the more exuberant. "It will be a rest to get to a quiet abode again," Macdonald wrote her mother from London in 1925, "I believe Vie wd go on tripping forever."[94] But they both had a grand time on their voyages, and they both declared themselves younger than they were to any official who needed to know.[95]

In those years of retirement, the memory of war ebbed and flowed like the tides around Macdonald's native province. She attended Armistice Day services in full regalia, complete with decorations and medals. People knew her always in relation to the war, for even out of uniform "Miss Margaret," as the neighbours referred to her, was "looked up to": she had the bearing and directness of an officer. When abroad, she floated on the currents of memory. She visited wartime friends, laid wreaths at cenotaphs in England, paid homage to the Canadian dead in France. English colleagues echoed the gestures with gifts of commemorative books and even personal visits. The new head of QAIMNS sent Macdonald a copy of *Reminiscent Sketches* by English nursing sisters, signing it "with love" and "in memory of our work together 1914–1919." Maud McCarthy sent her Elizabeth Haldane's new book, *The British Nurse in Peace and War*, inscribed "To Canada [her name for Macdonald] with love,"[96] and McCarthy travelled to Canada in 1926 and 1928 on the waves of reminiscence to be part of public memorials to Canadian nurses.

For the more private gatherings – local reunion dinners of the fledgling Overseas Nursing Sisters' Association, for example – Macdonald was always in demand as guest speaker. When she could not be there she sent greetings, summoning memory from the sea of drifting attention with such words as "The warmest recollections of the happiest of comradeships," or, quoting Hamlet, "So long as memory holds a seat in this distracted globe, we shall meet in spirit this night, consecrated to so many memories."[97] In 1928 she timed her return from a winter spent in California to be present at meetings of Overseas Nurses in Victoria, Vancouver, and Toronto. "Too strenuous really for my quiet taste," she remarked to a friend about the luncheons, teas, drives, and dinners organized in her honour, as if ten years after the war and her own strenuous part in it, she needed stillness to retain the full force of memory.[98]

Something stirred her in 1932 to request official confirmation from the American government of her own memories of her Spanish-American War involvement.[99] But three years later she refused to allow the Canadian prime minister to put her name forward for the Order of the British Empire, in spite of Lady Astor's suggestion to R.B. Bennett that he do so.[100] Was this her usual modesty, or might she have been caught in one of memory's undercurrents? Three of her nursing sisters had already been given the award, all of them subordinate to Macdonald, and two – Ethel Ridley and Edith Rayside – quite close to her.[101] So she may have considered the suggestion as coming too late.

By then, the memory of First World War nurses had been well anchored in marble. Macdonald drifted in and out of the preparations for a permanent memorial to Canada's nursing dead, but she was the one who unveiled the sculpture in the main hall of the Parliament Buildings in Ottawa in the summer of 1926. Before she had even returned from England in 1919, the Canadian National Association of Trained Nurses (yet to change its name to the Canadian Nurses' Association) began pondering some means of honouring the memory of the forty-seven nurses who did not return. It took two years to decide on the nature of the memorial and even longer on the form, location, design, and funding. In 1921 Macdonald had "a very definite idea as to what form this memorial should take, and through what channels subscriptions might flow," but for some reason she took umbrage at the way things were going, arrived late for the annual meeting of the association in Quebec City, and kept her ideas to herself. She and President Jean Gunn appear to have rubbed each other the wrong way, and the report of the meeting reads as if there had been much soothing of Macdonald's ruffled feathers. Part of the soothing was to place her on the national committee for the project.[102] She declined to be convener, and perhaps just as well, for she attended only one of the nine monthly meetings – all held in Toronto – before she left Ottawa in the summer of 1922. Nonetheless, she shared in the decision to have a sculpture of some sort located in the Parliament Buildings; to get it there required persuading the prime minister himself.[103] She then kept up with the project by mail from Bailey's Brook, completing the list of nursing dead by contacting British and American officials about the Canadians in their nursing services.[104]

Perhaps she was the one to suggest inviting Maud McCarthy to come from England for the unveiling; the two of them were the featured speakers at the event. She certainly urged her nurses to come to Ottawa for the ceremony, and in uniform: "I consider uniform superior in taste, dignity and style and by far the most fitting dress for such an occasion. What could present a more charming picture to the eye than a storming of the Capital by the Bluebirds?" She did allow that some might have outgrown their uniforms and be reluctant to purchase a new one, but she reminded them – perhaps revealing her own intention – "What an advantage to have always on hand so honoured a burial dress!" And then she added the orders she was so used to giving: "No skirt should be more than seven or eight inches from the ground [this at a time when women were chopping their skirts along with their hair, Macdonald herself having done the latter]. Decorations and medals should be properly mounted on a bar ... Get out that old button stick and shine, shine, shine." She wanted her "warrior sisters" present in fine military form.[105]

Two hundred and fifty former bluebirds came to Ottawa for Macdonald's unveiling of the sculpture. Fifty of them, as well as Macdonald herself, were wearing the service uniform of the CAMC nurses, the one depicted on the bas-relief. The sculpted marble panel in the grand hallway leading to the Parliamentary Library is a serene but crowded sweep of Canadian history, designed to link nursing with the development of Canada. Two military nurses on the left side of the panel hover over a wounded soldier. The nurses' stance and uniform echo the religious presence of a New France nun on the right side of the panel. She is caring for an aboriginal infant while a warrior looks on suspiciously. Linking them across the panel and across time is the allegorical figure of Humanity, in female form, her outstretched arms embracing the tableau of women's service and devotion, and offering it to another allegorical figure, this time male, holding history's book of records.[106] As a piece of mortuary sculpture, the panel is appropriately ethereal and reverential; the female figures make it so. As a depiction of Canadian history, or of Canadian women, it is more mythical than realistic, typical of commemorative statuary of the time. Macdonald's words at the ceremony are the verbal equivalent of the sculpture:

The purpose of the Memorial is to show respect and affectionate admiration and to preserve to future generations the memory of these heroic Nurses. Everyone will admire the grace and simplicity of the panel which the genius of Mr Hill has designed and will admit also that the setting is well chosen. Here in the House of Parliament where twelve years ago these Nursing Sisters were first called into martial life a tablet now records their fame and perpetuates the memory of women who are linked forever with Canada whose children they were and to whose traditions they have added a glorious page.

We are become the custodians of a great heritage. Willing and unafraid these Nurses entered into the valley of the shadow of death. Tho they died young these lives were crowned with achievement. To live but a short time, but pass away animated by high physical and moral courage, by noble purpose in a great cause is to attain one of the highest efforts of which life is capable. The memory can never be tarnished. No thought of advantage came to their minds; detached from all consideration of personal gain they saw only the light shining clear on the path of duty – the duty to alleviate suffering and to protect the weak. Our deepest and final thought must be one of gratitude for so dear a memory. And today we will all join in acknowledging a common debt to the life and high example of these valiant Army Nursing Sisters.[107]

Language for the dead, the heartfelt but sculpted language of commemoration. Words like hers were repeated around countless memorials across Canada and worldwide in the 1920s. She repeated them herself whenever possible. None of the words and none of the memory prevented the nations from warring again.

In the remote Bailey's Brook corner of the world in the late summer of 1939, the Macdonalds prepared for war. Macdonald herself had been in Germany in 1938 and must have seen the signs. Now she, her sister Vie, and brothers Ronald, Bill, and Donald held their breath around the radio and over the newspapers in the Moydart dining room. They spread out maps of Europe on the large table and pondered military moves. Their worry, tension, perhaps even excitement – they were, after all, a military family – spring up from the terse entries of Dr Ronald's diary:

22 August	Sensation caused in Europe by announcement of non-aggression pact between Germany and Russia
24 August	European crisis fast developing – War seems almost inevitable
25 August	War seems imminent. Britain ordered all nationals out of Germany
27 August	British cabinet meeting to consider a note from Hitler
1 September	German troops marching into Poland. World War inevitable.[108]

Before the war was even declared, Macdonald, now age sixty-six, wrote to the Ministry of National Defence to offer her services "in a military capacity in the event of an emergency." Only four days passed before the adjutant general turned her down: "Your patriotic offer, which is fully appreciated by this Department, has been recorded for future reference should circumstances arise necessitating further consideration."[109] Had she really expected a positive response? Her former nursing sisters received similarly worded rebuffs.[110] Age alone would eliminate most of

Nurses' memorial, Parliament Buildings, Ottawa

Margaret Macdonald (centre) and Maud McCarthy at the unveiling
of the nurses' memorial

them. In Macdonald's case, even reducing her age by a few years, as she was in the habit of doing, would not have brought her anywhere near the age limit of forty-five. There was always home duty – although nothing official came to her that way either – but that would not be the same. Macdonald wanted to be overseas.

She had to content herself with local volunteer work. Along with others, she manned the registration booth in Antigonish in August 1940 as part of the Canada-wide listing of all available manpower.[111] She spoke to nursing graduates in the town and echoed her speeches of the 1920s in praise of army nursing. Without quite saying so, she was hoping to attract another generation of her "elect of war."[112] She followed the progress of the war intently and took an interest in plans for postwar social welfare.[113] She sent packages of food to her friends in England.[114] But it was all make-do; she longed to be more involved. Close acquaintances knew of her distress: "I can quite appreciate how much you would like to be back in the present fray," wrote an old family friend, "and with your war record I don't see why they don't make a place for you – what are sixty odd years against your indomitable spirit?"[115]

Perhaps to keep herself busy in the early years of the war, Macdonald returned to the task of writing a history. At the request of the Overseas Nursing Sisters' Association in 1940, she agreed to tackle "Nursing in the Great War 1914–1918" as part of the Canadian Nurses' Association project on the history of nursing in Canada.[116] She had in fact continued to toy with the idea of a history ever since the nurses' silence and the army had cut off her first effort. In 1922 she had provided Dr Maude Abbott of McGill University with material for her series of lectures on the history of nursing.[117] In 1924 she had promised to write something about the nursing sisters for a planned brief history of the Canadian Nurses' Association (1908–25), intended for publication in 1926 to coincide with the unveiling of the memorial. But five months before the unveiling Macdonald had informed the CNA that she had "decided to prepare a book on the Nursing Service during the War" and therefore was "unable to send any contribution to the Association."[118] Seven years and still no book later, Macdonald was considering a request from instructors in nursing at the University of Toronto to help gather material on the history of nursing for an eventual textbook; they had asked her to provide information on army nursing during the war. Before she agreed, she wanted to know from army headquarters whether she would have access to material. Perhaps she was dissuaded by the official reply – only in Ottawa, only in the office of the historical section, and only during office hours[119] – for nothing more was heard from her.

In 1934 one of her nurses, Mabel Clint, produced a personal account of wartime nursing: *Our Bit: Memories of War Service by a Canadian Nursing Sister*. Macdonald gave it fine praise, stating that its publication represented "a red-letter day for the members of the nursing profession ... Reading it one may fancy one's self as occupying an orchestra chair; for those who viewed war nursing from afar the tremendous unrehearsed panorama will prove absorbing and enlightening, whilst to those who were of the cast, memory will be stirred to its depths."[120] Yet she must have wondered how Clint had managed to complete a manuscript and she had not. The overall story of the nurses was clearly too much for her, and unlike Clint, who had seen active service, she could not bring herself to tell only her own story. Since hers was an administrative story, she always considered it secondary to the real work of her nurses. She ought, then, to have known better in 1940 and turned down the request of the Overseas Nurses' Association.

Instead, she tackled the history once more. Reportedly "thrilled with the prospect of preparing this work,"[121] she contacted three of her war-time colleagues for assistance, pulled out what material she had, reread her speeches from the early 1920s, perused the Clint book with pencil in hand, and culled her own memories. "Had I but the wit to have kept a Diary how simple all wd. have been," she bemoaned early in the task.[122] But a year later she still had nothing to show for her labours. To the dismay of those who asked about her progress, she pleaded distance from documents, a winter-long flu, and preoccupied colleagues: Ethel Ridley had not responded at all, Edith Rayside was going blind, and Elizabeth Smellie had her hands full as matron-in-chief in Ottawa. After giving herself nightmares, Macdonald finally admitted that the task could not be done.[123] She might have added other excuses: her war work, the busy summers at Bailey's Brook with family and visitors, the annual disruption of moving into town for the winter. But what she was unable to say, perhaps because she would not admit it to herself, was that her heart simply was not in it.

In reply to the veiled criticism that "our work has been delayed considerably," she did agree in the winter of 1942 to answer a few, mostly factual questions.[124] Even to get that out of her required a second urging. What she eventually submitted from memory (she was in New Glasgow) was a three-page memorandum containing some of the factual material requested and a few reflections, along with a two-page chronology of her career, a one-page tribute to Georgina Pope, and a one-page list of overseas matrons.[125] When she offered to come to Montreal and assist in assembling material, she was politely turned down.[126] Was it her doing – or lack thereof – that accounts for there being only one sixteen-page chapter on the Great War in *Three Centuries of Canadian Nursing* when the book eventually appeared in 1947? Only one item from her chronology and four from the memorandum were included; the rest of the chapter draws on material gathered by the Overseas Nurses' Association after Macdonald withdrew from the project.[127]

And where exactly was her heart in those early years of the Second World War? It was in England. "How I wish I was 'over there' now," she confided late in 1940. "It is the only place where one cd. feel she was of some use."[128] Early the next year she let her heart dictate a long-delayed letter to Lady Astor:

Had I followed inclination, since the outbreak of the war, Cliveden – dear, lovely Cliveden – would have had a bombardment of letters. Naught but the fear of imposing on time that must be already too fully occupied restrained me. Now the impulse is so strong that I must tell how constantly you are in mind. I fancy you flitting about in your old-time, gay, inimitable manner – cheering up patients, nurses and everybody within range, those of high as well as low degree. And I'm sick at heart at not being one of the number.

That vile bug-bear – the Army Age Limit – knocked everything from under my feet. So I must stay at home doing the dull, drab daily round of war work – distanced war work.

Of course, the Canadian women are all heart and soul engaged in doing what they can to help and we're not doing so badly.

I delight in the thought of you having the hospital again and envy the Canucks to whom you are extending hospitality and all sorts of pleasures.

Shortly ago I was at Ottawa where I lunched with Lady Perley; your ears must have burned that day! We talked so much of you and your unceasing kindnesses. Certainly no one ever appreciated nor more enjoyed visiting Cliveden than did I. My spirit must haunt the place forever … To you I am everlastingly indebted for so many happy days and occasions – oftimes I marvel that it happened to me …

When this hellish war is over you will see me again – meanwhile I do hope you keep a little memory of me, and be sorry a bit that I'm not over there this time!

I suppose Wissie has made you a grandmother; it is hard for me to realize that even Michael is now a young man. On an off day perchance you might get your Sec. to send me a line telling of your various doings, of all the children etc etc – all little crumbs wd. be so acceptable. Was the St. James Sq. house damaged? the stories we read thrill us to the innermost wick – I mean the way all are carrying on in the blitz-es. What a happy war was the last by comparison.[129]

In spite of her promise, Macdonald never did see Lady Astor or Cliveden again. The first possible occasion to return to England after the war would have been the spring or summer of 1946, and something more powerful than her seventy-three years kept her home. Her heart, the heart that was so resistant to writing a history and had so wanted to be in England during the war, was giving way. "Acute myocarditis and coronary sclerosis," intoned the doctor learnedly after the fact, the second being the more known and recognizable disease at the time. As a result of it, she probably had pain in the chest, limited mobility, fatigue[130] – enough to prevent a trip to England. In June 1948 she went into St Martha's Hospital in Antigonish where, in spite of trailing intravenous tubes as she walked the halls with a young nurse, she still had considerable verve. She charmed the nurse with stories of her military experience, and she chided the dietician about hospital food – army food had been better.[131] By midsummer she was in hospital again, this time in New Glasgow, where she dictated her will to her sister Vie. Its only hint of a life led elsewhere was her bequest of a ring "to my friend of the first great war Miss Bo[u]lter."[132] And then, at her request and with the permission of her brother Dr Ronald, she gathered up memories and echoes and went home in anticipation of the last silence.

Moydart House, Bailey's Brook
Pictou County, Nova Scotia, 7 September 1948

She is in her own room now, upstairs and around to the left. Not the same room as that of her birth but the same house. The room is orderly and feminine, reflecting its inhabitant. White walls and white curtains, tied back to frame the two windows, catch the early morning light. To the south lie the front garden, the gravel road, and the meadow beyond. The old schoolhouse is off to the right, the one where she learned to read and cipher so long ago. She could see it if she were sitting at her desk below the south window, just as she would be able to make out the shape of Egnaig –

brother Ronald's summer home – partially hidden in the copse behind the meadow. The other window faces east, looking over the side lawns of Moydart and up the hill of the gravel road past the old buildings of her father's store – now used as a garage for farm vehicles and the family car, which she never learned to drive. Below the window is her prie-dieu for morning and evening prayers. No question of kneeling anywhere now. No need to get up even from the bed along the north wall to see what the day will bring. She knows what to expect of this day. Besides, she knows the view from the windows by heart. She can trace the path of the brook back up its course into the hills that bound Bailey's Brook on the south. And she can follow it north, in her mind's eye, two miles to the sea – the sea that had taken her to New York, Panama, South Africa, England, Europe – the same sea that always brought her home again. Back where she began. Twenty years as a girl in this house, twenty-five as a retired army nurse. Thirty years in between to test her wings beyond the meadow, beyond the hills, beyond the sea.

She is prepared for this last journey. Her Catholic faith is the only baggage she will require, and all her life it has proved both portable and sustaining. Father Dugald MacEachern, the parish priest, will be in any minute now to administer the last rites. He and her cousin Father Jerome Chisholm and eleven other priests will celebrate the solemn requiem mass at the Lismore church. She will wear her military uniform, the navy dress one, for this final trip; it is hanging ready in the cupboard at the foot of her bed. The women of her family are with her: sister Vie, who has spent so many days and nights watching over her from the rocking chair by the east window; sister-in-law Elizabeth and niece Mairi, summoned from Egnaig early this morning. All three of them are kneeling by the bedside, murmuring prayers for the dying. The men are downstairs, brother Donald and nephew Ronald. Her brother Bill has gone ahead of her, dead just two years ago at the age of sixty. Brother Ronald is in Montreal, where her niece Elizabeth, his second daughter, has recently begun nursing school. Unbeknown to any of them, he will join his sister in death five days later. For the moment, the images of her three brothers remain with her as they have always done, in a linked silver frame, the only picture in the room. She is at peace. She believes in the everlasting life. She is free to go.

Physically, she did not travel as far in death as she did in life – just down to the sea for the funeral service at St Mary's, Lismore, on 10 September and then back up to join her parents in the tiny cemetery at Mount St Mary's, east a mile and a half along the gravel road from her home.

Macdonald's east-facing window on the left, second floor

There her tombstone makes her eleven days older than she was. How she would have laughed! And then, as if to make sure she stays put, a granite boulder now marks the end of the gravel road half a mile west of her house. On it an inscription from the 1980s records that a young woman had gone forth from this locality to become someone remarkable.

In September 1948 that remarkable woman, that imperial daughter with her yen for wars, went forth once again, this time in response to "the last clear trumpet call of God."[133]

Postscript

There is a distinction, even to Nova Scotians, to the
D.D. Macdonalds of Bailey's Brook which perhaps
epitomizes the best in Scottish endeavour, moreso
from the reticence which has cloaked their deeds.[1]

For twenty-five years, Vie Macdonald carefully guarded her sister's correspondence in the family home at Bailey's Brook. On visits to their sister
Kate in Montreal, she would take packets of letters for the two of them to
enjoy. They reread the letters and shared their recollections of all those
years, all those wars, all that travel and fun. And then, shortly before she
died in 1974, Vie Macdonald, who had kept the home fires burning in war
and peace, tossed her sister's letters into the flames.

Echoes of the Great War

Speech by Margaret Macdonald
12 June 1920

To one whose work had long been almost entirely for and with men, the prospect of going to a war in charge of a party of one hundred odd women promised to be more alarming than novel – so alarming, in fact, that my first step was one of protest. I declared my incompetency to assume responsibility for, what then seemed, so enormous a number of nurses. Instead of assurance or sympathy I was reminded of a soldier's first duty – obedience. Denied a crumb of comfort, I took up my new duties with the same degree of liking one has for a cold plunge. However, long before the hundred odd had developed into a Corps of twenty-five hundred odd, confidence had succeeded fear, and novelty was swallowed up by a positive greed.

The more I knew of nurses the more of them I wanted to know. To gather all into the ranks of the elect of war became my hobby. An organization that expands gradually is easy of control. One grows along with it and finds that one thousand are quite as readily administered as one hundred; two thousand as two hundred and so on. In the Army, and for the reason that everything – almost one's mind – is governed by rule, difficulties of administration are, perhaps, not so frequently encountered. Still, with all the regulations in the world, there are bound to arise circumstances to which no rule applies. A law must be created to suit the occasion. Then comes in that indispensable quality possessed by nine-tenths of our Canadian women – initiative. When instant action is desired, decision must be prompt but sufficiently deliberate to permit of a few moments' intensive thought. Even under circumstances of the most pressing urgency, concentration of thought is the imperative requirement. It is surprising how much the mind can receive and dispatch in sixty or ninety seconds.

But to go back to September, 1914, and the troopship s.s. *Franconia*, upon which we began our voyage to the seat of war; a voyage that was subsequently to lead many of the nurses to theatres of war along Mediterranean shores. Here owing to the colour of their uniform they became known as "The Bluebirds."

It was in the spirit of enthusiastic adventure that the majority entered upon an Army career. But, sooner or later, – and more soon during a war – to all comes a deepened sense of a serious responsibility.

The voyage on the *Franconia* was enlivened, as voyages are, by music, song and dance. Looking about one remarked the calm, cheerful and confident faces of the soldiers; the happy, smiling nursing-sisters plainly betraying an instinctive feeling of comradeship. Notwithstanding the apparent gaiety an undercurrent of sadness was easy of detection. To all must have occurred the thought – to which not a few gave expression – that he or she might never again set foot on Canadian soil: the reflection served but to foster a greater optimism, with a grim determination not to fall short in their respective duties.

In this connection the remark of a young soldier to me, after his baptism of fire, was probably symbolic of the will of all. He said, "My only fear is for loss of courage."

The picture of this modern Armada – the First Canadian Contingent – being convoyed across the Atlantic has so many times been portrayed that [it is] unnecessary for me to touch upon. Until locality was plainly discernible, all, save the authorized officials, were quite in the dark as to the port of disembarkation. Surmise and speculation and that giant monster, rumour, made puppets of all.

The story of the Russian troops passing through England, (one of the greatest fabrications of modern times) was a mole hill in comparison to the mountains we swallowed at sea; yes, and on land, both during the war and long after. Officials in the highest to those in the most menial posts fell victims. All were ready to believe anything and everything. Conversation began and ended with surmise as to when the war would cease.

The most nearly correct prediction in this regard, I think, was the following from the pages of *Punch*:

My wife's sister's son heard a policeman on his beat,
Say to a housemaid in Downing Street,
That he knew someone who had a friend,
Who could tell when the war was going to end!!

The most thrilling of voyages came to an end in the most picturesque of fashions. Creeping up the "Hoe" to safe berth at Devonport, our armed escort was exchanged for a running fire of welcomes. From the banks and piers lined with people, from ships gaily beflagged in honour, from mast-head to hull, from every conceivable corner of the harbour of Devonport rang out shrill siren, sturdy shouts and melodious cheers. Our reception from the Motherland might readily have been mistaken for that accorded victors returning from war. Such scenes of enthusiasm we were not again to witness until Armistice Day, more than four years later.

During the voyage the distribution of the Nursing-Sisters had frequently been a matter of conjecture. This question was answered immediately the pilot came on board. Accompanying him was Sir Edward Ward, the bearer of an invitation from the Board of Governors, St Thomas' Hospital, London, asking us to be the guests of that institution for a few weeks. I caught a fleeting glance of relief on the face of the Director-General. Troops are easily marched to camp, but a hundred women, whose services are not immediately required, are not so easy of disposal!

When the *Franconia* docked two ladies came on – one a Canadian, the wife of a British officer; the other, the present Lady Astor, who represents in Parliament what was then her husband's constituency. Her object was to obtain permission for all on the ship to go up to her house for luncheon and tea. Every available motor car and char-a-banc in Plymouth had been chartered, and arrangements were made for a drive thro' the "Lorna Doon" country as well. We had considered the invitation to the hundred odd nurses evidence of magnanimous hospitality, so you may imagine how we looked upon an invitation extended to fifteen hundred troops.

I may say that Lady Astor's interest in Canadians – especially 'Tommy' – began that day; never ceased during the war, and still goes on, judging from the inquiries I receive as to the addresses of numbers of nursing-sisters, officers, and men whom she helped to convalescence.

The Military Authorities decreed that the men must at once entrain for camp, and we for London, so there was to be no joy-riding at Plymouth. Hasty adieus were made at the ship. This boat was later torpedoed in the Mediterranean and I may tell you that many were the sighs of relief that followed it to its watery grave. The Nursing-Sisters who had gone over in 1914 became known as the "Mayflowers"; those who followed were "Cauliflowers." The origin of the last named I have never been able to trace. You can see an amiable form of jealousy was bound to arise. Sometimes the Mayflowers were apt to assume an air over the Cauliflowers. The latter took it good naturedly, knowing full well that thro' no will of their own they were not of the first hundred. So when the poor, old *Franconia* went down, the Cauliflowers exclaimed. "Thank Heaven the Ark of the Mayflowers has disappeared from our horizon."

We arrived at Waterloo Station, London, at midnight. Here we found motor transport to take us to St Thomas' Hospital where a hot supper awaited us. Among our happiest recollections of the Great War, the two weeks spent at St. Thomas' is outstanding. Nothing that might add to our enjoyment was lacking, in fact, we were like to die of hospitality. From various British organizations and from individual sources we were deluged with attentions and invitations. Managers of the leading theatres showered us with tickets, not once but continuously. Everything of interest in and about London must be shown us. Whatever, of small or great moment, undertaken by the Mother Country is carried to a finish with a characteristic polish and perfection of detail.

I needn't tell you that some of us found we were quite the country cousin. Still our faux pas were not too glaring. It added to the merriment to find, for instance, a sister mistaking the tube station at Oxford Circus for a theatre or movie and solemnly asking for orchestra seats. The wax figures at Madame Tussauds were frequently addressed, and perhaps not the least amusing feature of this was the wrath of the victim at her own mistake. On the London omnibus ten shilling gold pieces were, at night, often given in lieu of a six-penny bit. Discovering the loss later we forgave the conductor believing his sight to be as short as our own.

It is undoubtedly true that when pleasure becomes a duty it almost ceases to be a pleasure. The nursing-sisters began to clamour for work; they had come Overseas for that purpose and were not to be cheated of it. Until such time as Canadian hospitals were opened the nursing-sisters were distributed in various British hospitals. This provided useful occupation and gave opportunity to acquire an insight into the routine and workings of Military hospitals, with which few were familiar. It also provided occasion, of which full advantage was taken, for the Canadian to cross swords with her English sister. It took fully a year's acquaintance to understand and appreciate one another.

During the two weeks we were enjoying London our men were anything but holidaying on Salisbury Plains. The cold, drizzling weather was largely responsible for the discomforts and illness that shortly followed, and it was not long before an s.o.s. reached us. Probably you have heard of the Canadian "Tommy" looking out from his tent upon a sea of Salisbury mud and flood, and exclaiming, "Well, if this is the Country we've come to save from the 'Boche,' why don't they let him have it?"

The first Canadian hospital was opened at Bulford, near Salisbury. I suppose it was the best possible under the circumstances, but it was the worst nightmare I ever saw, so I shall not dwell on it. The Nursing-Sisters had their full share of hard work and discomfort. This was endured uncomplainingly. They were soldiers and as such had not anticipated down beds. Meningitis, pneumonia and minor ills soon became prevalent in camp. The increasing number of cases necessitated the opening of two more hospitals in the neighborhood.

By November over fifty of the nursing-sisters were on duty at Salisbury and the other fifty had been distributed in Imperial hospitals in France. I had established an office in London, from whence was directed necessary changes in nursing personnel, etc. I devoted much time to furthering my knowledge of Army and Civilian Hospitals; then formulated a scheme for nursing organization to meet the needs of what might prove a protracted war. Rules and Regulations governing the service had to be drawn up; provision made for the care of sick and convalescent sisters; hours of recreation and holidays for the well ones received equal consideration.

Incidentally I tried to find out how the war was being run! The effort was vain. The Imperial policy was to shroud everything in Mystery. No doubt this was a wise precaution because it presumed great knowledge. Probably, if the truth were confessed, English Army officials at that time were carrying on in almost an entire fog. For the contingencies that arose there had been no precedent. The thing to do under such conditions seemingly is to convince outsiders of one's own superior knowledge. Even this attempt to conceal what was perfectly obvious to the eye, did not lessen our awe of the War Office!

When the nursing-sisters went to work the hospitality which I previously remarked by no means ceased. The Honourable Mrs. Graham-Murray – whose work in connection with clubs for soldiers must be well known to you – offered, rent-free, her residence in Chelsea as a Rest

Home for our nurses. There was nothing in the Canadian Army Regulations to cover the maintenance of such a place. I appealed to the Red
Cross Commissioner. He encouraged me sufficiently to say that given
an estimate of the cost per month, he would consider the proposition.
I wanted that house more than anything I ever saw, so I set about inter-
viewing the butcher, the baker, the candle-stick maker, etc. Plate, glass,
linen, light, gas, servants, and last but not least, the probable number
of convalescent sisters had to be computed.

All this was rather a joke on me who had ever preached but never
practised domesticity. However, the result of my calculation was the
immediate assuming by the Red Cross Society of all the responsibility
in regard to maintenance. For the first six months the actual cost did not
vary more than a few dollars from my original estimate. Later on came
the need for larger Rest Homes but I think none ever attained the
popularity of the charming one in artistic Chelsea.

These Rest Homes served as well a sentimental purpose. Thereby were
provided Canadian Homes from which nursing-sisters might be given in
marriage. These events were made the occasion of as much merriment as
possible. Roughly speaking about 15% of our Nursing-Sisters married
Overseas, and an equal proportion since returning home. Like domesticity I always advocated matrimony but never had the opportunity of putting it into practice myself!

Now I shall transport you to scenes of an entirely different character –
to the most advanced point to which a nurse's duty takes her in war – a
casualty clearing station. These hospital units, usually from six to fifteen
miles behind the front line of trenches, may be established in tents, in
huts, chateau, a school, factory or other suitable building. As the name
implies they were simply clearing houses for the wounded. Here wounds
were dressed, patients sorted and transferred to Ambulance Train by
which they were carried to the Base, then later to the United Kingdom
by hospital ship.

Casualty clearing stations were grouped three within an area. The system of operation was that on the same day No. 1 received patients, No. 2
discharged patients, and No. 3 cleaned and prepared to receive patients
the following day and vice-versa. A large placard by the roadside guided
approaching ambulances as to which was the receiving hospital. During
and immediately following a battle these hospitals were filled and stretch-
ers overflowed to the lawn [underlined and questioned in text] outside.
Surgeons, Nursing-Sisters and Orderlies worked quickly, cheerfully and
unsparingly. Hours of duty frequently averaged 18 out of the 24 but none

ever murmured on that score. Often gas masks had to be worn: the roar of the guns became at times deafening. There was no slackening of work; it must be carried on during air-raids and under shell fire.

Once when our hospital near Adinkerke was being shelled – and the aim was alarmingly accurate – the nursing-sisters were obliged to retire to a corn-field for the night. In order to expose the smallest number possible to the risk of shell fire, the Officer Commanding decided to reduce the staff. There was much congratulation on the part of those elected to remain, and great resentment on the part of those being sent to safety. I never knew women so keen to court danger. And so it always was over there. Night after night was uncomfortably spent in dug-outs, yet their spirits never flagged. Never once was it necessary to ask for volunteers. The truth is that at no time during the whole war were there sufficient danger posts to meet the demand from the Sisters. Even the torpedoing of our hospital ship, with its tragic loss of life, served but to increase the number of applicants for that duty.

With the army there are always periods of rest. During such times hospital work is not so strenuous, tho' there are always patients. The sisters, in times of leisure, spent their off-duty hours in visiting the surrounding country. There was invariably a nearby town or city which held something of interest.

No hospital is complete without its pet patient. This is usually a minor or a man recovering from a serious illness. By way of showing gratitude for the care received, the first idea is to help sister in her work. Most convalescent patients can be amazingly helpful in assisting to care for the sick. In their tender regard for less fortunate pals their hands, tho' roughened by manual labour, can become as gentle as those of a woman.

In one instance, a youth just beyond conscripted age, known as "Wee Jock" (In the Army all Scots are known as "Jock") had been in Hospital for some time. In child-fashion he grew attached to the sisters and more especially to the Matron who kept him occupied with odd chores, and incidentally out of harm's way. (Harm's way being the stern medical officer who returned patients to duty at the earliest possible moment.) When it came "Wee Jock's" turn to go, the Matron, recognizing sadness in the air, said, "I don't know how we're going to run the hospital without you, Wee Jock." Turning his head to hide the tears that would come, the reply came in trembling voice, "Dinna ye greet, Matron, Wee Jock'll no forget ye." It was with an effort the Matron controlled her smile.

Tragedy and Comedy ever walk hand in hand. You have all, I am sure, at the most serious of moments experienced a sense of the ridiculous.

Nowhere is this more apparent than during a war, or among people living on the edge of a volcano.

I recall one of the numerous air-raids in London. I happened to be staying at a Ladies' Club. About 2 A.M. we congregated in the dining room. Most of us had slipped coats over our night attire. One member strolled in fully dressed, as if for the street, wearing white kid gloves and carrying a small hand bag. Another, with an elaborate dressing gown, wore a piquant boudoir cap from which peeped the most golden of curls. In the daylight I discovered this good lady to be of quite senior years and her hair grey; so the curls we envied had been just a part of the cap. I admired all the more the vanity which was not to be frightened away by the Hun in the air. It is amazing how calm one can remain whilst hovering on the brink of eternity. Soldier-like, one grew to look upon danger in a detached sort of way; quite realizing it but feeling evil would befall the other fellow rather than one's self.

To my mind one of the most astonishing features of the war was the manner in which women, in every sphere of life, shouldered responsibilities formerly borne by men. They undertook and excelled in almost every branch of man's work. One of the immediate results was the development of a dormant self-reliance and self-confidence. This is now proving a helpful wholesome factor in the readjustment of national affairs. There is no limit to the capability of women. A greater tolerance and more active sympathy is everywhere in evidence. Sex disqualification is dying hard but the end is not far off. Women by their own efforts have at last attained the place which was for long denied them, and the result is women with an extended knowledge and understanding are proving better wives, mothers and Empire builders. The scheme of things has so advanced that the leisured social butterfly no longer views with disdain her sister worker. Rather she aspires to the same class.

An acquaintance Overseas, a lady of title, ancestral homes, money and its accompaniments, once said to me, "I should willingly exchange everything I possess for your record of war work." My poor work that was so paltry in comparison to the big things that were being done! But I think the war awakened in this good lady, as it has in many others, a sense of usefulness that will never more be satisfied to sit back with folded hands.

We are now being told that great crises confront the immediate future; famine and financial failure is threatened. If this is the case, (which I doubt) pessimism is not the remedy. If the people who keep telling the awful things that are going to happen to us would only realize how much better the world is than ever before; if they would deal out equally enormous doses of optimism, it would do far more towards regaining the lost balance than all the threats on earth. Obstacles are not overcome by sitting down bemoaning them. Work now is recognized as the chief remedy for existing social ills. Of this there is full share for all. For the woman who must earn a livelihood the choice and variety of field has never been so great. For the woman who elects to marry – undoubtedly a higher [handwritten above: nobler] calling – the opportunity for a mutually helpful, happy assumption of responsibility has never been more apparent.

We hear and read much of the value of the Franchise but not nearly enough is said of the grave and serious obligation it imposes. The vote is not a thing to be treated lightly and jocularly. Women have proved themselves worthy of trust and confidence. They must now seek in all earnestness to fit themselves for office. Were I asked what qualifications I consider essential to a woman entering public life, I should say: –

A strong faith; high ideals [handwritten above: patriotism &]; a balanced judgment; the power to eliminate the ego; dignity; an ardent enthusiasm [handwritten: good digestion] and a touch of humour. All this in a sound body will carry her far along the road to success remembering ever that "life is not a cup to be drained but a vessel to be filled."

Now I am wandering from my subject. Perhaps it may interest you to hear how one Canadian woman was affected by English people. By virtue of my office I was, on several occasions, privileged to meet their Majesties, the King and Queen. Once I travelled on the Royal train from London to Portsmouth but my greatest surprise was on being commanded to attend at Windsor Castle. Arriving there at 11.30 A.M. and leaving at 3.30 P.M. gave ample time for what in Celtic is known as a "Cailey." Nothing could exceed the kindly thought and graciousness of the Royal host and hostess. Always on meeting them one becomes conscious of their genuine interest in and earnest solicitude for the welfare of their subjects. The zeal with which their majesties undertook a more than full share of war work was astounding. It surely served as an inspiration to workers as well as slackers. [handwritten in upper margin: Can. nurse nursed the King] [handwritten addition to sentence: More than anything they seemed to be good parents]

I was also privileged to meet representatives of all classes of English society. Friendship and acquaintanceship extending over five years – and especially in times of stress – develops quickly. Many were the English homes I visited. The impression received was always of the ideal home life. There is a most refreshing simplicity and lack of pretence [handwritten above: & ostentation] about their mode of living. The children too,

I think, have a happier childhood than do ours. They are given every consideration but remain natural and wholly unspoiled.

But I must no longer impose upon your time. In conclusion I should like to tell you one of my favourite stories – concerning nurses – I need scarcely add. When No. 1 Canadian Stationary Hospital landed at Mudros in August, 1915, conditions there were about as bad as could be. The heat was intense, the flies and dust quite beyond anything before experienced. Water was scarce and that available was so highly chlorinated as to make of even tea an ill tasting medicine. Baths were out of the question. Dysentery and malaria raged. Many of our staff became sufferers. Unfortunately one matron and one sister succumbed. You may imagine the outlook as anything but cheering.

One day, seated on board benches, (there being no chairs) the sisters were dilating upon the merits of friendly France from which they had come and the demerits [handwritten above: to the detriment] of Mudros. They were blue and depressed; hot and thirsty with little prospect of real relief from either. Suddenly one sister in earnest solemn tone remarked, "I have but one regret." All became alert and put the usual query. "It is for a strawberry I left on my plate at Boulogne"! The laugh that followed revived the will and spirits of all. The reflection from the strawberry at once cast a rosy hue over the future, dispelling the momentary gloom.[1]

Notes

1 St Francis Xavier University, Antigonish, Nova Scotia, Archives (hereafter SFXA), Macdonald Family Collection (hereafter MFC), RG 1, file 10, photocopy of first two pages of New Testament listing, in D.D. Macdonald's handwriting, the names and birth dates of all the children. A similar list, with the odd discrepancy, is D.D.'s "Family Record and Memoirs," a seven-page typescript dated January 1890 in the possession of Ronald St John Macdonald Jr of Halifax. In spite of its title, the document lists only the names of D.D.'s children and the public positions he held. Four tombstones, also with some discrepancies of dates, mark the graves of seven Macdonald family members in Mount St Mary's cemetery, Bailey's Brook. In the "Family Record," D.D. spells Margaret's middle name Ste Clotilda. On the rare occasions when Macdonald filled in the C of her middle name, she wrote Clotilde or even Chisholm, her mother's family name.

2 SFXA, MFC, RG 1, file 8, Dr Ronald St John Macdonald, typescript, "Macdonalds of Egnaig, Moidart, Scotland," n.d. [1930s]. See also, Cameron, *Pictou County's History*, 17.

3 If nothing else, the story of D.D., Flora, and Mary, going back now one hundred and fifty years, reveals a strain of romance in and about the Macdonald family. It was told to me by three different people in the Bailey's Brook

area in 2001 and 2004: Macdonald neighbour Wilma Burke, Macdonald relative Father Greg MacKinnon of St Francis Xavier University, and an unrelated businessman/local history buff, Ronnie D.D. Macdonald of Antigonish. A shortened version, with only the D.D.-Mary encounter at the wedding in St Andrew's, appears also in Barry, "The Macdonald Family of Bailey's Brook," 20, citing an even closer oral history source: Mary McMaster Fairbanks of Antigonish, the daughter of Margaret Macdonald's younger sister Kate McMaster. According to Rankin, (*History of the County of Antigonish*, 98), D.D. had an uncle in St Andrew's; it may therefore have been a cousin's wedding that drew D.D. and Mary together. Rankin also has numerous Macdonalds and Chisholms marrying. The genealogy that anchors part of the story is a twenty-two-page document, "The Descendants of Paul Chisholm," by Roderick A. Chisholm of Hamilton, Ontario, which was provided to me by Chisholm Lyons of Burlington, Ontario, grandson of Sir Joseph Chisholm, who was Mary Elizabeth Chisholm Macdonald's younger brother and therefore Margaret Macdonald's uncle.

4 Joseph Howe, "Eastern Rambles no. 11," *Novascotian*, 18 August 1830, [1], 257.

5 Ibid. See also *Place Names and Places of Nova Scotia*, 30; Meacham, *Illustrated Historical Atlas of Pictou County Nova Scotia* (1879), 73. In the 1930s Margaret Macdonald's brother Ronald lovingly gathered the history, geography, agriculture, and institutions of Bailey's Brook (without, unfortunately, much about his own family) in a series of handwritten notes and an untitled and incomplete typescript for a book. This material is now in the possession of his son Ronald St John Macdonald Jr of Halifax. For ease of reference, I have adopted the title of the first section of that typescript to refer to the entire text: "Old Bailey's Brook."

6 Three visits to Bailey's Brook, two in the spring and summer of 2001 and one in the spring of 2004, gave me this sense of place. Father Greg MacKinnon accompanied me once in 2001, and on another occasion that same year I was able to meet with lifelong residents Wilma Burke, Dougal and Carmie Macdonald, Mary MacGillivray, and, from nearby Avondale, Catherine Anderson. Historians Tony Mackenzie and Del Muise facilitated these encounters. In 2004 I met Helen and Don Brown, newly retired back to Bailey's Brook, as well as Don Butler and Bernard MacDonald, and renewed my acquaintance with Wilma Burke. I greatly appreciate the hospitality and the information all these people so gladly shared with me.

7 SFXA, MFC, RG 1, file 9, D.D.'s handwritten recording of "firsts" [1905].

8 D.D. had nine children; the one missing from his list of eight classically educated offspring is probably the ninth and youngest, Donald Duncan,

who would be about fourteen at the time of his father's list and quite possibly still at the local school. In D.D.'s will, written in 1903, he made provision for "a course in some good agricultural school" for his youngest son, who presumably was not yet showing signs of his subsequent legal calling. See Pictou County Land Information Centre/Registry of Deeds, Last Will and Testament of Donald D. Macdonald, 22 December 1903.

9 The total cost for the boat harbour he estimated at $5,000, and he had received a grant of $2,000, thanks to the influence of two Liberal politicians: E.M. Macdonald, MLA for Pictou County, and Colin McIsaac, MP for Antigonish (SFXA, MFC, RG 3, file 4, D.D. Macdonald to Margaret Macdonald [hereafter MCM], 17 May 1902).

10 Barry, "The Macdonald Family," 12–17, drawing on material in MFC, RG 1, file 14. Most of the Barry essay on the Macdonald family is in fact a classification and index to MFC.

11 SFXA, MFC, RG 1, file 9, handwritten note of D.D. Macdonald [1905]. D.D.'s use of language – "he" instead of "I" – suggests a distancing from his earlier self.

12 Unidentified clipping from a Halifax paper, dated by hand 28 February 1906 (the date D.D. died), contained in a family scrapbook in the possession of Ronald St John Macdonald Jr, who kindly lent it to me for lengthy perusal. Judging from a handwritten label "1916," now unglued from the spine of the book, Margaret's sister Vie Macdonald constructed this particular scrapbook. The chronologically jumbled contents are not limited to that year or, indeed, to Margaret. I shall refer to this source as the Macdonald Family Scrapbook (hereafter MFS) to distinguish it from other scrapbooks with an archival reference in the MFC at SFXA.

13 SFXA, MFC, unclassified obituary file, undated obituary of Mary Elizabeth Chisholm Macdonald from the *Halifax Chronicle*. According to the inscription on her tombstone, Mary died 24 June 1927.

14 The specific details of this sketch are drawn from R. St J. Macdonald, "Old Bailey's Brook," notably the first section, and a later section "Schools and Teachers" which contains a handwritten copy of a teacher's contract from the late 1850s as well as a list of all the teachers until the late 1880s. Twenty male signatories to the contract subscribed amounts varying between one and twelve shillings in order to pay the teacher eight shillings per "scholar." D.D. Macdonald is among the subscribers (eight shillings), although he had no family at the time. The men also contracted to board the teacher and to provide firewood for the school. The photograph, marked "c 1887" (but more likely taken later, because of the presence of a four- or five-year-old Willie Macdonald, who was born in 1886), captures

and names on the back thirty-six young people, ranging from very big to very small. Two of them may be teachers, one male, one female. The latter is identified as Adele Macdonald, and she did teach at Bailey's Brook sometime in the late 1880s (Barry, "The Macdonald Family," 25). The names of the other Macdonald children are underlined, and some are recognizable as the offspring of Mary Chisholm and D.D. Macdonald, but the one indicated as Margaret ("Maggie") does not ring true, either in size or appearance and also because of the likelihood that she was elsewhere at the time (SFXA, MFC, Photographic Collection, Acc 95-31-619).

15 SFXA, MFC, unclassified obituary file, undated obituary of Mary Elizabeth Chisholm Macdonald from the *Halifax Chronicle*. The young orphan was Janet McGregor Macdonald, born in 1892, and easily confused in the census of 1901 as a younger Macdonald child. She later became a nurse and served overseas during the First World War. The Chisholm daughters, Mary's five nieces, aged between two and ten, were orphaned when their mother Frances ("Fanny") Affleck, died in childbirth in 1903. Their father had them cared for and educated at the Sacred Heart Convent in Halifax during the school year and brought them to his sister's home in Bailey's Brook for the summer. The son of the eldest of these girls, Father Greg MacKinnon, is a major source of information about the Macdonald family, information he acquired from his mother.

16 This presentation of the Macdonald children draws on a number of sources: SFXA, MFC, RG 1, file 10, and RG 5 finding aid; Barry, "The Macdonald Family"; R. St J. Macdonald, "Old Bailey's Brook," notably the section "Macdonalds of Egnaig, Moidart, Scotland"; an obituary of Margaret Macdonald in the *Eastern Chronicle*, 16 September 1948; and conversations with Father Gregory MacKinnon, Antigonish, 7 May 2001 and 15, 17, and 20 April 2004.

17 Interview with Elizabeth Macdonald Podnieks of Toronto, daughter of Margaret's brother Ronald, 22 January 2001.

18 Library and Archives Canada (hereafter LAC), RG 150, Ministry of the Overseas Military Forces of Canada, II-3, Canadian Expeditionary Force (hereafter CEF), personnel files, box 6752-26, attestation paper of Margaret C. Macdonald. Even these documents can be unreliable: her birth date, for example, is recorded as 1879 when it was in fact 1873.

19 SFXA, MFC, RG 3, file 98, "Echoes of the Great War," MCM speech to the Catholic Women's League, Toronto, 12 June 1920, 14. See appendix.

20 SFXA, MFC, RG 2, file 10, MCM to D.D. Macdonald, 30 August 1900.

21 Madge Macbeth, "Nursing Matron Margaret Macdonald," *Canada Monthly* 17 (January 1915): 174. Macbeth prefaced her comments with

the remark that Macdonald was "born with an aptitude for nursing."

22 Pictou County Genealogy and Historical Society, Acc 97-198, Stella Maris Church and Convent, Property Case Study Summary, n.d., [1980s?], which includes a two-page historical account of the convent school with this unidentified quotation from a newspaper of 1884. The school opened in 1880 with forty-three pupils, nine of whom were boarders; it ceased to take boarders in 1950 and closed in 1970.

23 Barry, "The Macdonald Family," 24–5. Marcella Macdonald, born in 1869, would therefore have been among the first pupils at Stella Maris and one of the initial nine boarders. Adele, born in 1871, was at Stella Maris 1884–86. Barry does not give the dates for Margaret's schooling.

24 Ibid., 24.

25 Corcoran, *Mount Saint Vincent*, 11–13; MacLean, *Bishop John Cameron*, 80–5.

26 Ray MacLean makes the Thompson-Affleck connection (ibid., 81), and I have pieced together the Affleck-Chisholm-Macdonald connection with one of those "ah ha!"s that keep historians going. MacLean's Johanna Affleck is Corcoran's Sister Mary Helena Affleck.

27 SFXA, MFC, RG 3, unfiled document, Scrapbook of Maggie C. Macdonald. Judging from the remaining contents (some items appear to have been removed), the scrapbook covers the years c 1890–1911, albeit in a very scattered fashion. Indeed, the title page, locating Margaret at the Mount, is stuck into the scrapbook, suggesting its possible origin in some earlier keepsake.

28 *Halifax Herald*, 6 July 1892, and the Halifax *Morning Chronicle*, 6 July 1892, both record the medal and the prizes, but the first paper lists the French prize and the second the Christian doctrine prize. Neither paper's account of the "closing exercises" is clear about whether Margaret actually graduated. Her name is not among the six of the "graduating class" in the *Chronicle*; nor is it in the following grouping, "Senior Division"; rather, it appears in the "Middle Division." The fact that thirty years later she helped create an alumnae association for the Mount suggests that she did indeed graduate.

29 SFXA, MFC, RG 5, file 47, Fanny Affleck Chisholm to her sister-in-law, Mary Macdonald, 4 December 1891. Judging from the Chisholm family genealogy, this letter would have been sent just a month after Fanny's marriage to Joseph Chisholm.

30 Gibbon and Mathewson, *Three Centuries of Canadian Nursing*, 112; Corcoran, *Mount Saint Vincent*, 81.

31 SFXA, MFC, RG 4, file 5, Diary of Ronald St John Macdonald, 29 March,

17 April, 30 June [mid-July], 16 August 1893. This diary of Margaret's thirteen-year-old brother hints at her comings and goings without saying where she is or what she is doing. The diary does suggest that she spent most of the summer of 1893 at home in Bailey's Brook. It is tempting to think she may have spent another year (1892–93) at the Mount, but there is no mention of her in the Halifax newspaper coverage of the school's closing exercises in 1893 (*Chronicle* and *Herald*, 28 June 1893).

32 The first story came via Margaret's niece and nephew, Mairi Macdonald and Ronald St John Macdonald Jr of Halifax, in discussions I had with them, 13 May 2001; the variant is from their sister Elizabeth Podnieks of Toronto in a telephone conversation, 21 June 2000. The second version was recounted to me by Father Gregory MacKinnon of Antigonish, 7 May 2001.

33 Hensley, "Canadian Nurses in New York," 161–8. A biographical sketch of Hensley is in Morgan, ed., *Canadian Men and Women of the Time* (1898), 458. She may have been asked or inspired to write this piece because of the appearance of numerous articles in American women's magazines of the 1880s and 1890s "extolling the virtuousness and rewards of nursing." See Reverby, *Ordered to Care*, 93.

34 Hensley, "Canadian Nurses in New York," 169. The hospital with the quota was Bellevue, and the one with the older age requirement was New York Hospital, a private institution not to be confused with the public New York City Hospital (ibid., 167).

35 Gibbon and Mathewson, *Three Centuries of Canadian Nursing*, 157, 148, 158.

36 Mottus, *New York Nightingales*, 81–2.

37 SFXA, MFC, RG 3, Scrapbook of Maggie C. Macdonald, S. Halliman to MCM, 25 September 1893.

38 Ibid., incomplete letter from MCM, "To Whom It May Concern," 2 October 1893.

39 Reverby, *Ordered to Care*, 48; Mottus, *New York Nightingales*, 112. Mottus studied the nursing schools of Bellevue, begun in 1872, and the New York Hospital, begun in 1880, the only two, it seems, with extensive records. Judging from Reverby's study of the nursing entrants to three Boston hospitals, Macdonald had more education than most.

40 Burgess, *Nurses, Patients, and Pocketbooks*, 35. Burgess acknowledges that her figures may be conservative, 34.

41 Darche, "Proper Organization of Training Schools in America," 93. Darche, the superintendent at Macdonald's nursing school, was proud of the nurse's role in this advance. Feminist historians of nursing have empha-

sized instead the subordinate place, even creation, of nurses, in this medical system. See, among others, Reverby, *Ordered to Care*, and Melosh, *"The Physician's Hand."*

42 Quoted in Duffy, *A History of Public Health in New York City*, 187. Such young women were also more obedient to paternal authority, which in a hospital setting was exercised by doctors.

43 SFXA, MFC, RG 3, Scrapbook of Maggie C. Macdonald, 142, character reference from Father Andrew McGillvray, parish priest of St Mary's Church, Lismore, Nova Scotia, 15 August 1893.

44 The last line of Margaret's first (incomplete) letter home gives the figure (ibid., 2–3, MCM, "To Whom It May Concern," 2–3 October 1893).

45 Dock, "The Relation of Training Schools to Hospitals," 16. Her speech was delivered to the nursing section of the International Congress of Charities, Correction, and Philanthropy held in Chicago in 1893 at the time of the world's fair.

46 James, "Isabel Hampton and the Professionalization of Nursing," 64.

47 SFXA, MFC, RG 2, file 9, MCM to D.D. Macdonald, [22–3 October 1893].

48 Ibid.

49 Ibid., file 8, MCM to D.D. Macdonald, 15 October 1893, and file 15, MCM to Mary Macdonald, 1 February 1894.

50 Ibid., file 8, MCM to D.D. Macdonald, 15 October 1893.

51 Ibid., file 9, MCM to D.D. Macdonald, 18 January 1894.

52 Ibid., file 8, MCM to D.D. Macdonald, 18 December 1893.

53 Ibid., file 9, MCM to D.D. Macdonald, 1 January 1894.

54 Ibid., MCM to D.D. Macdonald, 18 January 1894.

55 SFXA, MFC, RG 2, file 15, MCM to Mary Macdonald, 1 February 1894.

56 Darche listed the subject matter of first and second year in her speech to the International Congress in June 1893 ("Proper Organization of Training Schools," 103).

57 SFXA, MFC, RG 2, file 9, MCM to D.D. Macdonald, 7 June 1894.

58 SFXA, MFC, RG 3, Scrapbook of Maggie C. Macdonald, 140–1, *inter alia*, 153, 137.

59 SFXA, MFC, RG 2, file 15, MCM to Mary Macdonald, 1 January 1894.

60 Ibid., file 9, MCM to D.D. Macdonald, [22–3 October 1893]. She repeated the injunction at the top of another letter to him, 22 February 1894. The fact that only fifteen letters were preserved from a two-year period suggests that someone took her at her word. The sketch of Margaret at work and play is drawn from these letters and from her scrapbook.

61 Such a career path, limited to very few nurses, is outlined in Mottus, *New York Nightingales*, 154–5. The staff at New York City Hospital in 1896

consisted of a superintendent and an assistant superintendent, five supervising nurses, and six head nurses (SFXA, MFC, RG 3, Scrapbook of Maggie C. Macdonald, 92: unidentified press clipping entitled "Commencement Exercises" and hand-dated 5 June 1896, the year after Macdonald's graduation). This small staff directed the work of the sixty or so student nurses who, along with the still present untrained female help, some male nurses, and male orderlies, did the ward work of the thousand-bed hospital.

62 SFXA, MFC, RG 3, Scrapbook of Maggie C. Macdonald, 10 (tucked into an envelope), "New York City Training School Registry for Nurses: Rules and Regulations," 16 November 1893.

63 According to her biographical entry in Morgan, ed., *Canadian Men and Women of the Time* (1912), 682, she was the recording secretary.

64 SFXA, MFC, RG 2, file 9, MCM to D.D. Macdonald, 22 October 1893.

65 Duffy, *History of Public Health in New York City*, 165.

66 Mottus, *New York Nightingales*, 153.

67 SFXA, MFC, RG 3, file 81, "It was with a feeling …" MCM speech to graduating class in nursing, Hospital for Sick Children, Toronto, 19 November 1920.

68 SFXA, MFC, RG 3, Scrapbook of Maggie C. Macdonald. Envelopes and telegrams in the scrapbook reveal four different addresses, and there were likely many more. For example, she probably relinquished her lodgings when she went home to Nova Scotia for vacation, as she did twice between 1895 and 1898 (Barry, "The Macdonald Family," 27–8).

69 Reverby, *Ordered to Care*, 110.

70 Melosh, *"The Physician's Hand ,"* 115. Collections of Lillian Wald Papers are in the Special Collections at Teachers' College, Columbia University, and in the New York Public Library, but I have been unable to discern any link to Macdonald.

71 SFXA, MFC, RG 2, file 9, MCM to D.D. Macdonald, 29 February 1894.

CHAPTER TWO

1 St Francis Xavier University Archives (SFXA), Macdonald Family Collection (MFC), RG 3, file 82, "Light and Shade in Army Nursing," 1, Margaret C. Macdonald (MCM) speech [to recent graduates of St Martha's Hospital School of Nursing, Antigonish, Nova Scotia, 194?]. Sister Clare Marie Lyons of the Sisters of St Martha in Antigonish confirmed my guess of the location. She also kindly combed her memory and the Antigonish *Casket* to determine that the occasion was likely a graduation banquet (correspondence, 2 May, 19 May, 17 July 2003).

2 Pictou County Land Information Centre/Registry of Deeds, Last Will and Testament of Margaret C. Macdonald, 1 August 1948.

3 See, for example, McClintock, *Imperial Leather*.

4 Father Gregory MacKinnon, in a conversation 7 May 2001, recalled this retort of MCM to his mother.

5 Summers, *Angels and Citizens*, 97–8, 112, 114. See also Hay, *One Hundred Years*; Haldane, *The British Nurse*; and DeGroot's introduction "Arms and the Woman" in DeGroot and Peniston-Bird, *A Soldier and a Woman*.

6 Sarnecky, *A History of the U.S. Army Nurse Corps*, 13, 25–6, 39–40, 42, 60–1.

7 George M. Sternberg, Surgeon General, United States Army, printed circular letter in response to the 1,500 offers of medical assistance, 25 April 1898. The presence of this letter in the Macdonald Family Scrapbook (MFS) is the clue to Macdonald's having applied at the very beginning of the war.

8 Sarnecky, *A History of the U.S. Army Nurse Corps*, 30–4, 38; Sarnecky, "Nursing in the American Army," 59–61; McGee, "Women Nurses in the American Army."

9 Musicant, *Empire By Default*, 647–50.

10 Her contract is in MFS.

11 Gillett, *Army Medical Department*, 186–91; *Harper's Weekly*, 10 September 1898, 890, 891–3, and 17 September 1898, 908–9, contain a brief description and illustrations of Camp Wikoff. Other evidence of the presence of journalists comes from the letterhead of Macdonald's note home: "Headquarters of the *Brooklyn Daily Eagle* Camp Wikoff."

12 Musicant, *Empire by Default*, 649.

13 SFXA, MFC, RG 2, file 15, MCM to Mary Macdonald, 5 September 1898.

14 Gillett, *Army Medical Department*, 189, 191.

15 SFXA, MFC, RG 2, file 15, MCM to Mary Macdonald, 5 September 1898.

16 Library and Archives Canada (LAC), RG 9 II A3, Ministry of Militia and Defence, vol. 20, file "South African War Records Applications 1899–1900 Nurses," W.S. Fielding to F.W. Borden, quoting D.D. Macdonald, 6 January 1900. This is the source for the continuing – and I now think erroneous – references to Macdonald's having served on the *Relief*. See, for example, Nicholson, *Canada's Nursing Sisters*, 38, and Miller, *Painting the Map*, 451.

17 Macdonald's biographical sketch in Morgan, ed., *Canadian Men and Women of the Time* (1912), does not mention the *Relief*. Nor does the "Official Statement of Service," preserved in MFS and signed by C.H. Bridges, Major General, the Adjutant General [U.S. Army], 1932. The

National Archives and Records Administration in Washington (NARA) does not have a record of Macdonald in the papers of the Office of the Surgeon General (Army), RG 112, Series 148, 149, 150 (contract nurses, Spanish-American War).

18 MFS, SO no. 27 from U.S. Hospital Ship *Relief* by order of Major Torney, signed by A.O. Bradley, Major, Brigade Surgeon, U.S.V. Adjutant *Relief*, 16 September 1898.

19 MFS, written on the outside of the folded-in-three contract and dated 19 September 1898.

20 SFXA, MFC, RG 2, file 9, MCM to D.D. Macdonald, 7 June 1894.

21 Ibid., file 15, MCM to Mary Macdonald, 5 September 1898.

22 Ibid. This oath did not entail becoming an American citizen; indeed, it may have been just an employment requirement, indicating her willingness to abide by U.S. Army rules. My thanks to Michael Piva for explaining the many possible meanings of oaths in American employment practices.

23 Sarnecky, *A History of the U.S. Army Nurse Corps*, 48.

24 MFS, Captain A. Benoit, Department of Militia and Defence, telegram to MCM, 22 December 1899.

25 LAC, RG 9 II A3, vol. 20, file "South African War Records Applications 1899–1900 Nurses." Macdonald's application is not in this file.

26 "Joseph Pope," in Morgan, ed., *Canadian Men and Women of the Time* (1898), 826–7, and (1912), 910.

27 "Francis Gordon Forbes," in Morgan, ed., *Canadian Men and Women of the Time* (1898), 343–4, and (1912), 408. The dates, family names, and locality all suggest the relationship which Miller states but does not document (*Painting the Map*, 450). See also G. Pope, "Reminiscences," 570. Pope's article is a slightly updated version of her official report on service in South Africa contained in Canada, *Sessional Papers* 35a (64 Victoria A1901), pt II, "Report B," 63–5. Extracts from this report were published in the *British Journal of Nursing*, 19 October 1901, 320–1.

28 "Sarah Elizabeth Russell," in Morgan, ed., *Canadian Men and Women of the Time* (1912), 984; "James Russell," ibid., (1898), 896, and (1912), 983.

29 "Marcella Richardson," ibid., (1912), 939; "Hugh Richardson," ibid.; "Hugh Richardson," *Dictionary of Canadian Biography*, 14: 870–1. The article's author, Thomas Flanagan, makes no mention of Richardson's military daughter.

30 Obituary, Deborah Hurcomb, *Canadian Nurse* 3 (April 1907): 205; "George Perley," in Morgan, ed., *Canadian Men and Women of the Time* (1912), 897.

31 "Report of Major General on the South African Contingents," in Canada,

Sessional Papers 35a (62 Victoria 1899), pt II, 7, telegram from Joseph Chamberlain, Colonial Secretary, to Lord Minto, Governor General, 23 October 1899.

32 Pope, "Report B," in Canada, *Sessional Papers* 35a (64 Victoria A1901), pt II, 63.

33 SFXA, MFC, RG 3, file 47, Carrie Land, Honorary Secretary, Imperial Order Daughters of the Empire, Toronto, to MCM, 10 May 1902.

34 The four nurses had the company of more than thirty men of equivalent or higher rank: fourteen officers of the Royal Canadian Field Artillery; ten others travelling as "attached officers" until they reached South Africa, where they would join their own units; the *Laurentian's* officers (captain, purser, first officer, doctor, etc.); and five non-military men on their way to join the British Army Postal Corps. See Miller, *Painting the Map*, 167, 457; Canada, *Sessional Papers* 35a (64 Victoria A1901), pt II, 78.

35 Miller, *Painting the Map*, 169.

36 MCM, "Army Nursing," 358.

37 Instruction no. 8 of "Instructions for Medical Officers on Hired Transports to the Cape," in Canada, *Sessional Papers* 35 (64 Victoria A1901), 50.

38 Pope, "Reminiscences," 565.

39 LAC, MG 30 D209, John McCrae Papers, McCrae to his mother, 20 January 1900, "Saturday, 1 week out of Halifax" [28 January 1900], 7 February and 4 June 1900. In the letter of 28 January McCrae enclosed a sketch of his table setting. Major Hurdman, who was the senior military officer on the *Laurentian*, presided at the table; presumably, Major G.H. Ogilvie, the other major aboard, did the same at the second table with the two other nurses and other officers.

40 LAC, MG 30 D209, John McCrae Papers, McCrae to his mother, 25 January 1900, [28 January 1900]; Morrison, *With the Guns*, 36–7, 41; Miller, *Painting the Map*, 170, 457. Seventeen hundred letters were posted on the *Laurentian*.

41 SFXA, MFC, *The Span O' Life: A Tale of Louisbourg and Quebec*, by William McLennan and J.N. McIlwraith (New York: Harper 1899) in an uncatalogued box of books that belonged to Margaret Macdonald. Signatures of fellow passengers adorn the front and back soft-leather covers – those of eight of her table-mates and nine others, no nurses among them. Along the spine, in a handwriting not that of Macdonald, appears "Royal Canadian Artillery en route for S. Africa Transport 'Laurentian' Feb 15 1900 Lat. 29.55 Long 14.26." The tie around the book has served to retain – until the SFXA archivist catalogues (and separates!) the material – some tucked-in memorabilia, two pieces of which relate to John McCrae: a copy

of his poem "The Song of the Derelict" from the *Canadian Magazine* and a small studio portrait by the Montreal photographer William Notman.

42 Morrison, *With the Guns*, 46, 52–3. Morrison was borrowing and rendering plural the phrase "a gentleman in kharki ordered South" from Rudyard Kipling's poem "The Absent-Minded Beggar." My thanks to Karen Smith, head of Special Collections at Dalhousie University Library, for locating the poetic source of the phrase. Morrison was dismayed that the library of the *Laurentian* had "not a set of Kipling, in fact, only one or two volumes of his least interesting works" (36).

43 Miller, *Painting the Map*, 451; Pope, "Reminiscences," 566; D. Hurcomb, "Report F," 17 January 1901, in Canada, *Sessional Papers* 35a (64 Victoria A1901), pt II, 153. Morrison's chapter, "Preparing for the Front," has a final paragraph about the nurses at Rondebosch, whose experience he describes as all very jolly and easy (*With the Guns*, 56). Sidney Browne became the first matron-in-chief of the Queen Alexandra's Imperial Military Nursing Service in 1902 and then of the Territorial Force Nursing Service, formed in 1908.

44 Hurcomb, "Report F," in Canada, *Sessional Papers* 35a (64 Victoria A1901), pt II, 153–4.

45 Morrison, *With the Guns*, 112.

46 LAC, MG 28 I 157, Association of Medical Officers of the Militia Papers, vol. 1, Minute Book, 41, speech of Army Inspector General Sir Percy Lake to AMOM, Ottawa, 26 February 1909.

47 SFXA, MFC, unsigned letter to "Dear Bombadier" in an envelope addressed to MCM at Dames Institute Hospital, Bloemfontein, 28 May 1900, tucked into her copy of *The Span O' Life*. The letter writer, quoting Horace, was bored by lack of military action and he grumbled about the British: "The next time I go to war for the blooming British empire I will want a written guarantee that it is *war*."

48 Hurcomb, "Report F," in Canada, *Sessional Papers* 35a (64 Victoria A1901), pt II, 153–4, is the source for the nurses' work at Bloemfontein and also for the account in Nicholson, *Canada's Nursing Sisters*, 38–9, and Miller, *Painting the Map*, 451. Miller is the only source for Hurcomb becoming ill, but the *Canadian Nurse* 3 (April 1907): 205 did report her premature death. Denison's *Memoirs*, 71–3, recounts Horne's illness dramatically.

49 SFXA, MFC, RG 2, file 15, MCM to Mary Macdonald, 8 June 1900. General Kelly-Kenney (1840–1914) was an Irish-born career soldier with the British military. In South Africa he was in command of the 6th Division of the British forces. The Roberts women are the two daughters and the wife of

the British commander-in-chief, Lord Frederick Roberts. Dr Chisholm is Macdonald's maternal uncle, the brother of Mary and Joseph. He remained in Scotland after his medical studies in Edinburgh and returned to Nova Scotia later. He is buried at Marydale, and a tall monument there was subsequently moved by Vie Macdonald to a more prominent position in the cemetery at St Andrew's, where it is still visible. The Macdonald letter quoted here is one of only four communications to her family that remain from her first year in South Africa, January–December 1900.

50 LAC, McCrae Papers, J. McCrae to his mother, 4 June 1900.

51 LAC, McCrae Papers, Diary of John McCrae, 29 June 1900; J. McCrae to his mother, 28 June 1900. Morrison records another tea party, in *With the Guns*, 140.

52 LAC, McCrae Papers, Diary of John McCrae, 29 June, 1 July, [4 July], 10 July 1900.

53 SFXA, MFC, RG 3, file 3, J. McC[rae] to MCM, 9 July 1900. Clare Barry misread the shortened signature of this letter as J.M.A. and classified it as such in the finding aid to MFC, which forms the major part of her BA thesis on the Macdonald family. By comparing the handwriting with known manuscripts of McCrae in LAC, I was able to determine that the writer was indeed John McCrae.

54 LAC, McCrae Papers, Diary of John McCrae, 10 July 1900.

55 SFXA, MFC, RG 2, file 10, MCM to D.D. Macdonald, 30 August 1900.

56 Ibid.

57 Pope, "Report B," in Canada *Sessional Papers* 35a (64 Victoria A1901), pt II, 64; Nicholson, *Canada's Nursing Sisters*, 39; Miller, *Painting the Map*, 452.

58 LAC, McCrae Papers, Diary of John McCrae, 7, 8 August 1900, re visiting the nurses. On 30 August he noted the new headgear: "The helmets made the men look much smarter than the hats ever could & we were glad we had them."

59 Summers, *Angels and Citizens*, 209.

60 SFXA, MFC, RG 2, file 10, MCM to D.D. Macdonald, 30 August 1900.

61 Ibid., MCM to "Toots"[sister Floss?], 22 September 1900.

62 Ibid., MCM to D.D. Macdonald, 30 August 1900.

63 Hurcomb, "Report F," in Canada, *Sessional Papers* 35a (64 Victoria A1901), pt II, 153.

64 Pope, "Reminiscences," 568.

65 Macdonald was in Pretoria from 20 July to 23 November 1900, during which time the Irish Hospital became No. 19 General Hospital. Becher was in South Africa as matron of No. 19, although the precise dates of her

being there are not indicated in her service file at the National Archives in London (hereafter TNA), WO 399/501. As for McCarthy, her third posting in South Africa was at No. 19, where she served under Becher. McCarthy's service file (TNA, WO 399/12912) does not give precise dates either, but she recalled meeting Macdonald in Pretoria. See LAC, Nursing Sisters' Association (hereafter NSA), vol. 1, file 22, Maud McCarthy to Jean Browne, 28 May 1926. Pope also mentions McCarthy's presence at Pretoria, but not that of Becher ("Reminiscences," 568). I believe there are sufficient hints, nonetheless, to place all the women in Pretoria at some point while Macdonald was there. None of the records of the British hospitals in South Africa could be located in Britain.

66 SFXA, MFC, RG 2, file 10, MCM to D.D. Macdonald, 30 August 1900. She had intended to write something for the *Eastern Chronicle* of New Glasgow.

67 Ibid., MCM to "Toots," 22 September 1900.

68 Ibid., MCM to D.D. Macdonald, 30 August 1900. Her sister Adele, a CND nun in Montreal, had expressed pro-Boer views, encouraged perhaps by French Canadians in the same congregation. Margaret added to her father, "She had the same sentiment about the Spanish-American War and most likely has droll ideas about the Chinese War too."

69 SFXA, MFC, RG 2, file 10, MCM to "Toots," 22 September 1900.

70 The permit, dated 24 October 1900, is in MFS.

71 No first-hand records of this incident exist and the story has been repeated so often as to become almost apocryphal. The *Casket* of Antigonish, 22 November 1900, mentioned only that Macdonald had been "badly injured by a shell" in the Transvaal, information that the paper probably received from her family. Just before Christmas, the New York *Sun* carried a fuller account based upon a cable and letters to Macdonald's friends in the city announcing her wound "early in the autumn," but as the paper acknowledged, "even these reports are somewhat incomplete" ("The Daughter of a Highlander," New York *Sun*, 23 December 1900, third section, 4). Macdonald's connection with the New York City Hospital Training School for Nurses would seem to be the reason for the the story being carried at all. The *Montreal Daily Star* reprinted the story verbatim (5 January 1901, 7) without acknowledging the source. There are also some unidentified and undated press clippings about this incident in Vie Macdonald's scrapbook (hereafter VMS) about her sister Margaret (SFXA, MFC, RG 5, file 18). The press accounts take considerable licence with Macdonald's experiences in South Africa, attaching her "to the column that went to the relief of Kimberley" (when in fact she arrived there one month later) and then having her on Lord Roberts's staff and accompanying him "in all his fighting to

Pretoria," which is just wrong. She arrived in Pretoria six weeks after the fall of the city to the British and was never on Lord Roberts's staff, much less with him in his fighting. The story of the wound found its way, thanks probably to D.D. Macdonald, into a tiny brochure, *The Book of the Macdonald Society* (Glasgow: Celtic Press [1902]), now in the possession of Ronald St John Macdonald Jr. The wound cannot have been too serious because there is no mention of a shoulder scar in Macdonald's military file of the First World War.

72 SFXA, MFC, RG 2, file 10, MCM to "Toots," 22 September 1900.

73 Ibid., MCM to D.D. Macdonald, 8 November 1900; Hurcomb, "Report F," in Canada, *Sessional Papers* 35a (64 Victoria A1901), pt II, 154; Pope, "Reminiscences," 568. A discrepancy exists between Macdonald's note to her father and Pope's recollections. According to the note, Macdonald knew before they left for Natal that they would not be going to England. Pope's recollection was that because of breaks in the train lines, the nurses returned too late from Natal to Pretoria to make the connection to the Cape in time for a ship to England. According to Miller, the British authorities' offer that all the Canadians of the Second Contingent return to Canada via England was turned down because the men wanted to get home quickly (*Painting the Map*, 284).

74 Miller, *Painting the Map*, 282–3.

75 Ibid., 284–5; Graves, *Crown of Life*, 77. McCrae must have persuaded the nurses to participate, for there was a "ladies' concert" on New Year's Eve. The Montreal *Gazette* had access to the ship's log and reported the event, 9 January 1901, 1.

76 *Montreal Daily Star*, 9 January 1901, 10, covered the arrival of the *Roslyn Castle* in Halifax and described all seven nurses in this fashion, but it may be particularly apt for Macdonald, whose bright pink cheeks had drawn attention since at least her nursing-school days.

77 LAC, RG 9 II B4, vol. 13, Register, Army Medical Services 1898–1908, 92. In order, the names were Pope, Forbes, Affleck, Russell, Hurcomb, Horne, Macdonald, Richardson, and two newcomers who had not been in South Africa, Eleanor Fortescue and Mary Birmingham.

78 "Nova Scotia Nurses Volunteer for South Africa – Miss Forbes of Liverpool, and Miss MacDonald, of Bailey's Brook, Are Anxious To Go," Halifax *Morning Chronicle*, 2 December 1901, 3. In spite of the headline, the brief article is more about men volunteering for service.

79 Report of the Deputy Minister, Militia and Defence, in Canada, *Sessional Papers* 35a (2-3 Edward VII, 1903), pt I, 8.

80 *Morning Chronicle*, 2 December 1901, 3. The two other nurses keen to go

to South Africa again were Hurcomb and Affleck. As for the remaining three who had been in South Africa but had not volunteered, the *Chronicle* offered the following explanation: Miss Horne was "sick at home," Miss Russell was "with an invalid in Egypt," and Miss Richards[on] was "already attached to the [British] Army Medical Corps in South Africa."

81 LAC, MG 27 II B1, Minto Papers, vol. 8, Borden to Minto, 9 January 1902. See also Borden to Minto, 23, 24 December 1901, 4 [January], 7 January 1902.

82 Ibid., Borden to Minto, Fri. evg. [10 January 1902].

83 Ibid., Borden to Minto, 14, 17, 23 January 1902. In none of the correspondence does an actual list of names appear. See also, Nicholson, *Canada's Nursing Sisters*, 41–2.

84 Miller, *Painting the Map*, 397–8. The two ships could accommodate 957 men, but only 901 sailed, along with more than 1,000 horses (ibid., 393).

85 SFXA, MFC, RG 5, file 3, MCM to Florence Macdonald, 18 February 1902.

86 Ibid., MCM to D.D. Macdonald, 4 March 1902. Arthur N. Worthington had been the surgeon major with the Canadian Field Artillery in South Africa in 1900.

87 Miller, *Painting the Map*, 454–5.

88 Pope, "Report on Service of Nursing Sisters," in Canada, *Sessional Papers* 35a (2–3 Edward VII 1903), pt II, 65–6. See also Worthington's report on the Canadian Field Hospital (ibid., 55–65). Both Pope in her report and Macdonald in her correspondence refer to their hospital as No. 19 Stationary, as do Amy Scott and Margaret Smith in 1914, when they indicate their previous military experience on their attestation papers for the Canadian Expeditionary Force (LAC, RG 150, boxes 8711-40 and 9086-2.) Presumably, Nicholson's reference to the hospital as No. 18 (*Canada's Nursing Sisters*, 43) is a misprint.

89 SFXA, MFC, RG 2, file 15, MCM to Mary Macdonald, 25–6 March 1902; file 11, MCM to D.D. Macdonald, 18 April 1902; and RG 3, file 1, MCM to Donald Macdonald, 28 April 1902. Her father's admonition about health and religion came to her in a letter of 14 February 1902 (ibid., RG 3, file 4).

90 SFXA, MFC, RG 3, file 1, MCM to Donald Macdonald, 28 April 1902.

91 Ibid., and MCM to Donald Macdonald, [May 1902]; and RG 2, file 15, MCM to D.D. Macdonald, 9 May 1902.

92 SFXA, MFC, RG 2, file 15, MCM to Mary Macdonald, 25–6 March 1902; file 11, MCM to D.D. Macdonald, 18 April 1902; file 15, MCM to D.D. Macdonald, 9 May 1902.

93 Worthington Report, in Canada, *Sessional Papers* 35a (2-3 Edward VII 1903), pt II, 61.

94 Miller, *Painting the Map*, 413.

95 Pope may have thought that the Royal Red Cross decoration she received in 1902 for her services in South Africa (*British Journal of Nursing*, 8 November 1902, 378) would give her entry to the British nursing service, but her application was not accepted (Nicholson, *Canada's Nursing Sisters*, 43–4).

96 MFS, letter from Dr Anita Newcomb McGee, President, Spanish-American War Nurses, to MCM in Bailey's Brook, 1 March 1904. McGee had had an inquiry from the Nurses' Outfitting Association about Macdonald's request for uniforms, and McGee hastened to write her, thinking that an earlier letter with the State Department's negative decision must have gone astray. For information on the expedition, see Anita Newcomb McGee, *The American Nurses in Japan* and accompanying information, all part of an exhibition at the National Museum of Health and Medicine, and now available via the internet at: http://history.amedd.army.mil/ameddcorp/armynurse/ McGeeWHMspecial/McGee_in_Japan.html

97 MFS, letter from S.E. Redfern to MCM, 9 September 1904. The letter was addressed c/o Miss Cameron-Smith, 408 West 57th St., New York, and suggests temporary lodgings on Macdonald's part. Jean Cameron-Smith was later among the Canadian military nurses of the First World War.

98 The contract is in MFS, as well as the covering letter from D.I. Murphy, Secretary, Isthmian Canal Commission, to MCM, 12 September 1904. The promotion and pay raise to $720 a year are specified in SFXA, MFC, RG 3, file 48, Charles E. Magoon, Commissioner, Head of the Department of Government and Sanitation, to MCM, 12 June 1905. For the paid leave of absence and its unpaid extension, see MFS, H.D. Reed, Executive Secretary, Isthmian Canal Commission, Ancon, to MCM, 7 July, 7 September 1905. As a point of comparison for her pay, orderlies at Ancon Hospital in 1905 received an annual wage of $360 and doctors $1800 (*Annual Report of the Isthmian Canal Commission* [1905], 228–9, 309).

99 National Archives and Records Administration (NARA), RG 185, Records of the Panama Canal, Employment Card files, Service Record Card of Margaret Chisholm Macdonald.

100 *Annual Report of the Isthmian Canal Commission* (1904), 50; (1905), 60; Mears, *The Triumph of American Medicine*, 38.

101 *Annual Report of the Isthmian Canal Commission* (1904), 89; Mears, *The Triumph of American Medicine*, 38.

102 SFXA, MFC, RG 5, file 5, MCM to Vie Macdonald, 25 October 1904. See also *Annual Report of Isthmian Canal Commission* (1904), 88, and McCullough, *The Path between the Seas*, 416, 425.

103 Chamberlain, *Twenty-Five Years*, 13. See also McCullough, *The Path between the Seas*, 451–2, where he contends that the panic was "out of proportion to the actual seriousness of the epidemic"(452). As an illustration of hospital staff leaving Ancon because of yellow fever, McCullough cites an article from a New York paper about a returning nurse (451). The nurse in question, Miss A.A. Robinson, matron of the hospital at Colon, on the other side of the isthmus from Ancon, left after a year's service in Panama worn out by "the absolute stagnation of the mental and emotional life" (*New York Daily Tribune*, 6 July 1905, 5); nonetheless, the paper headlined her account "Fighting Yellow Fever." Between April and October 1905, there were 184 cases of yellow fever and 57 deaths. The highest numbers were in June and July (*Annual Report of the Isthmian Canal Commission* [1905], 6).

104 Ibid., 35.

105 NARA, Records of the Panama Canal, Macdonald's Service Record Card indicates that she was sick 15–22 April 1905 but does not name her illness.

106 The medical form completed at the end of her overseas service in the First World War records "Malaria 1905–6–7" (LAC, RG 150, box 6752-26). There is no hint of illness in the three letters from MCM to her sister Vie from Panama (SFXA, MFC, RG 5, file 5, 25 October 1904, 16 March 1905 and [early April 1905]).

107 *Annual Report of the Isthmian Canal Commission* (1905), 7, 35.

108 SFXA, MFC, RG 4, file 13, diary of Ronald St John Macdonald 1936–37 (in spite of the cover, which states 1934), piece of paper tucked in with the captioned snapshot glued to it: "Ancon, Canal Zone 1904: Miss Macdonald and Mr Luck."

109 SFXA, MFC, RG 5, file 5, MCM to Vie Macdonald, [early April 1905].

110 McCullough, *The Path between the Seas*, 424.

111 SFXA, MFC, RG 5, file 5, MCM to Vie Macdonald, 25 October 1904. Macdonald's phrasing refers to romance, not sex. She had been on the same ship from New York in September with the wife of General Jefferies. His name does not appear in Bennett, *History of the Panama Canal* or in any of the American biographical dictionaries.

112 SFXA, MFC, RG 5, file 5, MCM to Vie Macdonald, 16 March 1905.

113 Ibid., [early April 1905].

114 Ibid., 25 October 1904.

115 MFS, note signed "Jim" attached to the letter from H.D. Reed to MCM, 6 September 1905. Might Watkins be discernible in the illegible last name? A Dr James Watkins appeared in her scrapbook during her time in New York. Another (?) Jim, known to her family, is present in her letters from nursing school.

116 The name of Donald Macdonald of Egerton, halfway between Bailey's Brook and New Glasgow, was raised as a possible suitor by Ronnie Macdonald of Antigonish in a conversation, 10 May 2001. His assumption that the two were in Panama at the same time is questionable, although that does not preclude their knowing each other. Donald Francis Macdonald (1875–1942) worked for the Geological Survey of Canada from 1902 to 1911, during which time he completed undergraduate and graduate work in geology at American universities. He went to Panama in 1911 (long after Margaret Macdonald had left) and was there through at least some of the years of the First World War. Married to an American, he was appointed professor of geology at St Francis Xavier University in 1932 and taught there until 1940, when he returned to Panama to survey the canal and recommend improvements. He died there in 1942 (Bennett, *History of the Panama Canal*, 477; *Casket*, 15 September 1932, 22 August 1940, 4, 11, 18 June 1942).

117 SFXA, MFC, RG 5, file 5, MCM to Vie Macdonald, 25 October 1904.

118 *Annual Report of the Isthmian Canal Commission* (1905), 8.

119 "Ancon Hospital," 883.

120 MFS, unidentified press clipping from a Halifax paper. The handwritten date on the clipping, 28 February 1906, is the date of D.D.'s death, not the date of the press report. The *Eastern Chronicle*, 6 March 1906, carried a tribute to D.D. Macdonald.

121 Pictou County Land Information Centre/Registry of Deeds, Last Will and Testament of Donald D. Macdonald of Bailey's Brook, 22 December 1903.

122 Thereby hangs another tale about the Macdonald family. The tiny graveyard, a mile and a half east of the Macdonald home, was attached to Mount St Mary's Church, which is no longer standing. That church was the outcome of a three-year feud in the community, beginning in 1903, over whether to repair the existing church at Lismore or build a new one at Bailey's Brook. Thanks to D.D. Macdonald's friendship with Bishop Cameron and the latter's close ties to Rome, Bailey's Brook won out, and a lovely new church was built. Before it was completed, however, D.D. died and was therefore buried in the Lismore cemetery, where two Macdonald male children were already interred. But in his will he left two hundred dollars to his wife for an unspecified "special purpose," which may well have been the removal of his remains and those of the children from Lismore to the cemetery of the new church, something which happened in 1914, in spite of the local priest's disapproval. In 1917 fire destroyed the new church and rekindled the community feud. This time, a new bishop determined that the church would not be rebuilt; rather, the insurance monies from the fire would be used to refurbish the older church at Lismore, which is still in use

today. Memories of the feud linger in the community even in 2004. Father R.B. Macdonald, retired professor at St Francis Xavier University, shared his research on the story with me in conversations, on 16 July 2001 and 15 April 2004. The graveyard at Bailey's Brook (minus church) thus contains two gravestones that predate the church and the cemetery, that of D.D., to which his wife's name was added in 1927, and that of the seven-year-old Donald and the unnamed infant. Two newer ones postdate the church, that of Margaret Macdonald and the one that marks the burial site of her younger brother Donald and her sister Vie.

123 NARA, Records of the Panama Canal, Service Record Card. The entry for 16 April 1906 records the "18 days [leave] w.p. and 57 days w.o.p." Salary increases are registered 16 June and 1 October 1905.

124 SFXA, MFC, RG 5, file 5, MCM to Vie Macdonald, 25 October 1904.

125 Jones, "The Nursing Sister," 129. Rawling mistakenly takes these reserve numbers not only for reality but as permanent nursing members of the CAMC (*Death Their Enemy*, 54). Neither was the case. Even in 1914 at the outbreak of war, there were only five nursing sisters permanently employed in the CAMC.

126 SFXA, MFC, RG 3, file 49 contains a copy of Militia Order no. 269, 22 November 1906.

127 Nicholson, *Canada's Nursing Sisters*, 44.

128 Jones, "The Nursing Sister," 129; LAC, RG 24, Ministry of National Defence, vol. 6574, file HQ 1211-9-88, typescript extract from Marguerite H.L. Grant, "Historical Sketches of Hospitals in Halifax and Dartmouth," n.d., n.p.; G.C. Jones, "Report on Medical Services for year ending 31 March 1911," appendix A of Report of the Militia Council, in Canada, *Sessional Papers* 35 (2 George V 1912), 52. The Halifax garrison, the largest in Canada, numbered some 1,200 people in 1911–12: 60 officers, 21 warrant officers, and 1,119 non-commissioned officers and men. See Annual Report of the Militia Council year ending 31 March 1912, in Canada, *Sessional Papers* 35 (3 George V 1913), 19.

129 See Mann, ed., *The War Diary of Clare Gass*, 295, n.19. Maude Wilkinson's recollections do have a nursing sister in charge of a venereal ward at a Canadian military hospital in Salonika in 1916 (Wilkinson, "Four Score and Ten," November 1977, 20).

130 G.C. Jones, "Report on Medical Services," appendix A of the Report of the Militia Council, in Canada, *Sessional Papers* 35 (7–8 Edward VII 1908), 20–3, and (8–9 Edward VII 1909), 28–33. Subsequent reports do not list the ailments by hospital, and none of them enumerates the kinds of surgery performed.

131 Macdonald outlined this daily regime in a lecture to would-be military nurses, and one can assume that it reflected her own. See "Nursing Sister PAMC," lecture notes of Edith Hudson from the course in military training for nurses, Kingston, April 1914. Hudson's notes are in the possession of military collector and dealer Allan Kerr, MilArm Co. Ltd., Edmonton, and were brought to my attention and photocopied for me by Debbie Culbertson, 2002.

132 G.C. Jones, "Report of Medical Services for the year ending March 31, 1909," appendix A of Annual Report of the Militia Council, in Canada, *Sessional Papers* 35 (9–10 Edward VII 1910), 39.

133 Medical students who served as orderlies in some wartime hospitals constitute the exception to this description of orderlies. They served, for example, with the 10th Canadian Field Hospital in South Africa in 1902 and with No. 3 Canadian General Hospital (McGill) during the First World War.

134 SFXA, MFC, RG 3, file 80, "The Training of Our Orderlies," MCM, prewar speech, possibly given to a local branch of the Association of Medical Officers of the Militia. Accompanying the typescript of the speech is a letter dated 17 February to her brother Ronald in Montreal asking for any suggestions and for his copy of the program, which she had not yet received, "or at least the date & hour for my own Paper. I want to arrange in advance for my time." The February date on the letter corresponds with the timing of the annual meeting of the Association of Medical Officers of the Militia. But when she did give a paper there in 1913 (the name of the organization changed in 1912 to Association of Officers of the Medical Services of Canada), the organizers noted that it was a first for a nursing sister. The Minute Book of the Association (LAC, MG 28 I 157) records the annual meetings but has no record of a speech about orderlies. It does, however, mention the development of local branches as of 1909.

135 SFXA, MFC, RG 3, file 94, [Jean Cameron-Smith], "C.A.M.C. Nursing Service" [1917], 1. This text appears as well in LAC, MG 30 E45, Margaret C. Macdonald Papers, file "Memoranda." Lest it be mistaken for a text by Macdonald, extracts from it appear in files "Transcripts ch. 2" and "Transcripts ch. 3," where the inside cover of the file identifies Jean Cameron-Smith as the author.

136 LAC, Macdonald Papers, file "Memoranda," MCM typescript "Early Nursing Service," [1921?], 4; Nicholson, *Canada's Nursing Sisters*, 46. There is far more of "routine" and no mention at all of ethics in a list of very practical lecture topics for such a course taught by Georgina Pope at Halifax in 1909 (*Militia Orders*, 13 November 1908).

137 Drawn from the lecture notes of Edith Hudson. See note 131 above.

According to Hudson's notes, Macdonald gave two lectures, one on the daily round of a military nurse and the other on the regulations for patients. No trace remains of the "ethics of Army nursing," but one can assume it had much to do with appropriate behaviour of female nurses in close proximity to male soldiers. See also Pope, "Army Nursing," 599, and Cameron-Smith, "The Preparation of Nurses," 556.

138 LAC, Macdonald Papers, file "Memoranda," MCM, "Early Nursing Service," 4.

139 LAC, Macdonald Papers, file "Memoranda," Jean Cameron-Smith, "C.A.M.C. Nursing Service," 1.

140 The numbers of annual appointees to the reserve Army Nursing Service prior to the war can be seen in *Militia List* (1914), 315–16. The numbers jumped dramatically in the summer of 1914 (ibid., 318–20). The numbers of students in the training courses are reported in Canada, *Sessional Papers* 35 (1 George V 1911), 42; (2 George V 1912), 22; (3 George V 1913), 50; and (4 George V 1914), 17.

141 Annual Report of the Militia Council for the year ending December 31, 1906, in Canada, *Sessional Papers* 35 (6–7 Edward VII 1907), 2.

142 Macdonald went to Quebec City on 1 April 1909 to replace another nurse, Laura Eaton. See *Militia Orders*, no. 72(3) (1909); *Militia List* (1909). For the number of soldiers in the Quebec garrison see Annual Report of the Militia Council year ending 31 March 1912, in Canada, *Sessional Papers* 35 (3 George V 1913), 19.

143 Nicholson, *Canada's Nursing Sisters*, 46. Nicholson gives no source for the document "Report of Service Prepared by Matron M.C. Macdonald," which was finally located, untitled, in LAC, NSA, vol. 6, file 2 [1942]. In it, she recalls that "the application was unprecedented and occasioned great surprise in Army circles." Thanks to the support of Col. Guy Carleton Jones, the head of the CAMC, her request was granted.

144 She may even have wanted to accompany Canadian troops going to London as part of the festivities. The Canadian contingent of soldiers, chosen from across the country, sailed from Quebec aboard the *Empress of Ireland*, 2 June 1911. The extensive press coverage of the sailing and the arrangements made for the soldiers' well-being does not mention the presence of an army nurse, though there certainly would have been medical personnel on the ship (*Quebec Chronicle*, 2 June 1911, 3).

145 SFXA, MFC, RG 3, file 15 contains a form letter about seating for the coronation, 22 June 1911; file 17 contains a series of invitation cards to celebratory gatherings in the presence of members of the British aristocracy: Princess Louise and the Duke of Argyll, the Duke and Duchess of Con-

naught (he was soon to be governor general of Canada), and Lord and Lady Northcliffe.

146 Recollection of Father Greg MacKinnon, son of Mary Chisholm MacKinnon, in a conversation on 7 May 2001.

147 SFXA, MFC, RG 3, file 16, Clay Burton Vance to MCM, 18 July 1911. The very slight difference in shading of the typing of her name and that of the text of the two-page missive suggests a form letter, likely one for each of the signs of the zodiac (Macdonald was a Pisces).

148 Vie Macdonald wrote to her mother from Scotland, 2 October 1925, and commented on the beauty of the countryside: "You were right about Scotland, it is really lovely." She enclosed a ticket stub from a play "to remind you of the time you were here." Given family circumstances and the war, the most likely time for such a visit by Mary Macdonald would be 1911. Father MacKinnon had always assumed that his Aunt Mary had travelled to Britain after the war. However, the only year this could have been is 1923, when Margaret went; but earlier that year Mary Macdonald had been seriously ill, so travel was likely out of the question. I thank the Verhagen family, current owners of the Macdonald homestead in Bailey's Brook, for giving me Vie Macdonald's letter of 2 October 1925.

149 Morgan, ed., *Canadian Men and Women of the Time* (1912), 682. Macdonald probably wrote her own biographical sketch with its strong concluding antisuffragette statement.

150 For an overview of these reforms, see Macpherson, *History of the Great War: Medical Services*, vol. 1, chs 1 and 2.

151 In 1911 the 311 nurses of the QAIMNS were serving in Britain, South Africa, Egypt, Gibraltar, Malta, and Hong Kong (Hayhurst, "The Army Nurse," 366).

152 Thirty years later, Macdonald penned a curious remark about her two hosts: "Every *courtesy* was extended by these ladies (quite questionable!?)" (LAC, NSA, vol. 6, file 2 [1942]).

153 TNA, Military Records Information Leaflet 55, "British Army: Nurses and Nursing Services"; "The Army Nursing Service Reserve," letter to the editor from "An Old A.N.S.R.," *Nursing Mirror*, 16 December 1911, 190; Haldane, *British Nurse*, 167, 177.

154 Ann Summers details the development of the VADs, in *Angels and Citizens*, 237–70.

155 McCarthy had been matron at Connaught Military Hospital at Aldershot and at Queen Alexandra's Military Hospital at Millbank (TNA, WO399/12912, Service file of Maud McCarthy, W.L. Gubbins to Adjutant General, 10 February 1914).

156 SFXA, MFC, RG 3, Scrapbook of Maggie C. Macdonald. The name of the ship is written on an unidentified press clipping entitled "Shipping Intelligence" hand-dated 22 December 1911. See also LAC, Passenger Lists (microfilm T4741), *Grampian*, 22 December 1911 from Liverpool, arrived Halifax 30 December 1911. Macdonald's destination is listed as Quebec City. For J.S. Ewart, see Morgan, ed., *Canadian Men and Women of the Time* (1912), 381–2. Ewart's papers at LAC contain nothing of a personal nature.

157 Mackenzie, *Shoulder to Shoulder*, 179–83.

158 The speech was given to the annual meeting of the Association of Officers of the Medical Services, Ottawa, 25 February 1913, and subsequently published as "Army Nursing," *Canadian Nurse* 9 (June 1913): 357–9, which gives the delivery date as 26 February 1913.

159 Ibid., 359.

160 LAC, Association of Medical Officers of the Militia, vol. 1, "Minute Book," 25 February 1913, 123, 125.

161 Jones, "The Nursing Sister," 129.

162 G.C. Jones, "Report on Medical Services for year ending 31 March 1910," Report of the Militia Council, appendix A, in Canada, *Sessional Papers* 35 (1 George V 1911), 48.

163 G.C. Jones, "Report on Medical Services for year ending 31 March 1911," Report of the Militia Council, appendix A, in Canada, *Sessional Papers* 35 (2 George V 1912), 51. Jones's suggestion was not acted upon until the war years.

164 Macdonald was transferred from Quebec City to Kingston on 1 February 1914 (*Militia Orders*, no. 18 [1914]). Macdonald's own text, "Reserve Nursing Service," mentions the training courses at Niagara and Petawawa (LAC, Macdonald Papers, file "Transcripts ch. 2").

165 Between 1 April 1914 and 31 March 1915, sixty-six nurses attended a "Provisional School Army Medical Corps." Most of these would have been after the outbreak of war in August 1914; Macdonald's point had nonetheless been acted upon. See "Report of the Militia Council year ending 31 March 1915," appendix E, in Canada, *Sessional Papers* 35 (6 George V 1916), 28–9.

CHAPTER THREE

1 Numbers vary by source. Macdonald's own postwar accounting has 2,504 nurses with the overseas military forces, 447 serving in Canada, 190 in the imperial nursing service (from a larger number of 313, of whom 123 had

transferred to the CAMC) for a total of 3,141. See Library and Archives Canada (LAC), Macdonald Papers, file "Correspondence 1923," Margaret C. Macdonald (MCM) to W.R. Landon, 12 May 1922. She was not the matron-in-chief of the Canadian nurses in the imperial nursing service, so her flock would number 3,141 - 190 = 2,951. A.F. Duguid, in charge of the official history of Canada's part in the First World War, arrived at a similar total but with a slightly different breakdown: 2,411 nurses in the CAMC overseas (including those who had transferred from the British nursing service), 443 serving in Canada, and 229 who stayed with the British service, for a total of 3,083, of whom 2,854 were part of the Canadian Expeditionary Force (LAC, RG 24, vol. 1742, file DHS 4-24, Duguid to E.C. Ashton, 16 November 1932). The Progress Reports of the Medical Service 1917–19 only mention overseas "nursing strength" for 1918–19, the highest number of nurses during that period being 1,945 in September 1918 (LAC, RG 24, vol. 2546, file HQ 2069-E). Macdonald's own reports, "Resumé of Work of A.M.D. 4" [the nursing division of the medical corps], May 1917 – September 1919, was the source from which information was extracted for the Progress Reports of the Medical Service (LAC, Macdonald Papers, file "Transcripts ch. 4").

2 LAC, RG 24, vol. 6519, file HQ 398-8-158, Lorne Drum to A.F. Duguid, 8 October 1923. Drum was in Jones's office in the summer of 1914 and remembered the flurry of telegrams trying to locate Macdonald: "She was his choice for this important position, and he was going to have her or none." Drum, who had known Macdonald in South Africa and again in Halifax, clearly approved Jones's choice: "If my old Chief General Jones is not gratefully remembered for anything else ... he should be remembered for his discrimination and good judgment in selecting Nursing Sister Macdonald on the outbreak of the war, to be the head of our Nursing Services."

3 St Francis Xavier University Archives (SFXA), Macdonald Family Collection (MFC), RG 3, file 86, "In accordance with telegraphic instructions ..." 1. I believe Macdonald wrote this untitled piece covering the years 1914–15 sometime after the war, perhaps as part of her intended history of the nursing service. See chapter 5 for a discussion of the history.

4 G.C. Jones, "Report on Medical Services year ending 31 March 1913," Report of the Militia Council, appendix B, in Canada, *Sessional Papers* 35 (4 George V 1914), 58.

5 LAC, Nursing Sisters' Association (NSA), vol. 1, Canadian National Association of Trained Nurses, file 3, MCM to Jean Gunn, 29 August 1914; J. Gunn to Lt. Col. Fotheringham, 27 November 1914; J. Gunn to R. Borden, 21 December, 1914.

6 MCM, "In accordance with telegraphic instructions ..." 1. This proviso merely displaced the importuning and special pleading to the local level. Judging from a file from Military District No. 4 (Montreal) in 1917, nurses could move to the head of the line if they were personally acquainted with the officer in charge (LAC, RG 24, Ministry of National Defence, C-1-a, vol. 4468, file MD4 9-2-26).

7 A list divided by military district appears in LAC, RG 24, vol. 6936, file "Appointment of Nursing Sisters, First Contingent."

8 Morton, *When Your Number's Up*, 183.

9 LAC, RG 150, box 6752-26. Macdonald's attestation form is only partially completed, as if it were not necessary to submit officers to as close a scrutiny as ordinary soldiers. On the form in this box (but not on the copy used for the LAC website) some other hand has completed the year of birth by filling in "79" after Macdonald's "18." In fact, birth dates on many of the CEF attestation forms are unreliable.

10 What Pope thought of Macdonald's promotion over her head is unknown, but one can imagine a certain tension between the two. Father MacKinnon (conversation of 7 May 2001) recalled his mother mentioning the tension, but he had no details. No Pope papers exist. The War Museum has four letters: 1911, 1918. Pope's military file lists her postings in England and France from September 1917 to November 1918, when she was invalided home after suffering from neurasthenia and arteriosclerosis to the point of requiring three hospital stays during 1918 (LAC, RG 150, box 7901-51).

11 MCM, "In accordance with telegraphic instructions ..." 7, handwritten addition. In 1917 Macdonald told the chief paymaster that "as far back as September 1914, ladies with no hospital training whatever were, on the instructions of the then Honourable Minister of Militia and Defence, appointed Nursing Sisters, CAMC, CEF ..." Most became "home sisters," a combination housekeeper and den mother for the nurses' mess in a military hospital. Some of them Macdonald placed in clerical positions. See LAC, RG 9, Department of Militia and Defence, III B2, vol. 3435, file 7-2-0 (vol. 3), MCM to Chief Paymaster, 24 July 1917.

12 MCM, "In accordance with telegraphic instructions ..." 2.

13 One of the principal forms was the one-page attestation paper completed by all members of the CEF. Designed for soldiers, the form, once completed, "attested" to the name, place of origin, next of kin, military experience, religion, age, height, weight, eye and hair colour, size of chest, and any distinguishing marks of the individual. A doctor added his assessment of the state of health. Once signed and witnessed, the form bound the person to serve in the CEF for a year, or for the duration of the war (plus six months after its end) should it last longer than a year. These forms, for all Canada's

military nurses – and soldiers too – are in LAC, RG 150 II 2 Attestation Papers. They also appear as part of the military personnel file of each member of the CEF in LAC, RG 150 II 3, Canadian Expeditionary Force Personnel Files 1914–20. Most of the attestation forms are now accessible via the internet. Go to www.archives.ca and follow the links to Archivianet, Research, and Soldiers of the First World War.

14 LAC, Macdonald Papers, file "Correspondence 1923," Isabella Strathy McMurtry to "Scotty" [A.F. Duguid], 28 August 1923.

15 Clint, *Our Bit*, 4; Nicholson, *Canada's Nursing Sisters*, 51, drawing on Ridley's narrative of 1 July 1916 in LAC, Macdonald Papers, file "Memoranda."

16 Born in Belleville in 1878, Ridley was five years younger than Macdonald. She took her nursing training at the same school as Macdonald, the New York City Hospital, where she was acting superintendent at the outbreak of the war. She had also spent two years in the Philippines in charge of the American Red Cross Auxiliary. The two women likely met in New York, perhaps through their alumnae association. See LAC, RG 150, box 8271-51, attestation paper of Ethel Blanche Ridley; and "Canadian Nursing Service," *Nursing Mirror*, 22 January 1916, 329.

17 SFXA, MFC, RG 3, file 98, MCM, "Echoes of the Great War," 2. See also Clint, *Our Bit*, 6–7, 9–10; Nicholson, *Canada's Nursing Sisters*, 53–4, quoting a letter from Juliette Pelletier to her mother about the merry dancing and the now interesting, now boring lectures. Edith Hudson mentions the daily lectures, as well as "drill and gymnasium," in the wartime continuation of her notebook from her military nursing training with Macdonald in 1914 (see chapter 2, note 131).

18 LAC, MG 30 E8, John Jennings Creelman Papers, "Diary" [extracts of his letters home], 15 October 1914. Lt. Col. Creelman told his wife that he saw "dozens of hugging couples" on the *Franconia*, which was tied up beside his ship, the *Ivernia*, on arrival in England. He added a second-hand account that during the voyage the captain of the *Franconia* had had to declare the upper deck of the ship "out of bounds" after dark. If this was indeed the case, it is highly likely that Macdonald was the one who instigated the ban.

19 Quoted in Nicholson, *Canada's Nursing Sisters*, 43. The original is in LAC, NSA, vol. 6, file 2, MCM, tribute to Georgina Pope [1941].

20 Macdonald recorded this encounter in marginal notations in her copy of Andrew Macphail's essay on John McCrae, *In Flanders Fields*, 84, 85.

21 Graves, *Crown of Life*, 164–5. Whether they had been in touch since their time in South Africa in 1900 is unknown. McCrae's generally effusive correspondence with his family was very discreet about his women friends (ibid., 144).

22 John McCrae to Tom McCrae, 5 August 1914, quoted in ibid., 162.

23 SFXA, MFC, RG 3, file 98, MCM, "Echoes of the Great War," 4.

24 Ibid. and file 86, MCM, "In accordance with telegraphic instructions ..."
5–6.

25 Clint, *Our Bit,* 17; MCM, "Echoes of the Great War," 5; *Nursing Mirror,*
31 October 1914, 80.

26 MCM, "In accordance with telegraphic instructions ..." 3.

27 Ibid., 7.

28 The National Archives, London (TNA), WO 399/12912, military service file
of Emma Maud McCarthy, W.L.Gubbins to E.M. McCarthy, 11 March
1914; McCarthy to Gubbins, 12 March 1914; B.B. Cubbitt to the Secretary, the Treasury, 7 December [1914]. See also *Nursing Mirror,* 18 August
1917, 339.

29 MCM, "In accordance with telegraphic instructions ..." 9; LAC, RG 9 III
B2, vol. 3404, file 30-11-1 (vol.16), MCM to Adjutant General, OMFC, 28
February 1917, containing Routine Order no. 52 of E.A.H. Alderson, Com-
mander of the First Canadian Contingent, 4 November 1914.

30 The timing of these postings is pieced together from MCM's rather less
chronologically ordered account, "In accordance with telegraphic instructions ..." 8–9.

31 Ibid., 9.

32 This notion of Macdonald's not wishing to be under another woman's
authority comes from Mary Philpott of St John's, Newfoundland, in an e-
mail communication, 4 April 2003. Philpott is working on Newfoundland
nurses of the First World War. I have not found any documentation to support her contention, but it does seem plausible.

33 SFXA, MFC, RG 2, file 17, Ronald Macdonald to Mary Macdonald, 22 June
1918.

34 Beatrice Nasmyth, "Matron-in-Chief in Her London Office," Vancouver
Province, 25 March 1916. Thanks to Debbie Culbertson for bringing this
article to my attention. Lorne Drum was the deputy director of medical
services for a year and a half under Jones. He recalled Macdonald dealing
directly with Jones on nursing matters (LAC, RG 24, vol. 1742, file DHS
4-32, Drum to A.F. Duguid, 15 November 1923).

35 Andrew Macphail's lively account of the Bruce controversy in his *Official
History ... The Medical Services,* ch. 13, is circumspect about Jones (whom
he disliked) and hostile to Bruce. See also LAC, MG 30 D150, Andrew
Macphail Papers, vol. 4, Diary, 15 July, 24 and 27 August, 3 and 27 October, 19 November 1916. Herbert Bruce's sense that he, rather than Jones,
was the victim of politics, is evident in his *Politics and the CAMC* and in his

later memoirs, *Varied Operations*. Desmond Morton is more sympathetic to Bruce's criticisms of the CAMC than people of the time were. In his *Peculiar Kind of Politics*, ch. 5, 84–105, he places the Bruce affair in the context of the Canadian government's increasing unease with Sam Hughes as minister of the militia, and its decision to dismiss him and to create a Ministry of Overseas Military Forces of Canada, based in London and headed by George Perley. See LAC, RG 9 III A1, vol. 76, file 10-8-32A, "Observations on Memorandum of Colonel H.A. Bruce prepared by Lieut. Col. John McComb and Major M.H. Allan," 4, for the comment about the muddle created by Bruce in his short tenure as DMS.

36 LAC, MG 30 E3, William Baptie Papers, vol. 1, Herbert A. Bruce, "Report on the Canadian Army Medical Service," 64 and, for the paragraph about nurses, 66.

37 Bruce's proposed administrative reorganization of the CAMC adjoins ibid., 86.

38 LAC, NSA, vol. 6, file 2, MCM, "In 1914 the selection ..." [1942], 2–3. That this episode stuck in her memory after almost thirty years suggests its forcefulness. To her account, she added that Jones refused to recommend the transfer as not being in the best interests of the service.

39 Ibid. and SFXA, MFC, RG 3, file 80, MCM, "As it recurs" [1942?].

40 Pictou County Land Information Centre/Registry of Deeds, Last Will and Testament of Margaret C. Macdonald, 1 August 1948.

41 LAC, Macdonald Papers, file "Transcripts ch. 4," "Nursing Staff AMD 4"; SFXA, MFC, RG 3, file 25, J. Donovan to MCM, 20 March 1919. Macdonald identified Donovan on that letter as "My Head Stenographer." See also LAC, RG 9 III B2, vol. 3704, file 30-11-1 (vol. 18), MCM to Harriet Graham at No. 2 CCCS at Rémy Siding, 17 May 1917. The general correspondence from Macdonald's office is contained in ibid., vols. 3701–5, file 30-11-1 (vols. 1–23).

42 MCM, "Echoes of the Great War," 1.

43 SFXA, MFC, RG 3, MCM's wartime notebook. She sent home press clippings concerning herself, and her sister Vie pasted them haphazardly, with other MCM memorabilia, in the Macdonald Family Scrapbook (MFS). If there were other notebooks during the war, they have long since vanished.

44 See, for example, LAC, RG 9 III B2, vol. 3701, file 30-11-1 (vol. 2), MCM to DMS, 6 August 1915. She pointed out that the fifteen hospitals, two convalescent homes, and one rest home then in operation, as well as her own office, required total staffing of 630, whereas only 555 were in place.

45 "More Canadian Nurses for the War," *Nursing Mirror*, 23 January 1915, 281.

46 Wilson-Simmie, *Lights Out!* 11. Wilson had another probably useful contact in Ottawa, Dr H.G. Collins of the Geological Survey of Canada (ibid., 15). She mistakenly identifies him as head of the GSC, a position he did not occupy until 1920. Thanks to Denis St-Onge for tracking this information for me. Wilson's memoir leaves the impression that her joining the ranks of the elect occurred at the very beginning of the war; in fact her attestation paper is signed in London in May 1915.

47 Wilson-Simmie, *Lights Out!* 13.

48 Ibid., 20.

49 Maude Wilkinson was delighted with the matron-in-chief's attention to style ("Four Score and Ten," November 1977, 16).

50 Mann, ed., *The War Diary of Clare Gass*, xx, 13, 234–6. See also Fetherstonhaugh, *No. 3 Canadian General Hospital*, for a detailed history of the McGill hospital unit.

51 Wilkinson, "Four Score and Ten," October 1977, 28–9. Not surprisingly, when Bruce reported on the CAMC the following year, he found favouritism. He clearly knew whereof he spoke.

52 LAC, RG 9 III B2, vols. 3702 and 3703 contain numerous letters from nurses in these different units requesting transfer to the CAMC; in particular, see vol. 3702, file 30-11-1 (vol. 6), Elizabeth Reid to Sir George Perley, 27 April 1916. Reid was forthright with Perley: "I am very anxious to get into the Canadian Army Medical Corps, but one needs a little influence." Perley phoned Macdonald about the case and then sent Reid's letter together with an earlier one from the MP, Major Sam Sharpe. Macdonald replied that once Reid had completed her contract she would forward the application with a recommendation for approval (ibid., Perley to MCM, 28 April 1916; MCM to Perley, 29 April 1916). The two women were true to their word, and Reid's attestation paper has her joining the CAMC on 1 July 1916. See also vol. 3703, file 30-11-1 (vol. 12), MCM to Sir William Osler, 4 November 1916, and (vol. 10), MCM to Julia Hill, 14 September 1916.

53 LAC, RG 9 III B2, vol. 3702, file 30-11-1 (vol. 8), MCM to Matron Parsons of the Harvard hospital unit, 14 July 1916.

54 Macdonald wrote a sharp letter to the DGMS, Ottawa, urging him to clarify matters with his regional deputies (LAC, RG 9 III B2, vol. 3703, file 30-11-1 [vol. 13], MCM to Col. Potter, 28 November 1916).

55 Ibid., file 30-11-1 (vol. 12), MCM to Sir William Osler, 4 November 1916. Bruce had expressed his view that nurses who had already served overseas were "more or less tired out and stale" before he had completed his report and there is no mention of it in the report (LAC, RG 9 III A1, vol. 25, file 7-6-15, H. Bruce to Major General Carson, 15 September 1916). Bruce

appears to have put his views into practice once he became DMS in mid-October. See also LAC, Macdonald Papers, file "Transcripts ch. 4," log outline of highlights of Macdonald's London office, 1916, and RG 9 III B2, vol. 3703, file 30-11-1 (vol. 11), MCM to DGMS, Ottawa, 14 October 1916.

56 Ibid., file 30-11-1 (vol. 12), Tephi G. Best to MCM, 20 November 1916. Best joined the CAMC on 30 October 1917.

57 Macdonald appears sporadically in Linda Quiney's thesis on the Canadian VADS, "Assistant Angels." The thesis does not mention Bruce's interest in having VADS, which he expressed in *Politics and the CAMC*, 55, but not in his report of 1916. Also favourable to VADS was a longer-serving male colleague in Macdonald's entourage in London, Dr John George Adami. See "VADS and the Canadian Matron-in-Chief," *Nursing Mirror*, 25 August 1917, 356. The matron requiring a reminder about VADS was Katherine MacLatchy at No. 3 CGH in Boulogne (LAC, RG 9 III B2, vol. 3704, file 30-11-1 (vol. 19), MCM to K.O. MacLatchy, 19 May 1917). On masseuses, see Quiney, "Assistant Angels," 282–6, and LAC, MG 27 II D9, Albert Edward Kemp Papers, vol. 187, file 9, G.L. Foster, "Progress Reports of the Medical Services," 1 January 1917 – 31 March 1919, 11.

58 LAC, RG 9 III B2, vol. 3703, file 30-11-1 (vol. 11), MCM to Mrs Roberts Allan, 22 November 1916, in response to a query of 21 November 1916; vol. 3704, file 30-11-1 (vol. 17), MCM to Mrs Wickham, 10 April 1917, in response to a letter of 9 April 1917; (vol. 20), MCM to Alice Carr-Ellison, 25 June 1917, in response to a letter of 22 June 1917; vol. 3705, file 30-11-1 (vol. 23), MCM to V. Law, 8 August 1918, in response to a letter of 3 August 1918.

59 For example, ibid., vol. 3702, file 30-11-1 (vol. 3), MCM to Nursing Sisters B. Lamont and E.J. Stuart, 12 October 1915.

60 Ibid., MCM to ADMS, Canadians, Shorncliffe, 8 October 1915.

61 For example, the Westcliffe Canadian Eye and Ear Hospital at Folkestone and the Granville Orthopaedic Hospital at Ramsgate.

62 This administrative route is pieced together from the correspondence concerning postings of nurses in LAC, RG 9 III B2, vols. 3701–5, file 30-11-1 (vols. 1–23).

63 Ibid., vol. 3704, file 30-11-1 (vol. 22), MCM to K.O. MacLatchy at No. 3 CGH (McGill), Boulogne, 31 July 1917.

64 LAC, RG 9 III B2, vol. 3482, file 10-11-27, E.M. McCarthy to MCM, 30 July 1915.

65 Ibid., vol. 3704, file 30-11-1 (vol. 18), MCM to Matron A.C. Strong, No. 2 CSH at Outreau, 17 May 1917.

66 Ibid., vol. 3482, file 10-11-27, McCarthy to MCM, 9 June 1916.

67 Ibid., McCarthy to MCM, 24 August 1917; MCM to McCarthy, 28 August 1917. The approval route, traceable in the same file, went from McCarthy to the by then DGMS, British Armies in France, 29 August 1917, and from him to the DMS Canadian Contingents in London, 31 August 1917, with a carefully worded "Forwarded for favour of your remarks," presumably to avoid any implication that the British were requesting approval from the Canadians. The Canadian DMS nonetheless sent back his approval, 3 September 1917. With the omission of the War Office, this route is slightly shorter than earlier ones and may suggest some streamlining of communication.

68 LAC, Macdonald Papers, file "Transcripts ch. 6," E.M. McCarthy, "Report on Work in France of the Nursing Sisters of the Canadian Army Medical Corps" [1919], 4. This same item appears, along with reports by McCarthy on the other colonial nursing services, in TNA, WO 222/2134.

69 LAC, RG 9 III B2, vol. 3703, file 30-11-1 (vol. 11), Matron Ethel Ridley at Granville Hospital, Ramsgate, to Acting Matron-in-Chief, M.O. Boulter, 19 October 1916.

70 The example comes from ibid., vol. 3705, file 30-11-1 (vol. 23), 3 September 1917.

71 SFXA, MFC, RG 3, MCM Letterbook, Matron Harriet Graham at No. 2 CCCS, Boulogne, to MCM, 3 January 1916.

72 LAC, RG 9 III B2, vol. 3704, file 30-11-1 (vol. 22), MCM to the OC, No. 10 CSH, Eastbourne, 9 August 1917.

73 Ibid., file 30-11-1 (vol. 18), MCM to Matron A.C. Strong, No. 2 CSH, Outreau, 17 May 1917.

74 LAC, Kemp Papers, vol. 129, file B4, G.L. Foster to George Perley, 6 March 1917. Although signed by Foster, the letter reads like Macdonald and, given the initials at the bottom, MCM/MGC [Mary Gladys Coxall], was likely prepared by Macdonald for Foster's signature.

75 LAC, RG 9 III B2, vol. 3482, file 10-11-27, MCM to McCarthy, 19 June 1915; vol. 3678, file 29-11-1 (vol. 3), MCM to E. Ridley, 3 May 1918.

76 LAC, RG 9 III B2, vol. 3702, file 30-11-1 (vol. 8), MCM to Acting Matron O.F. Garland at Moore Barracks Hospital, Shorncliffe, 24 July 1916.

77 SFXA, MFC, RG 3, file 97, MCM, "1917" [1922?], 5.

78 LAC, RG 9 III B1, series 12, vol. 1686, file N-2-12, MCM to W.H. Delaney, 5 June 1916.

79 No. 1 CGH began on Salisbury Plain in England and then moved to Etaples in France. No. 3 CGH (McGill) came to England in May 1915, but only began operation in Camiers in France in July and moved to Boulogne in January 1916. See Mann, ed., *The War Diary of Clare Gass*, 18, 42–3, 84–5, 101–2, for the movement of the nurses of No. 3.

80 Nicholson follows the movements of the five Canadian hospital units in the Mediterranean in *Canada's Nursing Sisters*, ch. 5. Among Colonel Bruce's many complaints about the CAMC was the very sending of these hospitals to the Mediterranean when no Canadian soldiers saw action there. Even in France and England, Bruce wanted Canadians treated only in Canadian hospitals, something that was logistically impossible, given the nature of the war. The experience of Canadian nurses on Lemnos is described in each of the three published memoirs of nursing sisters: Bruce, *Humour in Tragedy*; Clint, *Our Bit*; Wilson-Simmie, *Lights Out!*

81 LAC, RG 9 III B2, vol. 3703, file 30-11-1 (vol. 11), Major [?] for Director of Personal (*sic*) Services, CEF, to DMS, Canadian Contingents, 18 October 1916.

82 Ibid., file 30-11-1, (vol. 13), Lt. Col. F.W. Ernest Wilson, A/DDMS Canadians, to A/DMS, 30 December 1916.

83 LAC, Baptie Papers, vol. 1, H.A. Bruce, "Report on the Canadian Army Medical Service," 66, and Macdonald's response in "Interim Report of Surgeon-General G.C. Jones," 144–5.

84 For example, Lt. Col. J.M. Elder, in charge of No. 3 CGH (McGill), as reported in LAC, RG 9 III B2, vol. 3490, file 11-1-3, MCM Inspection Report, France, 8 May 1917.

85 LAC, RG 9 III B2, vol. 3704, file 30-11-1 (vol. 21), Col. J.D. Courtenay, OC, Westcliffe Eye and Ear Hospital at Folkestone, to ADMS Shorncliffe, 28 June 1917. The letter wound its way via DMS London to Macdonald.

86 Ibid., file 30-11-1 (vol. 22), Lt. Col. Edwin Seaborne, OC, No. 10 CSH, Eastbourne, to MCM, 10 August 1917, in reply to a letter from MCM of 9 August in which she stated that two nurses who had been in England more than a year wanted to go to France.

87 Ibid., vol. 3482, file 10-11-27, MCM to McCarthy, 10 February 1917.

88 Ibid., vol. 3678, file 29-11-1 (vol. 2), MCM to OC, Westcliffe Eye and Ear Hospital, Folkestone, 31 December 1917, in response to a letter of Lt. J. White, A/Adjutant, for OC Westcliffe, 23 December 1917.

89 Ibid., vol. 3704, file 30-11-1 (vol. 19), MCM to OC [Col. G.S. Rennie], No. 2 CGH at Le Tréport, 7 June 1917, in response to a letter from him to DMS, 31 May 1917.

90 Ibid., MCM to Secretary (Adjutant General), 31 May 1917.

91 Ibid., vol. 3701, file 30-11-1, (vol. 1), MCM to Ethel Ridley at No. 2 CSH at Le Touquet, 23 June 1915.

92 LAC, RG 9 III A1, vol. 25, file 7-6-15, Lt. Col. Shillington, ADMS, quoting Matron Charleson with No. 1 CSH in Salonika, to Secretary, Headquarters, CEF, 26 October 1916.

93 LAC, RG 9 III B2, vol. 3678, file 29-11-1 (vol. 4), Nursing Sisters E.M. Kennedy to Matron Smith, 23 October 1918; E. Miller and D. Black to Matron Smith, 24 October 1918. The nurses' notes were passed to Mac-donald, who informed the adjutant general's office that those three as well as two others did not wish "to be transferred to the Home Establishment." However, a day later, following a telephone conversation [a command? or just a discussion of the impending end to the war?], she changed her mind and ordered their return to Canada (ibid., MCM to Secretary (Adjutant General), 5 and 6 November 1918).

94 Ibid., vol. 3677, file 29-11-1 (vol. 1), Murray MacLaren to MCM, 21 July 1915. Clare Gass, whose unit (No. 3 CGH [McGill]) had come to Europe on the same ship as No. 4 CSH in May 1915, was temporarily at No. 1 CGH at the same time. In her diary (19 July 1915) she recorded the arrival of these nurses: "Miss Flint's hens & hairpins have come. Quite a number of the French Canadians among them. They are the 'hairpins' I think" (Mann, ed., *The War Diary of Clare Gass*, 42). Her remark, coupled with that of MacLaren, suggests that language kept English and French Canadian nurses isolated from each other.

95 LAC, RG 9 III B2, vol. 3677, file 29-11-1 (vol. 1), Col. G.S. Rennie, ADMS Shorncliffe, to DMS, 23 February 1916. At the same time he complained about the shortage of nurses at Moore Barracks Hospital, Shorncliffe.

96 Ibid., vol. 3482, file 10-11-27, MCM to McCarthy, 13 June 1916; McCarthy to MCM, 24 June 1916; MCM to McCarthy, 27 June 1916.

97 Ibid., vol. 3703, file 30-11-1 (vol. 15), MCM to Matron C.A. DeCormier at St Cloud, 23 February 1917, in response to a letter from her, 16 February 1917.

98 Ibid., vol. 3704, file 30-11-1 (vol. 16), MCM to Matron DeCormier, 27 February 1917.

99 Ibid., vol. 3482, file 10-11-27, MCM to Maud McCarthy, 28 August 1917.

100 Ibid., vol. 3705, file 30-11-1 (vol. 23), MCM to OC, No. 6 CGH, 7 September 1917. Names are never a sure guide to mother tongue in Canada. Scottish and Irish names can camouflage generations of French Canadian families just as French Canadian names can shroud purely English-speaking individuals. Nevertheless, from the various lists of nurses overseas that can be found in the records of the Ministry of Militia and Defence, about one hundred French Canadian names can be culled. One would need to comb each of their military personnel files in LAC, RG 150 to try to determine whether French was their first language. A Nominal Roll of nursing sisters who "proceeded overseas" 1914–18 is in LAC, RG 24, vol. 1836, file G.A.Q. 9-27. Of the fifty-one women who were matrons or acting matrons

at one time or another during the war (Nicholson, *Canada's Nursing Sisters*, 232-3), three were definitely French Canadians. Five pages of Michel Litalien's book on the two French Canadian hospitals, *Dans la tourmente*, 83–90, deal with the nurses. He has looked at the attestation papers of all the original nurses of the two units and determined that 88% of the nurses at No. 4 CSH and 42% of those at No. 6 CGH were from Quebec (ibid., 86). Their names appear in ibid., 141-2, 145-6, 148, 150-1. Pierre Vennat touches briefly on the hospitals in his *Les "Poilus" québécois,* which is based solely on newspaper coverage in *La Presse.*

101 LAC, RG 9 III B2, vol. 3703, file 30-11-1 (vol. 15), MCM to Mrs Henn Collins, 23 February 1917.

102 Ibid., vol. 3702, file 30-11-1 (vol. 6), MCM to Col. J.A. Roberts, OC at No. 4 CGH in Salonika, 20 April 1916. Macdonald and Roberts had known each other since their return from South Africa in July 1902 aboard the *Winifredian.*

103 Ibid., vol. 3701, file 30-11-1 (vol. 9), MCM to Col. C.A. Hodgetts, Canadian Red Cross Commissioner in London, 11 August 1916. Whether anything came of this idea is unknown.

104 Ibid., vol. 3678, file 29-11-1 (vol. 4), MCM to ADMS, 27 November 1918. The nurse in question had written directly to the by then DGMS, General Foster, requesting a transfer to France.

105 Ibid., vol. 3703, file 30-11-1 (vol. 14), MCM to Adjutant General, 12 January 1917, in response to his query about Matron Violet Nesbitt, 11 January 1917. All Macdonald would say was that Nesbitt had been in France for twenty-one months and her replacement, Matron Edith Campbell, had been in England for two years.

106 Ibid., vol. 3482, file 10-11-42, ADMS to Chief Paymaster, 10 February 1916; Major J.R. Regan, Asst. Chief Paymaster to DMS, 16 February 1916; MCM to Chief Paymaster, 19 February 1916; Regan to DMS, 16 March 1916. The specific items that accumulated in Macdonald's office appear in LAC, RG 9 III B2, vols. 3701-3 (1914–16). Fewer such references occur for the years 1917–18.

107 Ibid., vol. 3453, file 7-2-2 (vol. 1), MCM to Matron J.B. Jaggard, 4 August 1915.

108 For example, ibid., MCM to Acting Matron, No. 1 CGH, 2 February 1915; MCM to Matron M.H. Casault, No. 4 CSH, 1 January 1916; MCM to OC, Granville Canadian Special Hospital, 10 February 1916; MCM to Officer in Charge of Claims and Allowances, 9 February 1916.

109 Ibid., vol. 3701, file 30-11-1 (vols. 1 and 2), contain correspondence and accounts related to the two hotels.

110 Ibid., vol. 3453, file 7-2-0 (vol. 1), MCM to Asst. Chief Paymaster, 24 June 1915. This file, with three fat "volumes," documents the complexities of paying the nurses. By early 1917, one of Macdonald's assistants, Mildred Forbes, was signing the routine notifications to nurses of their pay deposits.

111 Ibid., vol. 3703, file 30-11-1 (vol. 10), M.O. Boulter to Spirella Company of Great Britain, 8 September 1916, in response to a letter to MCM, 6 September 1916.

112 Ibid., vol. 3704, file 30-11-1 (vol. 20), Alice Carr-Ellison to MCM, 22 June 1917. With the exception of the plea from the two Canadians in India (see following note), the specific requests are gleaned from vols. 3701–4 (1914 to August 1917).

113 Ibid., vol. 3453, file 7-2-0 (vol. 3), Isabelle J. Neilly to MCM, 27 April 1919, reporting that she had received Macdonald's good news at the end of February in Bombay, although neither she nor her colleague Adair had yet received the pay adjustment. The case began with a letter from Neilly to MCM, 31 May 1918 (ibid).

114 Ibid., vol. 3704, file 30-11-1 (vol. 22), MCM to Mary Plummer, 2 August 1917, in response to a letter of 31 July 1917 from Plummer, who had made the request for a list of Alberta nurses on behalf of an unnamed male candidate. Plummer was with the Canadian Field Comforts Commission and had known Macdonald since at least 1914, when they both came to Britain on the *Franconia*. The closeness of their friendship is gauged by Plummer's addressing Macdonald by her second name, Clotilde. The *Nursing Mirror* noted MacAdams's candidacy ("Nurse-Candidate for Parliamentary Honours," 4 August 1917, 311). Catherine Cleverdon in *The Woman Suffrage Movement*, 74, has MacAdams mistakenly elected in June at the time of the provincial election and by a "purely male constituency." In fact, women in Alberta had had the provincial vote since April 1916, and therefore Alberta nurses overseas were part of the soldiers' vote that took place between 6 and 16 August 1917 under the auspices of the Alberta Military Representation Act. The results of that election were announced 18 September; Captain Robert Pearson and Nursing Sister Roberta MacAdams were elected with 4,286 and 4,000 votes, respectively, the number of votes indicating that MacAdams had the support of soldiers as well as nurses. My thanks for the electoral details to Debbie Culbertson of Edmonton, who is completing a book on MacAdams. Although Macdonald referred to her as "Nursing Sister," MacAdams was not in fact a trained nurse; she was a dietician, and was taken on with the CAMC as a "home sister."

115 For example, Matron Rayside with No. 2 CGH, 1 June 1915 – 9 October 1916, and continued by subsequent matrons until 30 April 1917 (LAC,

microfilm T10924); Matron Cora DeCormier with No. 8 CGH, June 1916 –
November 1918 (LAC, T10926); Matron MacLatchy with No. 3 CGH,
August, October–December 1918, January–April 1919 (LAC, T10924–5).
Some of these reports appear among the war diaries now available on the
LAC website. Care should be taken when accessing this material on the
web: names and dates are not always accurate.

116 *Instructions for Members of Canadian Army Medical Nursing Service,*
paragraph 19. These instructions, formalized 15 June 1917, were clearly in
operation long before. Macdonald referred to paragraph 19 in 1916
(LAC, RG 9 III B2, vol. 3677, file 29-11-1 [vol. 1], MCM to Matron Violet
Nesbitt at No. 1 CGH at Etaples, 28 January 1916). The Canadian War
Museum has an original printed version of the *Instructions*, as do the Macdonald Papers at LAC, file "Transcripts ch. 4." They are reproduced as
appendix 2 of Mann, ed., *The War Diary of Clare Gass*, 215–24.

117 LAC, RG 9 III B2, vol. 3677, file 29-11-1 (vol. 1), MCM to Matron Nesbitt
at No. 1 CGH, Etaples, 28 January 1916. Neither of the documents to
which Macdonald referred is in the file.

118 Ibid., vol. 3678, file 29-11-1 (vol. 2), M.O. Boulter to Matron Strong at
No. 2 CSH, Outreau, 19 September 1916; vol. 3704, file 30-11-1 (vol. 20),
M.O. Boulter to Matron Vivien Tremaine at Canadian Red Cross Hospital,
Buxton, 15 June 1917.

119 One example of such an amalgamated report is ibid., vol. 3678, file 29-11-
1 (vol. 4), undated but likely mid-October 1918, since the entire file is
organized chronologically. In it, three matrons comment on three nurses in
a fashion so brief as to suggest extracts from some longer missive.

120 LAC, Kemp Papers, vol. 129, file B4, General G.L. Foster to Secretary,
OMFC, 21 June 1918. See chapter 4 for details of this case, involving Nursing Sister Jean I. Bell.

121 LAC, RG 9 III B2, vol. 3678, file 29-11-1 (vol. 2), MCM to Matron Nesbitt
at No. 1 CGH, Etaples, 20 September 1916.

122 Ibid., vol. 3703, file 30-11-1 (vol. 9), MCM to Acting Matron Grace John-
stone, Kingscliffe Canadian Rest Home, Margate, 19 August 1916.

123 Ibid., vol. 3704, file 30-11-1 (vol. 22), MCM to Matron MacLatchy at No.
3 CGH (McGill), Boulogne, 31 July 1917.

124 Ibid., vol. 3705, file 30-11-1 (vol. 23), MCM to Matron Laura May Hubley
of No. 7 CSH at Arques, 5 September 1917. Macdonald's earlier instructions to Hubley had specified that CCS positions were to go to "good surgical Nurses and ones who have been longest in the Unit and are most
deserving in every way" (ibid., file 30-11-1 [vol. 22], MCM to Hubley, 24
August 1917).

125 Ibid., vol. 3703, file 30-11-1 (vol. 9), MCM to Matron Charlotte Macalister at Canadian Red Cross Special Hospital, Buxton, 7 August 1916.

126 Ibid., vol. 3704, file 30-11-1 (vol. 22), MCM to Matron Jean Urquhart of No. 2 CSH at Outreau, 4 August 1917.

127 The tours in France usually included all Canadian units; the tours in England often involved only one hospital. Hence the big difference in numbers. The numbers were compiled from references to the tours in LAC, RG 9 III B2, vol. 3490, file 11-1-3; vols. 3703–4; RG 24, vol. 2546, file HQ 2069-E, "Progress Reports of the Medical Services," 1917–1919; Macdonald Papers, file "Transcripts ch. 4," "Resumé of Work of A.M.D. 4"; TNA, WO 222/2134, Maud McCarthy, "Report on Work in France of the Nursing Sisters of the CAMC," 11. McCarthy did not capture all of Macdonald's visits to France, presumably because Macdonald did not always call on her.

128 SFXA, MFC, RG 3, MCM Letterbook, Gladys Coxall at No. 4 CGH in Salonika to MCM, 20 January 1916. The letter leaves the impression that Macdonald was "still contemplating [a] trip to the East." According to a postwar newspaper account, "Owing to the importance of her position she was not permitted to go to Gallipoli on account of the submarine warfare" (*Toronto Daily Star*, 9 February 1920, clipping in MFS). There were in fact no hospitals at Gallipoli itself, the sick and wounded being taken by ship to Lemnos. The Gallipoli campaign was abandoned in mid-December 1915.

129 LAC, RG 9 III B2, vol. 3702, file 30-11-1 (vol. 6), M.O. Boulter to Lady Drummond, 5 May 1916.

130 See in particular LAC, RG 24, vol. 2546, file HQ 2069-E, "Progress Reports of the Medical Services," April–December 1917. While in France in November 1917, Macdonald also visited some American hospital units. See RG 9 III B2, vol.3705, file 30-11-1 (vol. 23), MCM to Emily O. Boswell of Boston Nurses' Club, 10 November 1917.

131 Ibid., vol. 3490, file 11-1-3, MCM Inspection Report, France, 8 May 1917.

132 Ibid., MCM Inspection Report of No. 8 CGH, 9 August 1916; DMS Guy Carleton Jones to Senior Medical Officer [Col. Arthur Mignault], St Cloud, 10 August 1916.

133 Ibid., MCM Report on Royal Military Hospital, Devonport, 2 February 1917.

134 Ibid., DMS Guy Carleton Jones to Secretary, Quarter Master General Branch, OMFC, 7 February 1917; A.D. McRae, assistant QMG to DMS, 10 February 1917.

135 Ibid., vol. 3454, file 7-2-2 (vol. 3), Lt. Col. G.H.[?], Director of Personal (*sic)* Services, writing for the Adjutant General, Canadians, and citing DMS G.L. Foster's views, to the Secretary, War Office, 18 July 1917. Col. H.S.

Birkett of No. 3 CGH (McGill) responded obliquely to the inquiry about the employment of more women. He already had women anaesthetists and women as operating-room nurses. Women clerks, he was convinced, could not take the strain of long hours, often at night, to which his well-trained (male) clerks were now used (LAC, RG 9 III C10, vol. 4571, folder 5, file 1, H.S. Birkett to Assistant Adjutant General, Canadian Section, 3rd Echelon, GHQ, 20 June 1917).

136 LAC, RG 9 III B2, vol. 3490, file 11-1-3, MCM to DMS, 21 July 1917.

137 Ibid., G.L. Foster to OCS, Nos. 6 and 8 CGH, 24 July 1917.

138 Ibid., C.A. DeCormier to OC, No. 8 CGH, 29 July 1917.

139 Aldershot, Army Medical Services Museum (hereafter AMSM), QARANC Archive 43/1985, Maud McCarthy Papers, Annual Report of the Work of the Nursing Service in France, 1915, section "Visitors."

140 LAC, RG 9 III B2, vol. 3678, file 29-11-1 (vol. 2), MCM to Capt. H.W. Blaylock, Assistant Red Cross Commissioner, Boulogne, 13 July 1916.

141 SFXA, MFC, RG 3, file 98, MCM, "Echoes of the Great War," 6; LAC, MG 30 E160, Irene Peterkin Papers, Ruby Peterkin to Irene, 20 June 1915; MG 30 E510, Laura Gamble Papers, Diary, [10–11].

142 The Nursing Mirror captured some of the views. See, for example, "English Nurses and their Canadian Sisters," 4 August 1917, 301. A number of letters from nurses in LAC, RG 9 III B2, vols. 3701–5 refer to awkward situations with the British nurses.

143 LAC, Macdonald Papers, file "Transcripts ch. 4," [MCM], "Administration."

144 LAC, RG 9 III B2, vol. 3490, file 11-1-3, MCM to McCarthy, 22 April 1915.

145 Ibid., vol. 3482, file 10-11-27, McCarthy to MCM, 19 April 1916; MCM to McCarthy, 24 April 1916.

146 Ibid., MCM to McCarthy, 17 October 1916.

147 Ibid., MCM to McCarthy, 10 January 1917; E.H. Hordley, Acting Principal Matron, QAIMNS, BEF, to MCM, 29 March 1917; McCarthy to MCM, 21 April 1917.

148 Ibid., MCM to McCarthy, 26 October 1917.

149 AMSM, McCarthy Papers, Annual Report, 1917.

150 See chapter 4 for a longer discussion of this issue.

151 LAC, RG 9 III B2, vol. 3482, file 10-11-27, MCM to Mildred Forbes, Acting Matron of No. 2 CCCS at Rémy Siding, 10 January 1918. Forbes knew the normal practice from having worked in Macdonald's office in London from October 1916 to June 1917. She expressed her uneasiness in a letter to MCM, 5 January 1918.

152 AMSM, McCarthy Papers, Annual Report, 1917.

153 LAC, RG 9 III B2, vol. 3482, file 10-11-27, MCM to McCarthy, 7 December

1917. The names of Matrons-in-Chief M. Thurston of New Zealand and G.M. Wilson of Australia appear at the bottom of the letter.

154 Ibid., vol. 3490, file 11-1-3, MCM Inspection Report, France, 8 May 1917; vol. 3700, file 30-9-78, Surgeon-General [G.L. Foster] to Secretary, Adjutant General, OMFC, 30 September 1917; Memorandum of MCM, 13 November 1917.

155 AMSM, McCarthy Papers, Annual Report, 1917; LAC, RG 9 III B2, vol. 3482, file 10-11-27, MCM to McCarthy, 12 October 1917; vol. 3700, file 30-9-78, B.B. Cubitt for the Army Council at the War Office to Adjutant General, OMFC, 19 November 1917; McCarthy to MCM, 5 December 1917. McCarthy's report stated that 764 Canadian nurses were in France in October 1917, compared to 2,246 British professional nurses and 1,696 VADs. A different source had as many as 1,200 Canadian nurses in France in July 1917. See vol. 3678, file 29-11-1 (vol. 2), Col. H.A. Chisholm to Capt. Charleton of the adjutant general branch of the OMFC, 23 July 1917. Whatever the accuracy of the figures, part of the justification for a principal matron in France was the expectation that the number of Canadian nurses in France would increase.

156 LAC, RG 9 III B2, vol. 3678, file 29-11-1 (vol. 2), Ridley to MCM, 3 March 1918; MCM to McCarthy, 6 March 1918; McCarthy to MCM, 11 March 1918; MCM to McCarthy, 21 March 1918; the British DGMS in France and the Canadian adjutant general got involved that same day as did Macdonald's superior officer, DMS Foster; MCM to Ridley, 26 March 1918.

157 LAC, RG 9 III B2, vol. 3590, file 11-1-3, MCM to DMS, Canadians, 23 July 1918, two days after her return from France.

158 Ibid., vol. 3705, file 30-11-1 (vol. 23), e.g., Ridley Inspection Report, May 1918.

159 Ibid., vol. 3678, file 29-11-1 (vol. 3), MCM to E.B. Ridley, 3 May 1918.

160 Ibid., Ridley to MCM, 9 May 1918.

161 Ibid., Ridley to MCM, 21 June 1918; MCM to Ridley, 25 June 1918.

162 Ibid., vol. 3678, file 29-11-1 (vol. 2), correspondence between OMFC and DMS, 21, 23 April, 3 May 1917; RG 24, vol. 2546, file HQ 2069-E, Progress Report of the Medical Service, May 1917. The confidential files of Cains and Rayside would clear up the mystery around this appointment, for they are referred to in pencil on the letter of 23 April in the DMS-OMFC correspondence, but these files no longer exist. The appointment of Rayside as matron-in-chief in Canada has Nicholson mistakenly ending Macdonald's title and tenure in 1917 (*Canada's Nursing Sisters*, 231 and illustration 7, after page 80). Edith Rayside (1872–1950) was born in Lancaster, Ontario, and was one of the early women graduates of Queen's University (1896).

She trained at St Luke's Hospital, Ottawa, and nursed both there and in Mexico, where she had an administrative job. She was matron at No. 2 CGH at Le Tréport from mid-March 1915 to early October 1916 and then at Moore Barracks Hospital, Shorncliffe, until June 1917.

163 SFXA, MFC, RG 3, file 5, B[elfrage] G[ilbertson] to MCM (addressed as "My dearest Mac"), 1 July 1917. The wording of the letter suggests that Macdonald may have had to fight to get Rayside. She had certainly dragged her feet for at least three weeks in April and early May (partly because she was in France at the time) when Ottawa wanted the name for the matron's position. See the OMFC-DMS correspondence referred to in note 162 above.

164 SFXA, MFC, RG 3, file 57, "Annual Report Canadian Army Nursing Service," [Ottawa] 31 August 1918.

165 SFXA, MFC, RG 3, file 98, MCM, "Echoes of the Great War," 1.

166 The *Toronto Daily Star*, 9 February 1920 (MFS, press clipping), entitled an article on Macdonald: "Held Same Position All Through the War"; it added that she was the only Canadian staff officer to do so. The *Star* meant it as a compliment, but in fact what the paper was unwittingly revealing was the lack of mobility for women in the army. The very same remark was made about Maud McCarthy, with the same intention and the same revelation: "The only head of a department in the B.E.F. who remained in her original post throughout the war" (*Australian Dictionary of Biography*, 10: 218.

167 SFXA, MFC, RG 3, file 35, [Lady] Sybil Grey to MCM, [mid-November 1919].

168 MFS and SFXA, MFC, RG 3, file 82, "Some Aspects of War Nursing," MCM speech to a convention of the Graduate Nurses Association of Ontario, Ottawa, 8 April 1920. The *Montreal Star* reported the speech, with some misquotations: "Tells Services of War Nurses," 10 April 1920, 31.

CHAPTER FOUR

The title of this chapter was chosen long before I knew of the title of Cynthia Toman's thesis

1 Library and Archives Canada (LAC), RG 9 III B2, vol. 3702, file 30-11-1 (vol. 6), Margaret C. Macdonald (MCM) to Col. J.A. Roberts, OC at No. 4 CGH in Salonika, 20 April 1916; (vol. 5), MCM to Matron Casault at No. 4 CSH at St Cloud, 24 February 1916.

2 St Francis Xavier University Archives (SFXA), Macdonald Family Collection (MFC), RG 3, file 98, MCM, "Echoes of the Great War," 12.

3 SFXA, MFC, RG 3, file 82, "Comedies in War Tragedy," MCM incomplete speech [to the Catholic Women's League of Ottawa and Hull, 1921].

4 LAC, RG 9 III B2, vol. 3482, file 10-11-23, MCM to Sidney Browne, Matron-in-Chief, TFNS, inviting her to "come over here and have a cup of tea with us one afternoon," 23 February 1916.

5 LAC, RG 150, box 6752-26, MCM military personnel file, pay sheets 1916–17; RG 9 III B2, vol. 3453, file 7-2-1, J. Regan, Assistant Chief Paymaster, to MCM, 13 July 1915.

6 SFXA, MFC, RG 2, file 16, MCM to Mary Macdonald, 1 January 1916, and an undated and incomplete letter, MCM to Mary Macdonald [late March – early April 1917]. The "real tenant" of the apartment she had for a while was Lord Osborne Bearcleves, son of the Duchess of St Albans. Bearcleves was on the staff of Field Marshal Sir Douglas Haig and thus away on war service.

7 "Distinction has been won by these five women in widely different fields," *Women's Home Companion*, April 1918, 11 (clipping in Macdonald Family Scrapbook [MFS]).

8 SFXA, MFC, RG 2, file 16, undated and incomplete letter from MCM to Mary Macdonald [mid-April 1917], after she had spent a weekend at the Astor estate at Cliveden.

9 For an analysis of Canadian women travellers from this perspective, see Mann, "Travel Lessons."

10 Philistia, "At the Sign of the Maple," press clipping from an unidentified magazine, 2 December [1915], in MFS. Macdonald may well have met Kitchener in South Africa.

11 The hospital was a gift to Russia from Britain. Nursing Sister Dorothy Cotton, who had come to Europe with No. 3 CGH (McGill), went to Russia in November 1915 and three other CAMC nurses followed her. A nice collection of Cotton's letters from Russia is in vol. 8 of R.C. Fetherstonhaugh Papers, McGill University Library, Rare Books and Special Collections.

12 SFXA, MFC, RG 3, file 18, 25 January, 8 April, 27 June, and 6 September 1916.

13 SFXA, MFC, RG 2, file 16, undated page of a letter from MCM to Mary Macdonald [autumn 1916 or 1917].

14 LAC, RG 9 III B2, vol. 3482, file 10-11-23, has correspondence about these and smaller rest homes made available to Canadian nurses.

15 SFXA, MFC, RG 2, file 16, MCM to Mary Macdonald, [mid-April 1917].

16 *Nursing Mirror*, 22 January 1916, 319; SFXA, MFC, RG 3, file 98, MCM, "Echoes of the Great War," 14.

17 Musolf, *From Plymouth to Parliament*, 1–2, 8.

18 SFXA, MFC, RG 3, file 6, B[elfrage] G[ilbertson] to MCM, 10 December 1921: "I expect Mistress Astor misses your cheerful countenance!"

19 See University of Reading Library, MS 2421, Cliveden Visitors Books, 1914–19, for names of guests present at the same time as Macdonald. Macdonald was such a frequent visitor to Cliveden that she did not always sign the guest book. Her name appears 24 June 1915, 1 December 1917, and 12 October 1919, but not at Easter 1917, a visit she described to her mother, complete with the names of the other guests, most of whom *are* in the guest book for Easter – which in turn allowed me to date the letter in SFXA, MFC, RG 2, file 16, MCM to Mary Macdonald, as mid-April 1917. Nor does her name appear in June 1918, although a *New York Times* photo of 16 June 1918 captures her there – unidentified – with "Mrs Waldorf Astor and a group of British Colonial Soldiers" (MFS, press clipping). My thanks to Michael Bott, Librarian, University of Reading, for perusing the Cliveden Visitors Books at my request.

20 University of Reading, MS 1416, Nancy Astor Papers, M. Waedoualdy (*sic*: MCM) to Lady Astor, 30 January 1941. This letter and Lady Astor's reply of 15 March to "Maria" are filed under W in the Astor correspondence, a misreading by Astor's secretary of Macdonald's signature. The two letters appear in that same guise in Thornton's *Nancy Astor's Canadian Correspondence*, 294–7, and hence Macdonald is neither recognized nor identified. Only by chance and curiosity did I pursue the odd Waedoualdy name in Thornton's index to find Moydart House, Bailey's Brook, as the home address, so I knew it was Macdonald. Thornton was clearly not perturbed by such a peculiar name, but I went on puzzling even after identifying Macdonald: What ever could Waedoualdy mean? My thanks to Fiona Brown in Scotland, to whom I spelled the name over the phone; she immediately saw the upside-down Macdonald. How we both laughed!

21 The *Nursing Mirror* (NM) lauded Roberts for being, among other things, a great friend and supporter of nurses ("The Passing of Lord Roberts," NM, 21 November 1914, 129).

22 Edith Cavell (1865–1915) was the matron of a British Red Cross Hospital in Brussels. Arrested as a spy and accused of aiding British, French, and Belgian soldiers to escape, she was shot 12 October 1915. Her fate at the hands of the Germans was the stuff of much British wartime propaganda.

23 "The Memorial to Florence Nightingale," NM, 19 February 1916, 401–2.

24 "Anniversary Dinner of Canadian Nurses," NM, 10 November 1917, 103. Chairing the gathering was one of Macdonald's South African War colleagues, Margaret Smith, then the matron of No. 16 CGH at Orpington (*British Journal of Nursing*, 10 November 1917, 301).

25 "Nurses' Memorial Service," NM, 30 March 1918, 475.

26 "In Recognition of the Work of Matrons-in-Chief," NM, 26 October 1918, 47, and "The Luncheon to the Matrons-in-Chief," NM, 2 November 1918, 65.

27 "V.A.D.s and the Canadian Matron-in-Chief," NM, 25 August 1917, 356. The colleague was John George Adami, McGill University professor of pathology. During the war he was in charge of records in the office of the DMS in London in order to produce a history of the medical service. Only one volume, *War Story of the CAMC*, was completed.

28 SFXA, MFC, RG 2, file 16, MCM to Mary Macdonald, 1 January 1916.

29 LAC, RG 9 III B2, vol. 3701, file 30-11-1 (vol. 1), MCM to Ethel Ridley, 23 June 1915. See also LAC, Macdonald Papers, file "Transcripts ch. 4," MCM, "London Office" [1915], 5.

30 LAC, RG 9 III B2, vol. 3703, file 30-11-1 (vol. 15), Edith Rayside to MCM, 24 February 1917.

31 SFXA, MFC, RG 3, MCM Letterbook, undated letter (signature missing) to MCM, [January 1916]; Judge A.C. Galt of Winnipeg to MCM, 30 January 1916. The letterbook, a 9 x 8 x 1 in. leather-bound notebook with MSS embossed on the front, has seventy-two letters attached to the lined pages with strips of white sticky paper. Vie Macdonald wrote inside the front cover, "Royal Red Cross, Jan. 1st 1916." Journalist Beatrice Nasmyth reported Macdonald's RRC being in her desk drawer ("Matron-in-Chief in her London Office," Vancouver *Province*, 25 March 1916).

32 LAC, RG 150, box 6762-6, military personnel file of Ronald St John Macdonald.

33 Ibid., box 6770-20, military personnel file of William Chisholm Macdonald.

34 Ibid., box 6714-22, military personnel file of Donald D. Macdonald. Unusually, the medical documentation in this file is clearer than the military service record. For the erroneous report of his death, see Montreal *Gazette*, 6 October 1916, 5. By the time the *Casket* in Antigonish picked up the story, 12 October 1916, the family in nearby Bailey's Brook would have been reassured by a telegram from Margaret. The initial telegram announcing his death was addressed simply "D.D. Macdonald, Canada" but reached its destination.

35 SFXA, MFC, RG 5, file 3, Donald Macdonald to Florence Macdonald, 29 July 1916; RG 5, file 6a, Bill Macdonald to Vie Macdonald, [2, 6 or 8] March 1917; RG 2, file 18, Bill Macdonald to Mary Macdonald, 4 November 1917; RG 5, file 31, Donald Macdonald to Bill Macdonald, 12 June 1918. Also RG 4, file 6, Ronald St John Macdonald Diary, 8 October 1916,

5, 13 June and 11 September 1917. Some of Ronald's tiny diary books are loosely held in the MFC, not filed according to the index to the collection.

36 SFXA, MFC, RG 5, file 3, Donald Macdonald to Florence Macdonald, 29 July 1916.

37 SFXA, MFC, RG 3, MCM Letterbook, Harriet Graham at No. 2 CSH at Outreau to MCM, 3 January 1916. Her co-prankster was Margaret Marjory "Pearl" Fraser. Both of them came from New Glasgow, were known to Macdonald before the war, and came with her on the *Franconia*. Ronald Macdonald was at No. 3 CGH in nearby Boulogne. He had arranged to accompany Nursing Sister Alexina Dussault to tea at the home of a judge in Boulogne. "See here," Graham reported saying to Ronald, "Pearl and I are going to be awfully mad if you are coming up here to see Dussault, from Quebec and your own home people not being even asked for." She went on, "Well he enjoyed it and we had a great laugh. But poor Dussault didn't know what to say. She is an awfully nice girl."

38 SFXA, MFC, RG 2, file 17, Ronald Macdonald to Mary Macdonald, 22 June 1918.

39 Ibid., file 16, MCM to Mary Macdonald, 1 December 1918.

40 SFXA, MFC, RG 3, MCM Letterbook, Katherine MacLatchy to MCM, 2 January 1916.

41 Ibid., Buzz Benson to MCM, 30 October 1916.

42 LAC, RG 9 III B2, vol. 3678, file 29-11-1 (vol. 2), Mary Plummer to MCM [early July 1916]; SFXA, MFC, RG 3, file 5, B[elfrage] G[ilbertson] to MCM, 1 July 1917; Barry, "The Macdonald Family," 34, quoting a letter from Nancy Astor to MCM. The letter is not in the MFC file to which Barry refers. The fictitious title was no doubt a humorous reference to Macdonald's compatriot Max Aitken, who became Lord Beaverbrook in 1917, the name chosen from a waterway near his New Brunswick home. Macdonald's "ladyship" stuck, for in the 1920s, her former DMS was still using it (SFXA, MFC, RG 3, file 9, Guy Carleton Jones to MCM, 2 January 1924).

43 The "caravanning" holiday with an unnamed friend is referred to in SFXA, MFC, RG 3, file 5, B[elfrage] G[ilbertson] to MCM, 1 July 1917. The Irish trip, with Joan Arnoldi of the Canadian Field Comforts Commission, a woman who had come to Europe on the *Franconia* with Macdonald, is mentioned in the only diary that Macdonald kept – or that has survived: SFXA, MFC, RG 3, MCM Diary for 1919, 12–19 August 1919. A photo captured Macdonald, out of uniform and on horseback, at Cliveden (SFXA, MFC, photographic material, MCM photo album).

44 SFXA, MFC, RG 3, file 5, BG to MCM, 1 July 1917; MCM Letterbook, Gil to MCM, 13 January 1916. The identity of BG was a mystery for some time,

finally clarified after I sent a hunch to Michael Stansfield of the Archives and Special Collections of Durham University where the Grey family papers are held; he was able to identify her. The anecdote that Gil recounted came from Lord Osborne Bearcleves, Mac's landlord and a nephew of Lord Grey: an "illiterate sergeant had taken off the cable at H. Qrs. from the G.G. to the Canadians [after Vimy] as follows 'your immoral deeds in France will never be forgotten: now the gaol is in sight!'" (BG to MCM, 1 July 1917).

45 LAC, RG 9 III B2, vol. 3703, file 30-11-1 (vol. 13), Beatrice Nasmyth to MCM, 13 December 1916.

46 SFXA, MFC, RG 3, file 20, Edith McDougall to MCM, 26 May 1918.

47 LAC, RG 9 III B2, vol. 3702, file 30-11-1 (vol. 8), E[thel] R[idley] at Granville Canadian Special Hospital, Ramsgate, to MCM, 3 July 1916.

48 Thurston recalled such talks with nostalgia after the war (SFXA, MFC, RG 3, MCM Letterbook, M. Thurston to MCM, 26 September 1920).

49 SFXA, MFC, RG 3, file 19, Sr M. Dominic to MCM, 16 December 1917. The letter is signed "with grateful thanks [for a Christmas gift] and affectionate love." Sister Dominic was Julia Quinlan (1879–1952), superior of the convent and headmistress of the convent school [1915]–21. The convent – and school – in Devizes had five sisters during the war. It is now closed. Among the records at the Provincial House of the Sisters of St Joseph of Ancy in Newport, Wales, are day books, kept "at the whim of the keeper," and account books. Sr Marie de Montfort, who provided the information about Sr Dominic, kindly searched these records for me but could not locate anything related to Macdonald (telephone conversation, 28 August 2003, and e-mail communication, 24 May 2004).

50 Text in the possession of Ronald St John Macdonald Jr of Halifax. He told me his aunt loved this piece. Presumably she had sent it home to her family, for the original has "Xmas 1916" written at the bottom in Vie Macdonald's handwriting.

51 Colonel Oscar-Charles Pelletier, a career soldier and South African War veteran, may have known whereof he spoke when he tried to dissuade his daughter Juliette from joining the CAMC in 1914. He was unsuccessful and later regretted his remark, but the family remembered it down through the generations. My thanks to Juliette Pelletier's daughter, Marguerite Ramsey Mackinnon of Montreal, for this recollection of her mother. For details of Pelletier's nursing career, see Mann, ed., *War Diary of Clare Gass*, 270–1, n.14.

52 An illustration is the lengthy move of No. 3 CGH (McGill) from Dannes-Camiers to Boulogne in late 1915, early 1916. Some of the nurses went to

the Duchess of Connaught's Canadian Red Cross Hospital at Cliveden, others to Shorncliffe, and some stayed in camp (under guard!) while the OC resisted the idea of billets for them in Boulogne as adverse to discipline and morale. See Mann, ed., *War Diary of Clare Gass*, 79–103 (diary entries 11 November 1915 – 21 February 1916); LAC, RG 9 III C10, vol. 4571, file 1, folder 3, H.S. Birkett to MCM, 4 December 1915.

53 LAC, RG 9 III B2, vol. 3453, file 7-2-2 (vol. 1), MCM to Chief Paymaster, 23 September 1915 in response to a letter from his office to the DMS, 15 September 1915; vol. 3703, file 30-11-1 (vol. 9), G.C. Jones to Secretary, Headquarters, CEF, 17 August 1916; Quartermaster General to Chief Paymaster, 2 September 1916; vol., 3704, file 30-11-1 (vol. 18), J.M. Spencer, Assistant Quartermaster General to DMS, 8 May 1917.

54 LAC, RG 9 III B2, vol. 3701, file 30-11-1 (vol. 1), MCM to Matron Jaggard, 18 June 1915. Later that year Jaggard succumbed to the ghastly conditions on Lemnos – including the food – and died of dysentery (Nicholson, *Canada's Nursing Sisters*, 69).

55 Macdonald adapted for the army the position of home sister that Florence Nightingale had invented for the Training School at St Thomas's Hospital in the 1870s. As early as November 1914, Macdonald had a home sister in place at Bulford, Salisbury Plain (LAC, Macdonald Papers, file "Memoranda," MCM, "Mobilization," 3, and MCM, "No. 1 Canadian General Hospital," 1). See also LAC, RG 9 III B2, vol. 3678, file 29-11-1 (vol. 2), M.O. Boulter to Secretary, Headquarters, CEF, 12 and 18 September 1916; and ibid., vol. 3453, file 7-2-0 (vol. 3), MCM to the Chief Paymaster, 24 July 1917. In soldiers' parlance, a "housewife" denoted a small sewing kit, part of every soldier's gear.

56 LAC, RG 9 III B2, vol. 3702, file 30-11-1 (vol. 4), MCM to Matron Campbell at Duchess of Connaught's Canadian Red Cross Hospital, Cliveden, 9 December 1915; vol. 3703, file 30-11-1 (vol. 9), MCM to Matron Ridley at Granville Canadian Special Hospital at Ramsgate, 10 August 1916, in response to an undated query from Ridley about silk uniforms. The prohibition of jewellery is contained in the *Instructions for Members of the Canadian Army Medical Corps Nursing Service (when mobilized)*, no. 58.

57 LAC, RG 9 III B2, vol. 3703, file 30-11-1 (vol. 15), MCM sending theatre tickets to Matron Margaret Smith at Ontario Military Hospital, Orpington, 7 February 1917; Nicholson, *Canada's Nursing Sisters*, 97.

58 LAC, Macdonald Papers, file "Memoranda," MCM, "No. 1 Canadian General Hospital," 2; RG 9 III B2, vol. 3701, file 30-11-1 (vol. 1), MCM to Matron Rayside at No. 2 CGH at Le Tréport, 24 June 1915; Wilkinson, "Four Score," November 1977, 16.

59 LAC, RG 9 III B2, vol. 3701, file 30-11-1 (vol. 1), MCM to Matron Rayside, 24 June 1915.

60 Ibid., vol. 3702, file 30-11-1 (vol. 4), MCM to J.G. Colner, Secretary, Canadian War Contingents Association, 5 January 1916. Nursing Sister Clare Gass received veils and boots from a Montreal friend; others no doubt had family and friends assisting with the maintenance of their uniforms. See Mann, ed., *War Diary of Clare Gass*, 55 (entry for 23 August 1915), 226, 227.

61 SFXA, MFC, RG 3, MCM Letterbook, B.L. Neiley at No. 1 CCCS at Aire to MCM, 5 January 1915 (*sic*: 1916). I think this may be Captain Bayard Lamont Neiley, a dental surgeon from New Glasgow who later became the dental corps commander; if so, he should be added to Macdonald's list of male friends.

62 SFXA, MFC, RG 3, file 82, "Comedies in War Tragedy." The title of her speech sounds like a variation of *Humour in Tragedy* by Constance Bruce (no relation of Col. Herbert Bruce) published in London in 1918 with a preface by Lord Beaverbrook, something not likely acquired without an influential intermediary. Constance Bruce worked in Macdonald's office for two months, February to April 1918.

63 LAC, RG 9 III B2, vol. 3490, file 11-1-3, MCM, "Inspection Report," 8 May 1917. SFXA, MFC, RG 3, file 82, "Some Aspects of War Nursing," MCM speech to a convention of the Graduate Nurses' Association of Ontario, Ottawa, 8 April 1920, 2.

64 LAC, RG 9 III B2, vol. 3482, file 10-11-27, untitled mimeographed note from McCarthy to all matrons, 24 September 1917.

65 Ibid., McCarthy to MCM, 16 October 1917.

66 Ibid., MCM to McCarthy, 18 October 1917.

67 LAC, Macdonald Papers, file "Transcripts ch. 6," E.M. McCarthy, "Report on Work in France," 6.

68 LAC, RG 9 III B2, vol. 3705, file 30-11-1 (vol. 23), "A true Canadian man" to MCM, [mid-October 1917]; MCM to Matrons V. Nesbitt at No. 9 CGH, Folkestone, F. Wilson at Westcliffe Canadian Eye and Ear Hospital, and B.L. Smellie at No. 11 CGH, Moore Barracks, Shorncliffe, 17 October 1917; B.L. Smellie to MCM, 21 October 1917; F. Wilson to MCM, 21 October 1917. Matron Nesbitt's reply of 24 October 1917 is in vol. 3678, file 29-11-1 (vol. 2).

69 LAC, RG 9 III B2, vol. 3702, file 30-11-1 (vol. 5), Henriette Casault of No. 4 CSH at St Cloud to MCM, 4 March 1916. No reply is in the file.

70 Ibid., vol. 3482, file 10-11-27, McCarthy to MCM, 29 May 1916. See also McCarthy to MCM, 19 April 1916, and MCM to McCarthy, 24 April 1916.

71 Ibid., MCM to McCarthy, 5 June 1916.

72 Ibid., McCarthy to MCM, 22 August, 5, 17 September 1917.

73 Ibid., MCM to McCarthy, 3 January 1918, in reply to a note from McCarthy to MCM, 30 December 1917.

74 For example, LAC, RG 9 III B2, vol. 3705, file 30-11-1 (vol. 12), MCM to OC, No. 5 CGH at Salonika, 7 November 1916.

75 LAC, RG 9 III B2, vol. 3482, file 10-11-23 is a fat file documenting the complications and delights of convalescent homes for Canadian nurses. See, in particular, the exchange of correspondence between Col. C.A. Hodgetts of the Canadian Red Cross and MCM, 26 April, 10, 11, 12 May, 25, 30 June 1915. Macdonald's postwar recollections glossed over the struggle (SFXA, MFC, RG 3, file 98, MCM, "Echoes of the Great War," 7).

76 LAC, RG 9 III B2, vol. 3511, file 19-1-30, MCM to Col. Hodgetts, 6 June 1916.

77 Ibid., a flurry of correspondence between Hodgetts and MCM, 23, 29, 30, 31 August, 1 September 1917.

78 LAC, RG 9 III B2, vol. 3482, file 10-11-23, MCM to Hodgetts, 9 January 1918.

79 MFS, two unidentified press clippings refer to the reception and the accusation. Macdonald turned the taunt into a joke: "What would be said of her," she is quoted as saying about a nurse's club established in the home of Lady Minto in February 1918, "now [that the nurses] had a club which was such a fine background for *affaires de coeur*."

80 LAC, RG 9 III B2, vol. 3482, file 10-11-23, correspondence between MCM and Hodgetts, 8, 11, 15, 16, 18, 19 February 1918.

81 SFXA, MFC, RG 3, MCM Letterbook, Janet McGregor Macdonald at No. 1 CCCS at Aire to MCM, 18 January 1916.

82 Ibid., H.W. Blaylock to MCM, 8 January 1916.

83 An entire file at LAC, RG 9 III B2, vol. 3482, file 10-11-36, reveals the complexities of marriage in the nursing service and the puzzle it presented to military authorities, both imperial and Canadian. Clare Gass mentions the marriage of a number of nurses in her unit, No. 3 CGH (McGill). See Mann, ed., *War Diary of Clare Gass*. See also SFXA, MFC, RG 3, file 98, MCM, "Echoes of the Great War," and file 82, MCM, "Light and Shade in Army Nursing."

84 SFXA, MFC, RG 3, Scrapbook of Maggie C. Macdonald, 140.

85 Ibid., MCM Letterbook, Annie Strong at No. 2 CSH at Outreau, 10 February 1916. Strong sent Macdonald a pin and a ring at Christmas 1915; there is no indication of what sort of ring it was.

86 Sir Richard McBride, the agent general for British Columbia in London, acted as go-between for a Vancouver journalist who wanted his fiancée

returned to Canada. See LAC, RG 9 III B2, vol. 3702, file 30-11-1 (vol. 8), McBride to MCM, 20 July 1916; MCM to McBride, 21 July 1916; G.C. Jones to Director General, QMG2, Medical Service, War Office, 21 July 1916. There is no indication in the file that Nursing Sister Mary L. Cobb had requested the move.

87 LAC, RG 9 III B2, vol. 3482, file 10-11-36, Matron F. Wilson with No. 5 CGH in Salonika to MCM, 5 June 1916; MCM to Wilson, 21 June 1916. The nurse in question then resigned from the CAMC (M. Milligan to DMS, 17 July 1916).

88 Ibid., MCM to DMS, 25 January 1917. Her reference to nursing as a divinely appointed mission comes from SFXA, MFC, RG 3, file 81, "It was with a feeling of much exhilaration ... ," MCM speech to graduating nurses at the Hospital for Sick Children, 19 November 1920.

89 SFXA, MFC, RG 3, file 98, MCM, "Echoes of the Great War," 9.

90 LAC, RG 9 III B2, vol. 3482, file 10-11-36, MCM to DMS, 25 January 1917.

91 Ibid., G.C. Jones sent Macdonald's recommendation and rationale to the adjutant general [P.E. Thacker], 26 January 1917, and he replied 5 February with the ruling: "I am to inform you that it has been ruled that Nursing Sisters will not be permitted to marry and still retain their appointments in the Canadian Army Medical Corps."

92 Ibid., MCM to Major J.A. Fortier, 8 May 1917, in response to a letter from him, 24 April 1917.

93 LAC, Macdonald Papers, file "Transcripts ch. 4," "Résumé of Work A.M.D. 4," July 1917 – August 1919. Overall numbers of married nurses are hard to come by. A list from 1916 named twenty-four nurses married to officers in the CEF (RG 9 III B2, vol. 3703, file 30-11-1 [vol. 13], MCM to Chief Paymaster, 1 December 1916). Macdonald herself used very imprecise numbers to say that "ten percent of the Canadian nurses who went overseas were happily married," that "marriages in the service overseas ran into many hundreds," and that "about 15% of our Nursing Sisters married Overseas and an equal proportion since returning home" (MFS, unidentified press clipping from an Ottawa paper, hand-dated 1921; SFXA, MFC, RG 3, file 82, MCM, "Light and Shade in Army Nursing"; file 98, MCM, "Echoes of the Great War"). All that can be said with any certainty is that most nurses were and remained single.

94 These specifications did not appear in print until 13 December 1918 in a circular letter from Edith Rayside, Matron-in-Chief in Canada, to the General Officer Commanding in each of the military districts in Canada (RG 9 III B2, vol. 3705, file 30-11-1 [vol. 23]). Canadian army officials in both England and Canada had, however, been fussing over the question since at

least January 1918 (RG 9 III B2, vol. 3482, file 10-11-36). A list of resignations for marriage between 1 April and 12 October 1918 reveals the names of thirty-seven women, fifteen of whom married doctors in the CAMC (RG 9 III B2, vol. 3678, file 29-11-1 [vol. 4]).

95 SFXA, MFC, note of niece Mairi Macdonald of Halifax in MCM's copy of Andrew Macphail's *In Flanders Fields*. Her sister, Elizabeth Macdonald Podnieks of Toronto, used the phrase "love of her life" in an interview, 22 January 2001, without identifying McCrae. Mairi and her brother Ronald filled in the story in an interview, 12 May 2001. Second cousin Chisholm Lyons of Burlington, grandson of Margaret Macdonald's maternal uncle Sir Joseph Chisholm, also knew the story and recounted his version in a telephone conversation, 19 June 2003.

96 John McCrae to Janet McCrae, 27 August 1916, quoted in Graves, *Crown of Life*, 226.

97 Ibid., 226. Graves lists John Prescott's *In Flanders Fields* in her bibliography, but she does not repeat his speculation, based on two letters of Lady Osler, about an engagement between McCrae and Nona Gwyn. Gwyn was a sister of Jack McCrae's sister-in-law, Mrs Amy (Tom) McCrae. Prescott discounts his own speculation (111–12) with the prefatory comment, some forty pages earlier, that McCrae "was so charming and was such a hero to his generation that several women came forward after his death to say that they had been engaged to him" (70). Whatever the nature of the McCrae-Macdonald relationship, she would never have done that.

During the war, McCrae's friend and colleague at No. 3 CGH (McGill), Dr Edward Archibald, reported breezily to his wife on his matchmaking efforts: he had Nursing Sister Sophie Hoerner in mind for Jack (McGill University, Osler Library of the History of Medicine, Edward Archibald Fonds, letters from Edward to Agnes Archibald, 1915–16). Sophie Hoerner's letters at LAC make no mention of this.

98 SFXA, MFC, pencilled note of McCrae to MCM, Saturday [31 October 1914], pinned into her copy of Macphail's *In Flanders Fields*. By piecing together information in Graves, *Crown of Life*, 175, about McCrae's being in London that weekend, I was able to date the note. Devizes is just north of Salisbury Plain and in 1914–15 was the location of the officers' mess for the 1st Brigade, Canadian Field Artillery, McCrae's unit.

99 Mann, ed., *War Diary of Clare Gass*, 76 and 277–8, n. 49.

100 Ibid. Matron MacLatchy described the Christmas dinner of 1915 at No. 3 CGH and added as an aside "(I think he [Jack McCrae] has had a change of heart)" in what may be a reference to such behaviour (SFXA, MFC, RG 3, MCM Letterbook, K.O. MacLatchy to MCM 2 January 1916).

101 Graves, *Crown of Life*, 247–9.

102 MFS, press photo dated 25 February 1918.

103 SFXA, MFC. Without telling them why, I quizzed a number of Macdonald relatives and acquaintances as to the likelihood of Vie Macdonald's inventing the story of a romance between her sister and John McCrae. None of them could attach fabrication to Vie's vibrant personality.

104 "Fairy dust" is Carol Shields's phrase, from her analysis of a very similar story about Jane Austen, including a sister as the source (*Jane Austen*, 105).

105 In order of presentation: LAC, RG 9 III B2, vol. 3704, file 30-11-1 (vol. 16), Matron Jean Urquhart at Canadian Military Hospital, Hastings, to MCM, 23 March 1917; vol. 3453, file 7-2-0 (vol. 2), Acting Matron Cora A. DeCormier at No. 8 CGH, St Cloud, to MCM, 3 October 1916; vol. 3677, file 29-11-1 (vol. 1), Lena I. Boyd to MCM, 3 November 1915; MCM to Ethel Becher, 4 November 1915; Matron M.S. Rammie of No. 2 Australian Imperial Military Nursing Service at Netley to MCM, 9 November 1915; DGAMS to DMS Canadians, 13 November 1915; vol. 3704, file 30-11-1 (vol. 16), Matron S.C. MacIsaac at No. 9 CSH, Bramshott, to MCM, 7 March 1917; (vol. 21), Acting Matron B. Smellie at Moore Barracks Hospital, Shorncliffe, to M.O. Boulter, 5 July 1917; (vol. 16), Matron MacIsaac to MCM, 7 March 1917.

106 Ibid., vol. 3704, file 30-11-1 (vol. 17), MCM to Matron Jean Urquhart, 27 March 1917.

107 LAC, MG 27 II D9, Kemp Papers, vol. 129, file B4, Jean I. Bell to A.E. Kemp, 14 October 1918. The file contains numerous letters from and about Nursing Sister Bell, 10 April 1918 – 29 March 1919. Bell's political connection was through her brother-in-law, A.E. Fripp, a Conservative member of parliament.

108 Macdonald recalled this action with considerable pride as late as the 1940s (SFXA, MFC, RG 3, file 80, "As it recurs").

109 LAC, RG 9 III B2, vol. 3705, file 30-11-1 (vol. 23), Brigadier General Delmé Radcliffe to Sir Arthur Stanley of the Joint War Committee of the British Red Cross/Order of St John, n.d., enclosed in a letter from Alfred Keogh, DGAMS to G.L. Foster, DMS, Canadians [early October 1917].

110 Ibid., Keogh to "My dear Foster."

111 Ibid., MCM to Major Johnson, 1 December 1917.

112 Ibid., as relayed by the civil assistant, DGAMS to Foster, 28 February 1918. The file contains numerous letters of inquiry and explanation and umbrage about this alleged incident from early October 1917 to 28 February 1918.

113 Public Archives of Ontario, MU 7809, Merriman Papers, F951, Bertha

Merriman with No. 1 CSH in Salonika to her family in Hamilton, 8 April 1916.

114 LAC, RG 9 III B2, vol. 3705, file 30-11-1 (vol. 23), Matron Ridley's report of an inspection she and Macdonald made, 12 July 1918, at No. 6 CGH at Joinville-le-Pont. Ridley to MCM, 29 July 1918.

115 Ibid., vol. 3490, file 11-1-3, MCM to A.M.D., [12 August 1918], in reference to Nos. 2 and 10 CSH, both then on the French north coast.

116 Ibid., vol. 3482, file 10-11-27, MCM to McCarthy, 12 October 1917. The air raid on the British No. 58 General Hospital at St Omer occurred during the night of 31 October/1 November 1917. A staff nurse and two VADS were killed, and another staff nurse died of wounds (Macpherson, *History of the Great War … Medical Services*, 2: 167).

117 In the early years of the war, Macdonald wrote numerous letters of reassurance to anxious relatives. See, for example, LAC, RG 9 III B2, vol. 3702, file 30-11-1 (vol. 4), MCM to Stuart Kidd, 28 December 1915; (vol. 5) MCM to Mrs Primrose, 26 February 1916; vol. 3482, file 10-11-23, MCM to the mother superior at the Convent of the Sacred Heart in Point Grey, BC, 22 July 1916; vol. 3703, file 30-11-1 (vol. 9), MCM to J. Paris, 26 August 1916; (vol. 10), MCM to Mrs N.C. Armstrong, 14 September 1916.

118 Ibid., vol. 3705, file 30-11-1 (vol. 23), MCM to Fr A. Lombardini, 1 June 1918.

119 As early as 1920, Macdonald looked forward to the day when the nursing service would be designated a combatant one (SFXA, MFC, RG 3, file 82, MCM, "Some Aspects of War Nursing," [8 April 1920], 1).

120 Ibid., 3.

121 LAC, RG 9 III B2, vol. 3751, file "Hospital Ships."

122 LAC, Kemp Papers, vol. 147, file L10, Arthur James Balfour to A.E. Kemp, 13 July 1918. The official report is in the same file.

123 A copy of the pamphlet is in LAC, RG 9 III B2, vol. 3751, file "Hospital Ships." The pamphlet drew on the account in the *Canadian Daily Record*, 9 July 1918. The *Nursing Mirror* covered the story too: "A Crowning German Crime," NM, 6 July 1918, 199, and "The 'Llandovery Castle,'" NM, 13 July 1918, 220. The sinking of the *Llandovery Castle* was one of the cases submitted by Great Britain in the German war trials at the Supreme Court in Leipzig, May 1920. By then, the ship's commander had disappeared, but two lieutenants were tried and convicted (LAC, RG 24, vol. 1836, file GAQ 9-28c, Historical Section, "Hospital Ships Sunk"). The fourteen drowned nursing sisters were Christina Campbell, Carola Josephine Douglas, Alexina Dussault, Minnie Follette, Margaret Jane Fortescue, Margaret Marjory (Pearl) Fraser, Minnie Katherine Gallaher,

Jessie Mabel McDiarmid, Mary Agnes Mackenzie, Rena Maude McLean, Mae Belle Sampson, Gladys Irene Sare, Anna Irene Stamers, and Jean Templeman. A brief biography of Rena Maude McLean is in *Dictionary of Canadian Biography*, 14: 723.

124 SFXA, MFC, RG 2, file 16, MCM to Mary Macdonald [early April 1917]. She had expressed the same hope in February. See LAC, RG 9 III B2, vol. 3703, file 30-11-1 (vol. 15), MCM to S.H. Hallam, 16 February 1917.

125 LAC, Macdonald Papers, file "Transcripts ch. 4," "Nursing Sisters killed or died of wounds." According to this source, another seven died while on home service in Canada. See chapter 5, note 104, re numbers of nursing dead.

126 SFXA, MFC, RG 3, MCM Diary, 22, 27, 29 October 1919. The same diary records a visit to France as of 1 May 1919, but there is no mention of visiting graves. Lady Sybil Grey, in France in late 1919, supervising five hundred Women's Legion motor drivers, considered it a great honour to be asked by Macdonald to place wreaths on the French graves of Canadian nurses and to photograph the sites for her (ibid., RG 3, file 35, Sybil Grey to MCM, n.d. [1919]). It is just possible that the photograph of John McCrae's grave that is among Macdonald's effects was taken by Grey, for the handwritten identification on the back of the photo misspells McCrae, something neither Macdonald nor her sister Vie would have been likely to do.

127 Hilda Macdonald of Glendyr, Cape Breton, interview in *Cape Breton's Magazine*, 1 August 1983, 5.

128 The Victory Ball was held at the Albert Hall, 27 November 1918, in aid of the Nation's Fund for Nurses. It was the first such masquerade charity ball since before the war (*Times*, 28 November 1919, 9).

129 British elections were held 14 December 1918, the first in which women could vote. Lloyd George was re-elected.

130 SFXA, MFC, RG 2, file 16, MCM to Mary Macdonald, 1 December 1918.

131 LAC, T10926, War Diary, No. 3 CGH, 27 February 1919.

132 LAC, RG 9 III B2, vol. 3678, file 29-11-1 (vol. 4), Col. C.F. Wylde to DGMS, OMFC, 11 November 1918; MCM to E. Rayside, 17 January 1919; (vol. 5) MCM to DGMS Ottawa, 8 February 1919; Col. H.A. Chisholm to DGMS, Ottawa, 5 March 1919.

133 Ibid., (vol. 5), E. Rayside to MCM, 26 February 1919.

134 Ibid., E. Rayside to MCM, 15 February, 1 March 1919.

135 Ibid., Col. J.T. Fotheringham, A/DGMS, Ottawa, to DGMS, OMFC, 25 March 1919.

136 Ibid., E. Rayside to MCM, 15 February 1919.

137 Mottus, *New York Nightingales*, 159; Stimson, "Nursing in Government Services," 427–30.

138 LAC, NSA, vol. 1, file 7, Jean Gunn to Ethel Johns, 7 May 1918. The two women were, respectively, president and secretary of the CNATN and were alarmed at the prospect. They feared a too narrow curriculum and that it would be used to train VADS. In either case, the status of their professionally trained nurse members risked being undermined. Nothing came of the idea.

139 SFXA, MFC, RG 3, file 6, Ethel Hareda [? indecipherable signature] to MCM, 1 September 1918. It is unknown whether Macdonald pursued the matter but in any case the commandant's job went to Helen (Fraser) Gwynne-Vaughan in September 1918, and the WRAF itself was disbanded late in 1919.

140 LAC, RG 9 III B2, vol. 3678, file 29-11-1 (vol. 4), MCM to DGMS, Ottawa, 22 January 1919.

141 Ibid., (vol. 5), MCM to Matron B.J. Willoughby at No. 4 CGH, Eastbourne, 4 February 1919. The service gratuity amounts, tied to length of service, are outlined in LAC, RG 9 III B2, vol. 3705, file 30-11-1 (vol. 23), MCM to Mary S. Rundle, 26 March 1919.

142 LAC, Kemp Papers, vol. 131, file C9, G.L. Foster memorandum to Kemp, 29 July 1919.

143 SFXA, MFC, RG 3, file 90, MCM comments on Stimson's article, "Nursing in Government Services."

144 Ibid., file 95, MCM, "Casualty Clearing Stations," and, on second page, "Demobilization." Macdonald talked about the "family" of nurses in a chatty letter to Mabel Clint (LAC, RG 9 III B2, vol. 3702, file 30-11-1 [vol. 6], 17 April 1916). She described the nurses' mess as a happy community of women in her speech "Aspects of War Nursing," SFXA, MFC, RG 3, file 82. In file 57 of the same collection, her "A.M.D. 4 Report for 1919" refers to the army as parent.

145 LAC, RG 9 III B2, vol. 3678, file 29-11-1 (vols. 4, 5 and FD32) contain official correspondence about the movements of Canadian nurses to and in France, 18 November 1918 – 2 June 1919. Macdonald's own trip is recorded in SFXA, MFC, RG 3, MCM Diary for 1919, 1–15 May.

146 LAC, RG 9 III B2, vol. 3705, file 30-11-1 (vol. 23) contains a number of letters about this case, 3 July – 18 October 1919.

147 Ibid., vol. 3678, file 29-11-1 (vol. 5), MCM to E. Rayside, 11 September 1919; MCM to DGMS, Ottawa, 15 September 1919. The quotation is from the latter.

148 MCM speech to Association of Hospital Matrons, London, 28 June 1919. Both the *Nursing Mirror*, 12 July 1919, and the *Nursing Times*, 5 July 1919, carried an account of the speech, which the *Canadian Nurse* picked up as "The Canadian Matron-in-Chief on Work in France," 9 (September

1919): 1991–93. The *Halifax Chronicle* also took the speech from the *Nursing Times*, and a New Brunswick paper reprinted it from the *Chronicle* (clipping in MFS).

149 LAC, RG 9 III B2, vol. 3482, file 10-11-23, MCM to Hon. Mrs A. Henn-Collins, 17 June 1918.

150 LAC, RG 150, box 6752-26, MCM military personnel file. According to this file, she was in the Canadian Red Cross Officers' Hospital in North Audley Street, London, from 16 to 28 February 1919. Another file indicates that she was at the Daughters of the Empire Canadian Red Cross Hospital for Officers, 1 Hyde Park Place, a hospital which, after December 1918, was used for nursing sister patients (RG 24, vol. 1836, file G.A.Q. 9-28d, typescript "Medical Units organized in Ontario ..." 1).

151 SFXA, MFC, RG 3, MCM Diary, 1919. The undated press clipping, "Life and Character Reading February 26," has war news on the back but not enough to identify the year. A search through some of the London tabloids around that date in 1917 and 1918 did not produce the item.

CHAPTER FIVE

1 Margaret Atwood's juxtaposition of the words "remembrance" and "forgetting" in *Blind Assassin*, 14, inspired my phrase.

2 *Casket*, 25 December 1919; *Pictou Advocate*, 26 December 1919.

3 Nicholson, *Canada's Nursing Sisters*, 106–8.

4 St Francis Xavier University Archives (SFXA), Macdonald Family Collection (MFC), RG 3, file 63, M.N. Brotherhood to Margaret C. Macdonald (MCM), 12 January 1921.

5 Macdonald Family Scrapbook (MFS), press clipping; SFXA, MFC, RG 3, file 65, Dr Helen MacMurchy to MCM, 24 August 1921.

6 MFS, press clipping. Three Toronto papers covered the event: *Daily Star*, 1 September 1921, 29; *Evening Telegram*, 1 September 1921, 14; *Mail and Empire*, 2 September 1921, 10.

7 Corcoran, *Mount Saint Vincent*, 54–5.

8 MFS, press clipping dated 9 June 1924: "Dr Macdonald is Guest of Honour at Alumnae Tea." The tea was held at St Patrick's high school in Halifax on 7 June 1924. Unless otherwise specified, press clippings in MFS are the source for the occasions mentioned in this paragraph.

9 "Women's League Pay Honor to a Nurse," *Toronto Daily Star*, MFS press clipping dated 12 June 1920, the actual date of the speech. I was unable to locate the original, presumably because it appeared in a different edition of

the daily paper from the microfilmed one at the Robarts Library, University of Toronto.

10 MCM speech to Association of Hospital Matrons, London, 28 June 1919 (*Nursing Mirror*, 12 July 1919, 276).

11 SFXA, MFC, RG 3, file 82, "Some Aspects of War Nursing," 2, MCM speech to Graduate Nurses' Association of Ontario, Ottawa, 8 April 1920.

12 Ibid., RG 3, file 98, "Echoes of the Great War," 1, MCM speech to Catholic Women's League, Toronto, 12 June 1920. See appendix.

13 Ibid., RG 3, file 82, "Comedies in War Tragedy," 2-4, MCM speech [to Catholic Women's League, Ottawa, 1921].

14 Ibid., RG 3, file 81, "Without admitting too great a number ..." 1, MCM speech at Canadian National Exhibition, 1 September 1921. The text of the speech was subsequently published in the *Canadian Nurse*, 17 (November 1921): 704-7.

15 MCM, "Without admitting too great a number ..." 5.

16 SFXA, MFC, RG 3, MCM Letterbook, Mabel Thurston to MCM, 26 September 1920, in reply to one from MCM. There is no trace of Thurston papers in New Zealand archives, so Macdonald's own letter cannot be found. However, Thurston's reply gives a sense of it: "I agree with you that public memory is the shortest lived on record!!"

17 MCM, "Without admitting too great a number ..." 4.

18 The photo is in the Toronto *Mail and Empire*, 2 September 1921, 10, and a clipping of it is in MFS. The original photograph no longer exists.

19 MCM, "Without admitting too great a number ..." 6.

20 Darren Hawkins of Vancouver purchased these items in Newcastle, Ontario, and informed me of them in an e-mail communication, 12 October 2004. He kindly sent an electronic version of the two tributes which I believe he intends to give to the Canadian War Museum.

21 SFXA, MFC, RG 3, file 81, "It was with a feeling ..." 1-2, MCM speech to the graduating nursing class at the Hospital for Sick Children, Toronto, 19 November 1920.

22 "Matron-in-Chief Here," *Toronto Daily Star*, 19 November 1920 (clipping in MFS).

23 SFXA, MFC, RG 3, file 81, "In coming here this evening ..." 2, MCM speech to a group of [public health?] nurses [1921 or early 1922].

24 Ibid., file 98, MCM, "Echoes of the Great War," 12.

25 Ibid., file 81, MCM, "Without admitting too great a number ..." 2.

26 Ibid., file 98, MCM, "Echoes of the Great War," 12.

27 SFXA, MFC, RG 3, MCM Letterbook, Mabel Thurston to MCM, 26 September 1920. Thurston was referring specifically to the announcement that

military nurses were to be eligible henceforth for the Victoria Cross, the highest military honour for soldiers.

28 The bill then went to the House of Lords for final consideration before being enacted in December 1919. The connection between the war and these changes regarding women is the subject of much historical debate. Gerard DeGroot summarizes it briefly in *Blighty*, 126–39, 304–11, and 320–2. Susan Kingsley Kent offers a fascinating interpretation in *Making Peace*, notably ch. 4, "The Vote: Sex and Suffrage in Britain, 1916–18."

29 SFXA, MFC, RG 3, file 98, MCM, "Echoes of the Great War," 14, with the pencilled-in addition of the good digestion. The *Toronto Daily Star* quoted the list too and added, "These last two qualifications [good digestion and sense of humour], Miss Macdonald averred, would carry a woman far." "Women's League Pay Honor to a Nurse," *Toronto Daily Star*, 12 June 1920 (clipping in MFS).

30 The Toronto *Mail and Empire*, 2 September 1921, 10, attributed these words to Macdonald, although they are not in the text of her speech at the CNE.

31 The courts had first to determine whether women were in fact "persons" and hence qualified by the terms of the British North America Act to be named to the Senate. The Canadian courts said no and it took a final appeal to the then highest court for Canada, the Judicial Committee of the Privy Council in London, to obtain a favourable verdict. Macdonald must have followed the "Persons Case," and she knew Cairine Wilson, the first woman named to the Senate, but there is no record of her reaction. How she would enjoy the commemorative sculpture to the five women who pursued the case through the courts during the 1920s that now graces Parliament Hill!

32 *Toronto Daily Star*, 12 June 1920.

33 Library and Archives Canada (LAC), RG 150, box 6752-26, MCM military personnel file.

34 SFXA, MFC, RG 3, file 58, Monthly Reports, September 1918 – May 1920, signed ECR [Edith C. Rayside]. MFS, press clipping from the *Toronto Daily Star*, 9 February 1920, has her in Toronto as "Matron-in-chief Overseas" and Rayside as "Matron-in-chief in Canada." Another unidentified clipping from a Winnipeg paper has her there on 17 February as "matron-in-chief of CAMC" and Rayside as "matron-in-chief of the military hospitals in Canada."

35 SFXA, MFC, RG 3, MCM Letterbook, M. Thurston to MCM, 26 September 1920 ("Your flat sounds charming") and, in the same letterbook, an empty envelope addressed to MCM at 238 Gilmour St, postmarked 28 December 1920.

36 SFXA, MFC, RG 5, file 5, undated incomplete letter from MCM to Mary or Vie Macdonald. The degree was awarded 11 May 1920 (*Casket*, 13 May 1920, 6. MFS, telegram from H.P. Macpherson to MCM, 3 May 1920). According to the press reports (clippings, MFS), the first Canadian woman to receive an honorary doctorate was Aletta Marty, Queen's University, 1919. Three British women, all aristocrats, had received honorary doctorates (one from Queen's and two from McGill) before the First World War. Thanks to Suzanne Morton for bringing the McGill information to my attention and to Douglas Morren for checking the Queen's records.

37 MFS, telegram from H.A. Blaylock to MCM, 31 May 1920. The medal was instituted in 1912 in memory of Florence Nightingale, who died in August 1910. It was to be awarded annually to six nurses anywhere in the world who had "rendered exceptional service to the sick." None was given during the war, hence the forty-two nurses who were recipients in 1920. Macdonald was the only Canadian among them (Editorial, *Canadian Nurse*, 16 [July 1920]: 410).

38 LAC, RG 24, vol. 1742, file DHS 4-32, G.L. Foster to W. Gwatkin, 10 June 1920. The official authorization, dated 15 June 1920, is in the same file: "Miss Macdonald will report forthwith to the Historical Section." Foster's fussing over his own position went on from March to November 1920, when he retired. See LAC, Kemp Papers, vol. 142, file F23.

39 LAC, RG 24, vol. 1742, file DHS 4-32, A.F. Duguid, quoting E.A. Cruikshank, to the Deputy Chief of General Staff, 7 February 1923.

40 SFXA, MFC, uncatalogued material, MCM's copy of Adami's book, inscribed "To Matron-in-chief M. Macdonald with the writer's cordial good wishes. 12.XII.18."

41 A list of seventy-five files recorded as signed out to her from the Central Registry is in LAC, RG 24, vol. 1742, file DHS 4-32, R.M. Gorssline to Director of Historical Section, 17 May 1923. Central Registry did allow that other files might have been seen by Macdonald, but it was unable to provide a complete list. An attempt in 2004 to trace those files by means of the file number alone (all that is on the list) proved too much for the LAC database.

42 LAC, RG 9 III B2, vol. 3704, file 30-11-1 (vol. 17), MCM to N. Goodhue, 31 March 1917. Goodhue, at the Royal Victoria Hospital in Montreal, had requested an article on military nursing for the Canadian Society of Superintendents of Training Schools for Nurses. Macdonald declined because of the pressure of work and passed the assignment on to Cameron-Smith. Her article appeared as "The Preparation of Nurses for Military Work," *Canadian Nurse* 13 (September 1917): 556–8.

43 LAC, Macdonald Papers, file "Correspondence 1923," J. Cameron-Smith to MCM, 15 December 1917. In that letter, Cameron-Smith requests access to the matrons' diaries in order to "obtain accurate and detailed information and so enlarge and authenticate my notes." In reference to the material that Cameron-Smith sent along with her letter, Macdonald commented at the bottom of the letter, "Contains many inaccuracies." The connection between Cameron-Smith's appointment and the state of her health – synovitis in the knee joints – is clear from her military personnel file, LAC, RG 150, box 1415-47.

44 LAC, Macdonald Papers, file "Transcripts ch. 6," E.M. McCarthy, "Report on Work in France of the Nursing Sisters of the Canadian Army Medical Corps," 11.

45 SFXA, MFC, RG 3, MCM Letterbook, M. Thurston to MCM, 26 September 1920.

46 SFXA, MFC, RG 3, file 61, circular letter from MCM for Brigadier-General E.A. Cruikshank, Director of Historical Section, 15 October 1920. This item is not in Macdonald Papers at LAC.

47 SFXA, MFC, RG 3, file 61, Emily H. Crossley of Montreal to MCM, 31 October 1920; ibid., file 62, L.K. Harvie (née Stimson) of Coldwater, Ont., to MCM, 7 November 1920.

48 Ibid., RG 3, file 61, Agnes B. Davis (Mrs Thomas Sullivan) of Redondo Beach, California, to MCM, 15 November 1920; ibid., file 96, MCM's "Excerpts" identifies only one of five items as those of Agnes Davis, but the other four are attributable to her because of MCM's description of "anon" in the closing lines of her proposed chapter 3.

49 Ibid., RG 3, file 61, Alice E. Isaacson of Cedar Rapids, Iowa, to MCM, 7 November 1920. Isaacson's entire diary, from which she took the two accounts of soldiers, was eventually donated to the Canadian Nurses' Association and is now a separate fonds at LAC, R11203.

50 SFXA, MFC, RG 3, file 47, Nancy Astor to MCM, 9 December 1920.

51 LAC, RG 24, vol. 1742, file DHS 4-32, MCM to G.J. Desbarats, 15 July 1923. Other responses could well have disappeared over the years along with most of Macdonald's personal papers. Of six other items in MFC that might be viewed as responses to her request, three have no date and the others are dated 1916. It is likely therefore that these items came to Macdonald during the war (SFXA, MFC, RG 3, files 85 and 87). There are no responses from nurses among her papers at LAC and only one of a matron, that of K.O. MacLatchy, "No. 3 Canadian General Hospital" (Macdonald Papers, file "Transcripts ch. 6"). This piece was subsequently published in the *Canadian Nurse* 18 (July 1922): 414–18, and is reproduced as

"Matron MacLatchy's Recollections" in Mann, ed., *The War Diary of Clare Gass*, appendix six, 243–8.

52 For example, LAC, RG 9 III B2, vol. 3703, file 30-11-1 (vol. 12), MCM to Edith Horn, 2 November 1916, in response to a request for a speaker; (vol. 15), Elizabeth Breeze to MCM, 30 January 1917; (vol. 17), MCM to Nursing Sister Jessie Scott, 27 March 1917.

53 Ibid., Jessie Scott to MCM, 29 March 1917.

54 MFS, clipping from Quebec *Chronicle Telegraph*, hand-dated 2 June 1921 (unverifiable, given the illegible state of the microfilm copy of the newspaper at Bibliothèque nationale du Québec); Toronto *Evening Telegram*, 1 September 1921, 14.

55 The texts written by Macdonald can be determined in part by her style but also by the listing on the inside front cover of each file folder that contains transcripts for the chapter divisions of the history (LAC, Macdonald Papers).

56 An example is SFXA, MFC, RG 3, file 88, MCM, "No. 1 Canadian Stationary Hospital."

57 Ibid., file 94, MCM, "Canadian Army Nursing Service," annotated typescript with sixteen chapter divisions.

58 Ibid., file 66, MCM to Nursing Sister G.S. Allen in Victoria, 5 April 1922; MCM to Matron Olive Garland in Winnipeg, 24 April 1922; file 67, MCM to Mrs J.J. Fraser in Toronto, 24 April 1922.

59 Ibid., file 67, Georgie Fraser to MCM, 1 June 1922.

60 Ibid., file 25, Andrew Macphail to MCM, 22 August 1919.

61 Macphail, *Official History ... Medical Services*, "Ancillary Services," 224–30. The style alone reveals a different author. Macdonald knew about this use of her material, having been "called upon to supply material to Sir Andrew Macphail for the Medical History" in April 1922 (LAC, RG 24, vol. 1742, file DHS 4-32, A.F. Duguid to Deputy Chief of General Staff, 7 February 1923). Macdonald's originals for the Macphail book are in LAC, Macdonald Papers, file "Transcripts ch. 1," "Transcripts ch. 2," "Transcripts ch. 3" and in SFXA, MFC, RG 3, file 95, "Special Duties, Anaesthetics." Macphail edited these texts ever so slightly. See also LAC, MG 30 D150, Andrew Macphail Papers, vol. 3, file 26, draft of a letter from Macphail to Major General F.H. MacBrien, Chief of General Staff, 30 January 1923. Dave Campbell's study of Macphail's history notes the lack of thematic unity but not the different authors ("Politics, Polemics, and the Boundaries of Personal Experience: Sir Andrew Macphail as Official Historian," paper presented at the Canadian Historical Association annual meeting, Toronto, May 2002). For an example of Macphail's antifeminist

sentiments, see "On Certain Aspects of Feminism," *University Magazine* 13 (February 1914): 79–91, reproduced in Cook and Mitchinson, eds., *The Proper Sphere*, 300–9.

62 LAC, RG 24, vol. 1742, file DHS 4-32, Col. W. Gisborne to DGMS, 21 June 1922.

63 Ibid., MCM to D[G]MS [Col. J.W. Bridges], 6 August 1922.

64 Her pay and pension figures are revealed – indiscreetly – in a letter from A.F. Duguid to Lorne Drum, 21 October 1923 (LAC, RG 24, vol. 1742, file DHS 4-32).

65 Ibid.

66 Ibid., D. McNiven to MCM, 12 August 1922.

67 *Canadian Nurse* 18 (September 1922): 548. Macdonald's British colleagues would read the same thing in *Nursing Times*, 14 October 1922 (clipping in MFS).

68 LAC, RG 24, vol. 1742, file DHS 4-32, MCM to A.F. Duguid, 24 October 1922.

69 Ibid.

70 Ibid., A.F. Duguid to MCM, 29 November 1922.

71 Ibid., MCM to A.F. Duguid, 29 January 1923, in response to his of 24 January 1923 (copy of his letter of 29 November 1922).

72 Ibid., A.F. Duguid to Deputy Chief of General Staff, 7 February 1923. Tim Cook, of the Canadian War Museum, suggests that Duguid, who saw himself as the guardian of all war records, was overworked and understaffed. Apparently Macdonald was not his only problem author. Cook's book on the official histories is forthcoming from UBC Press.

73 Ibid., G.J. Desbarats to MCM, 16 February 1923.

74 Ibid., MCM to G.J. Desbarats, 24 February 1923.

75 Ibid., Desbarats to MCM, 22 March 1923; MCM telegram to Desbarats, 2 April 1923; Duguid to DGMS, 17 April 1923; R.M. Gorssline to Director, Historical Section, 19 April and 17 May 1923; R.J. Orde to Deputy Chief of General Staff, 28 May 1923; Desbarats to MCM, 2 June 1923; MCM to Desbarats, 15 July 1923; Duguid to Deputy Chief of General Staff, 3 August 1923 and reply 13 August 1923.

76 Ibid., A.F. Duguid to Secretary, Canadian Nurses' Association, 22 May 1926; Duguid to DGMS, 9 May 1933.

77 What remains of whatever material she kept is in SFXA, MFC, RG 3, files 57, 61, 67, and 83–99. The material she sent to Ottawa in February 1923 is in her papers at LAC, file "Memoranda." I have checked the two sets of material; some items are the same and some are not.

78 These "transcripts," placed by chapter according to Gorssline's outline, form the major part of the single small box of Macdonald Papers at LAC.

"Transcripts ch. 8" is missing; according to the outline, it would cover the Canadian nursing experience in the Mediterranean. Inside the front cover of each file is Gorssline's identification – title and author or source – of each transcript; from that it would appear that Macdonald was the author of less than one-quarter of the material in the file box. The remaining file of "Memoranda" in that box contains the material Macdonald sent from Bailey's Brook in February 1923. She told the deputy minister that she had sent all she had: 137 folios (LAC, RG 24, vol. 1742, file DHS 4-32, MCM telegram to G.J. Desbarats, 2 April 1923). Duguid made a list of the material received, "Index to Folios," 1 March 1923, now in file "Proposed Outline of History" in LAC, Macdonald Papers. However, the folios themselves are loose sheets in the "Memoranda" file and have probably been subject to some shuffling, either by Gorssline for his "transcripts" in the summer and fall of 1923 or by general handling since then.

79 Ibid., file "Correspondence 1923."

80 LAC, RG 24, vol. 6519, file HQ 393-8-158, Lorne Drum to A.F. Duguid, 8 October 1923.

81 LAC, Macdonald Papers, file "Correspondence 1923," Isabella (Strathy) McMurtry to A.F. Duguid, 28 August 1923, in reply to his letter of 25 August 1923.

82 Nor is it clear how this box of material got to the archives as her papers. Normally, such material would be part of the records of the Directorate of History, Ministry of National Defence and thus in RG 24. The archives' description of the Macdonald fonds has a mistaken provenance as well as the wrong birth date for Macdonald.

83 Vance, *Death So Noble*, and Eksteins, *Rites of Spring*, explore these issues brilliantly, if never from the nurses' point of view. Although Heilbrun's *Writing a Woman's Life* mentions neither nurses nor war, it is very suggestive about forms of narrative and language as handicaps to writing a woman's life.

84 Mann, ed., *The War Diary of Clare Gass*, contains numerous references to nurses resigning because of a sick parent in Canada. See also SFXA, MFC, RG 3, file 37, Flora H. Wylie to MCM, 7 February [1918?]. In this latter case, the ailing mother died, so Wylie was able to return to the CAMC.

85 The phrase is Heilbrun's, *Writing a Woman's Life*, 22.

86 SFXA, MFC, RG 3, file 68, M. Muir, Secretary of the Montreal Association of Overseas Nursing Sisters, to MCM, 28 October 1922. Thirty-eight signatures adorn this letter.

87 LAC, RG 24, vol. 6519, file HQ 393-8-158, Lorne Drum to A.F. Duguid, 8 October 1923.

88 McCarthy retired from the QAIMNS in September 1919 because of the

army age limit of fifty-five. In late June 1920 she became matron-in-chief of the Territorial Force Nursing Service for a year in order to reorganize it into the Territorial Army Nursing Service. Its retirement age was changed to sixty-two, and McCarthy thus kept her new job until 1925. See The National Archives, London (TNA), WO 399/12912, service file of Emma Maud McCarthy. Macdonald would have known of these developments: she saw McCarthy in London in 1919; she read the British nursing press; and the two may have corresponded.

89 SFXA, MFC, RG 3, file 9, Guy Carleton Jones (living in Italy) to MCM (addressed as "Lady Baileybrook"), 2 January 1924: "As there will soon be an election in Canada, so it appears to me, I suppose you will be running as a candidate, you ought to."

90 *Canadian Nurse* 18 (September 1922): 573. She reappeared as "honorary editor" of the section in October 1924 but does not seem to have been involved in what was mostly a listing of social gatherings of groups of former nursing sisters.

91 *Canadian Nurse* 18 (October 1922): 606.

92 SFXA, MFC, RG 4, notebook re Ronald St John Macdonald Jr. The Barry index to MFC has this item catalogued in file 8, but it is in fact loose among Ronald Sr's diaries.

93 Sources for this portrait are the diaries of Ronald St John Macdonald (SFXA, MFC, RG 4), three copies of the "Brook Bulletin," 1–7 February 1935, 11–17 January 1936, 20 January 1936 (ibid., uncatalogued material), and conversations I have had with Macdonald family members: Mairi and Ronald Macdonald Jr, Elizabeth Macdonald Podnieks, Father Greg MacKinnon, and Chisholm Lyons; and with Bailey's Brook neighbours: Wilma Burke, Dougal and Carmie Macdonald, and Catherine Anderson. I thank them for sharing their childhood memories with me.

94 SFXA, MFC, RG 2, file 16, MCM to Mary Macdonald, 27 November 1925.

95 LAC, microfilm T14803, Passenger Lists for the *Aurania*, which arrived in Halifax 13 December 1925. Macdonald's age is listed as 45 and Vie's as 35 when in fact the two were 52 and 46, respectively. Other sources for these post-retirement activities are SFXA, MFC, RG 5, file 18, Vie Macdonald Scrapbook (VMS), press clippings; RG 4, Diaries of Ronald Macdonald, 1936–38; RG 3, file 9, invitation card; RG 2, file 16, MCM to her mother, 27 November 1925; RG 3, file 41, press clippings from the *Times*, London, 4 July 1934, and, among the uncatalogued material, Macdonald's passport, issued 1934. Information also came from a letter of Vie Macdonald to her mother, 2 October 1925, lent to me by the present owners of Egnaig and Moydart; from conversations with Father Greg MacKinnon, 7 May 2001,

and with Mairi Macdonald and Ronald Macdonald Jr, 12 May and 18 August 2001; and from a bundle of old newspapers supplied to me by Ronald Macdonald Jr in 2001. The controversial book was that of Compton Mackenzie, *The Windsor Tapestry*, extracted in the *Sunday Despatch*, 26 June, 3 and 10 July 1938.

96 SFXA, MFC, uncatalogued material, MCM's copies of the books. The new head of the QAIMNS was A. Beadsmore-Smith, who had been Maud McCarthy's assistant in France.

97 *Canadian Nurse* 22 (January 1926): 35; ibid., 30 (January 1934): 37; Nicholson, *Canada's Nursing Sisters*, 110–11.

98 *Victoria Daily Times*, 16 April 1928, 6. The entire issue of the paper was included in a bundle of old newspapers given to me in 2001 by Ronald St John Macdonald Jr. See also SFXA, MFC, RG 5, file 8, MCM in Victoria to "Libs," 23 April 1928 (on back of a letter from "Cassie" to MCM and Vie Macdonald, 11 April 1928); RG 5, file 18, VMS, clippings from Victoria and Vancouver papers and program from the Toronto dinner, 8 May 1928.

99 SFXA, MFC, RG 3, file 46, Official Statement of Service provided by War Department, Adjutant General's Office, signed by Major General C.H. Bridges, 1932.

100 Thornton, *Nancy Astor's Canadian Correspondence*, 167–8, Nancy Astor to R.B. Bennett, 25 (*sic*) March 1935; SFXA, RG 3, file 78, part of a letter from R.B. Bennett to MCM, 18 May 1935; MCM to Bennett [May 1935]. This correspondence could not be traced in the Bennett Papers at the University of New Brunswick Archives except for the Astor letter, which is dated 21 March in that collection.

101 Ridley was awarded the CBE in January 1919, just before the Canadian government put a stop to Canadians receiving British honours. The ban was lifted briefly in 1934–35, which allowed the CBE to be awarded to Rayside and the approach made to Macdonald. A third Canadian nurse, Matron Bertha Willoughby, received the OBE in 1919.

102 *Canadian Nurse* 17 (July 1921): 414–15. Natalie Riegler's study of Jean Gunn draws on this same material without shedding any light on the tension between Gunn and Macdonald ("The Work and Networks of Jean Gunn," 295–301).

103 LAC, Nursing Sisters' Association of Canada (NSA), vol. 1, file 8, Minutes of National Memorial Committee, 28 October 1921 – 9 June 1922. The one meeting she attended was 24 March 1922. Along with two other members of the committee, she did however meet with officials of the Department of Public Works in Ottawa about the location of the sculpture (ibid., meeting of 10 March 1922). In the face of the officials' refusal, the nurses

then had two men of their business committee prevail upon Mackenzie King (ibid., meeting of 9 June 1922). See also *Canadian Nurse* 18 (August 1922): 483. The journal carried reports of the memorial committee through the 1920s.

104 LAC, NSA, vol. 1, file 8, Minutes of meeting of 9 September 1922. Precision about the number of nursing dead is hard to come by. Depending on the source, the number 47 can refer to all Canadian nurses who died overseas: 39 with the CAMC, 2 with the British nursing service, and 6 with the American Army Nurse Corps; elsewhere, a total of 46 refers only to members of the CAMC: 39 overseas and 7 on home service in Canada.

105 MCM, "A Message to the Nursing Sisters," *Canadian Nurse* 22 (July 1926): 367–8.

106 Guides in the Parliament Buildings were astonished by my desire to gaze at length at the sculpted panel. The *Canadian Nurse* recorded the unveiling, in vol. 22 (October 1926). See also Nicholson, *Canada's Nursing Sisters*, 103–6. A fascinating "reading" of this sculpture, to which I am indebted, is Kathryn McPherson's article "Carving Out a Past."

107 SFXA, MFC, RG 3, file 81, MCM, "Address given by M.C.M. on the occasion of the unveiling of Memorial to the N/Sisters who gave their lives in the 1914–18 War."

108 Ibid., RG 4, Diary of Ronald St John Macdonald [1939].

109 Ibid., RG 3, file 79, G.W. Cragghorn for adjutant general to MCM, 30 August 1939, in response to her letter of 26 August 1939.

110 Nicholson, *Canada's Nursing Sisters*, 113–14 quotes the response of the deputy minister, Department of National Defence, to the Overseas Nursing Sisters' Association of Canada, 6 September 1939. Five nursing sisters from the First World War served in the Second World War.

111 "National Registration," *Casket*, 22 August 1940, 12; SFXA, MFC, RG 4, Ronald St John Macdonald Diary, 19 August 1940.

112 SFXA, MFC, RG 3, file 82, "Light and Shade in Army Nursing," MCM speech to a banquet for graduate nurses of St Martha's Hospital, Antigonish [1942 or 1943]. Much of this speech is a collage of excerpts from her speeches of the early 1920s.

113 Ibid., RG 5, file 18, VMS, undated press clipping reporting Macdonald's presence at the Arts and Letters Club in New Glasgow. To that meeting she brought Montreal press coverage of the Beveridge Report on social security in Britain.

114 Ibid., RG 3, file 40, N. Fairhurst to MCM, 13 January 1945, thanking her and mentioning that "Beryl" had received a package too.

115 Ibid., file 14, Jo Nicol to MCM, 27 August [1940].

116 Ibid., file 93, Frances Upton to MCM, 7 October 1940.

117 LAC, RG 24, vol. 6519, file HQ 393-8-158, Jean Wilson, executive secretary of the CNA, to A.F. Duguid, 28 April 1926. The *Canadian Nurse* carried the Abbott lectures on war nursing monthly from March 1922 to May 1923.

118 LAC, RG 24, vol. 6519, file HQ 393-8-158, Jean Wilson to A.F. Duguid, 17 April 1926. Wilson conveyed her "dismay and disappointment" to Duguid (who probably muttered, "I could have told you so") and asked for his help. Before any was forthcoming, Wilson wrote again to say he need not bother: she now had the material Macdonald had prepared for Dr Maude Abbott and, because of Macdonald's own proposed book, the CNA would not "include a lengthy report of the Service in its record" (ibid., Wilson to Duguid, 28 April 1926).

119 Ibid., copy of a letter from Mary McCamus to MCM, 24 April 1933, with an appended note from MCM to D[G]MS Ottawa, 4 May 1933, who passed it on to Duguid for information about the availability of files, 6 May 1933. On that same note is the brief interaction between Duguid and DGMS A.E. Snell about the conditions, 9, 11, 15 May 1923.

120 MCM, "Our Bit," *Canadian Nurse* 30 (January 1934): 12. Macdonald's lightly annotated copy of *Our Bit* is among the uncatalogued material in SFXA, MFC.

121 LAC, NSA, vol. 6, file 3, Frances Upton to Grace Fairley (secretary-treasurer and president, respectively, of the Overseas Nursing Sisters' Association of Canada), 19 October 1940.

122 Ibid., MCM to Frances Upton, 12 November 1940.

123 Ibid., MCM to Upton, 4 July, 8 October 1941. Although she never said so to Macdonald, Upton let others know that it had been "a year of wasted time" (ibid., Upton to E.L. Smellie, 27 February 1942). She then took it upon herself to pull together the threads of the wartime history for the CNA project that had been underway since 1932. She approached ten individuals but heard from only six of them. Seventeen branches of the ONSA itself were more responsive. After her work was completed she confessed that the "work of assembling data ... was tedious and at times discouraging" (ibid., Upton to Anne F. Mitchell, 23 March 1944).

124 Ibid., Upton to MCM, 31 January 1942. The original of this letter is in SFXA, MFC, RG 3, file 93.

125 LAC, NSA, vol. 6, file 2 [March 1942]. The chronology of her career contains a number of errors. As for the memorandum, when read in conjunction with the MCM-Upton correspondence (ibid., file 3), it may provide a tentative dating of the document "As it recurs," in SFXA, MFC, RG 3, file 80. The document feels ever so slightly like a first stab at the memorandum.

126 SFXA, MFC, RG 3, file 93, Frances Upton to MCM, 27 February 1942.

127 Gibbon and Mathewson, *Three Centuries*, 296–7, 306–7. The task of writing about the nurses of the First World War has not become any easier over the years. Nicholson's *Canada's Nursing Sisters*, commissioned by the NSA in the 1970s, contains only three chapters on them. And in 2005 there still is no book-length study of Canada's military nurses in the First World War. For an exploration of some of the reasons, see Mann, "Where Have All the Bluebirds Gone?" Macdonald would be chagrined to know that a book on the Canadian VADs by Linda Quiney will appear before one on the nurses. Indeed, she would be chagrined to know that her own story has now been told before that of her nurses.

128 LAC, NSA, vol. 6, file 3, MCM to F. Upton, 12 November 1940.

129 University of Reading, Nancy Astor Papers, MCM to Lady Astor, 30 January 1941. See note 20 of chapter 4 for the peculiar filing of this letter. The entire letter, along with Lady Astor's brief but warm reply of 15 March 1941, is published in Thornton ed., *Canadian Correspondence*, 294–7. The Astor letter, with the remark, "I miss my old Canadians very much. The new ones are nice, but not in the least like the old ones," is also in SFXA, MFC, RG 3, file 7.

130 NSARM, Nova Scotia Vital Statistics, Death: Pictou County Book 5, no. 616, Death certificate of Margaret C. Macdonald. I thank Drs Maurice McGregor and Nadia Giannetti of McGill's Faculty of Medicine for interpreting the death certificate for me. The certificate added anemia and colitis as "other morbid conditions." Macdonald clearly had not been well for some time.

131 Sister Clare Marie Lyons of the Sisters of St Martha was the young nurse. "In the evenings after supper, I often went to her room and took her for a walk in the corridor. I was intrigued by her stories of her career as a military nurse" (letter to S. Mann, 2 May 2003). Theresa MacIsaac of Antigonish related the story about hospital food in a phone conversation, 13 July 2001. St Martha's Hospital destroyed all its records in the 1950s.

132 Nova Scotia, Land Information Centre/Registry of Deeds, Last Will and Testament of Margaret C. Macdonald, New Glasgow, 1 August 1948. The will is in Vie's handwriting, and two registered nurses witnessed the signing of the document, one of them being Mary J. Ross, later the director of nursing at Aberdeen Hospital, 1955–70. To various relatives and three neighbours she left a total of $6,150 and three sets of fifty common shares. The entirety of the Margaret Clotilde Macdonald trust fund as well as the remainder of her estate she left to her "beloved sister" Vie. The Eastern Trust Company that held her fund no longer exists, so it was impossible to

establish Macdonald's financial worth at the time of her death. And the Aberdeen Hospital no longer has its records from the 1940s.

133 The last line of the hymn "Oh Valiant Hearts," quoted in full in SFXA, MFC, RG 4 (*sic*: 3), file 73, Edith Rayside to MCM, 8 August 1927. Rayside had represented Canadian nurses at the dedication of the altar in the Memorial Chamber of the Peace Tower that summer. A book on the altar records the names of all Canada's war dead. I wish to thank Mairi and Ronald Macdonald for sharing their memories of their aunt's death, coming as it did just five days before that of their father.

POSTSCRIPT

1 SFXA, MFC, RG 4, file 26, obituaries of Dr Ronald St John Macdonald.

APPENDIX

1 SFXA, MFC, RG 3, file 98, speech of Margaret Macdonald to the Catholic Women's League, 12 June 1920.

Bibliography

ARCHIVAL SOURCES

ARMY MEDICAL SERVICES MUSEUM, ALDERSHOT, ENGLAND
Maud McCarthy Papers

DALHOUSIE UNIVERSITY ARCHIVES
Waldren Studios Photographic Collection

LIBRARY AND ARCHIVES CANADA
Government Documents:
   Ministry of Militia and Defence
   Ministry of National Defence
   Ministry of Overseas Military Forces of Canada
Personal and Association Papers:
   Association of Medical Officers of the Militia
   William Baptie
   Canadian Nurses' Association
   John Jennings Creelman
   Laura Gamble
   Sophie Hoerner
   A.E. Kemp

John McCrae
Margaret Macdonald
Andrew Macphail
Nursing Sisters' Association of Canada
Irene Peterkin
Cairine Wilson

McGILL UNIVERSITY
Osler Library of the History of Medicine:
  Edward Archibald Fonds
Rare Books and Special Collections:
  R.C. Fetherstonhaugh Collection

THE NATIONAL ARCHIVES, LONDON, ENGLAND
Ethel Becher, military service file
Maud McCarthy, military service file
Reports on Army Nursing Services in France

NATIONAL ARCHIVES AND RECORDS ADMINISTRATION,
  WASHINGTON AND COLLEGE PARK, USA
Office of the Surgeon General
Records of the Panama Canal

NOVA SCOTIA ARCHIVES AND RECORDS MANAGEMENT
F.W. Borden Papers
J.W. Carmichael Papers

PUBLIC ARCHIVES OF ONTARIO
Merriman Family Papers

ST FRANCIS XAVIER UNIVERSITY ARCHIVES, ANTIGONISH,
  NOVA SCOTIA
Macdonald Family Collection

WELLCOME LIBRARY FOR THE HISTORY AND UNDERSTANDING
  OF MEDICINE, LONDON, ENGLAND
Royal Army Medical Corps Muniment Collection

UNIVERSITY OF READING
Nancy Astor Papers
Cliveden Visitors Books

PERSONAL ARCHIVES
Alan Kerr, MilArm, Edmonton:
  Edith Hudson, CAMC, lecture notes and diary
Ronald and Mairi Macdonald, Halifax:
  Macdonald Family Scrapbook
  Ronald St John Macdonald, "Old Bailey's Brook"
  Newspapers and oddments

PUBLISHED SOURCES

GOVERNMENT DOCUMENTS
Annual Reports of the Isthmian Canal Commission, 1904–7. Washington:
  Government Printing Office 1905–8
Canada. Census of Canada
– *Sessional Papers*

MILITARY DOCUMENTS
*Instructions for Members of Canadian Army Medical Nursing Service
  (when mobilized)*. Ottawa: King's Printer 1918
Militia List. Ottawa: King's Printer, annual
Militia Orders. Ottawa: King's Printer, annual

NEWSPAPERS AND PERIODICALS
Canadian Nurse
Casket, Antigonish
Eastern Chronicle, New Glasgow
Halifax Herald
Halifax Morning Chronicle
Mail and Empire, Toronto
Nursing Mirror
Nursing Times
Times, London
Toronto Daily Star
Telegram, Toronto

BOOKS, THESES, AND ARTICLES
Adami, John George. *War Story of the Canadian Army Medical Corps
  1914–15*. vol. 1: *The First Contingent*. London: Colour and Rolls House 1918
"Ancon Hospital." Written by the Nursing Staff. *American Journal of Nursing*
  5 (September 1905): 881–3

Baer, Ellen D., et al., eds. *Enduring Issues in American Nursing*. New York: Springer 2001

Barry, Clare. "The Macdonald Family of Bailey's Brook." BA thesis (history), St Francis Xavier University 1979

Bennett, Ira E. *History of the Panama Canal, Its Construction and Builders*. Washington: Historical Publications 1915

Bruce, Constance E. *Humour in Tragedy: Hospital Life behind Three Fronts*. London: Skeffington [1918]

Bruce, Herbert A. *Politics and the CAMC*. Toronto: William Briggs 1919
– *Varied Operations*. Toronto: Longmans 1958

Burgess, May A. *Nurses, Patients, and Pocketbooks: Report of a Study of the Economics of Nursing*. New York: Committee on the Grading of Nursing Schools 1928

Cameron, James M. *Pictou County's History*. Kentville, NS: Pictou County Historical Society 1972

Cameron, Kenneth. *History of No. 1 Canadian General Hospital CEF*. Sackville: Tribune 1938

Cameron-Smith, Jean. "The Preparation of Nurses for Military Work." *Canadian Nurse* 13 (September 1917): 556–8

Cardinal, Agnes, Dorothy Goldman, and Judith Hattaway, eds. *Women's Writing on the First World War*. Oxford: Oxford University Press 1999

Catholics of the Diocese of Antigonish Nova Scotia and the Great War. Antigonish: St Francis-Xavier University Press, n.d.

Chamberlain, Weston P. *Twenty-Five Years of American Medical Activity on the Isthmus of Panama*. Mount Hope, CZ: Panama Canal Press 1929

Cleverdon, Catherine. *The Woman Suffrage Movement in Canada*. Toronto: University of Toronto Press [1950] 1974

Clint, Mabel. *Our Bit: Memories of War Service by a Canadian Nursing Sister*. Montreal: Alumnae Association of the Royal Victoria Hospital 1934

Cook, Ramsay, and Wendy Mitchinson, eds. *The Proper Sphere: Women's Place in Canadian Society*. Toronto: Oxford University Press 1976

Corcoran, Theresa. *Mount Saint Vincent University: A Vision Unfolding, 1873–1988*. Lanham, Md: University Press of America 1999

Crawford, Elizabeth. *The Women's Suffrage Movement*. London: Routledge 2000

Darche, Louise. "Proper Organization of Training Schools in America." In *Nursing the Sick 1893*, ed. Isabel Hampton et al., 93–103. New York: McGraw-Hill 1949

DeGroot, Gerard J. *Blighty: British Society in the Era of the Great War*. London: Longman 1996

– *The First World War*. Basingstoke, Palgrave 2001

DeGroot, Gerard J., and Corinna Peniston-Bird, eds. *A Soldier and a Woman: Sexual Integration in the Military*. Harlow: Pearson Education 2000

Denison, S.A. *Memoirs*. Toronto: Best 1927

Dock, L. "The Relation of Training Schools to Hospitals." In *Nursing the Sick 1893*, ed. Isabel Hampton et al., 12–22. New York: McGraw-Hill 1949

Doyle, Arthur Conan. *The Great Boer War*. New York: McClure, Phillips 1900

Duffy, John. *A History of Public Health in New York City 1866–1966*. New York: Russell Sage Foundation 1974

Eksteins, Modris. *Rites of Spring: The Great War and the Birth of the Modern Age*. Toronto: Lester & Orpen Dennys 1989

Elshtain, Jean. *Women and War*. New York: Basic Books 1987

Fetherstonhaugh, R.C., ed. *No. 3 Canadian General Hospital (McGill), 1914–1919*. Montreal: Gazette Printing 1928

Gibbon, John M., and Mary S. Mathewson. *Three Centuries of Canadian Nursing*. Toronto: Macmillan 1947

Gillett, Mary C. *The Army Medical Department 1865–1917*. Washington: Center of Military History 1995

Gorgas, Marie D., and Burton J. Hendrick. *William Crawford Gorgas: His Life and Work*. New York: Doubleday, Page 1924

Graves, Dianne. *A Crown of Life: The World of John McCrae*. St Catherines: Vanwell 1997

Haldane, Elizabeth. *The British Nurse in Peace and War*. London: Murray 1923

Hampton, Isabel et al. *Nursing the Sick 1893*. New York: McGraw-Hill 1949

Hay, Ian. *One Hundred Years of Army Nursing*. London: Cassell 1953

Hayhurst, A. "The Army Nurse." *Canadian Nurse* 7 (July 1911): 361–6

Heilbrun, Carolyn. *Writing a Woman's Life*. New York: Norton 1988

Hensley, Sophie M. "Canadian Nurses in New York." *Dominion Illustrated Monthly*, April 1892, 161–8

Hyatt, A.M. Jack, and Nancy Geddes Poole. *Battle for Life: The History of No. 10 Canadian Stationary Hospital and No. 10 Canadian General Hospital in Two World Wars*. Waterloo: Laurier Centre for Military Strategic and Disarmament Studies, Wilfrid Laurier University 2004

James, J.W. "Isabel Hampton and the Professionalization of Nursing in the 1890s." In *Enduring Issues in American Nursing*, ed. Ellen D. Baer et al., 42–84. New York: Springer 2001

Jones, Guy Carleton, "The Nursing Sister in the Canadian Militia." *Canadian Nurse* 3 (March 1907): 129

Kent, Susan Kingsley. *Making Peace: The Reconstruction of Gender in Inter-war Britain.* Princeton: Princeton University Press 1993

Litalien, Michel. *Dans la tourmente: deux hôpitaux militaires canadiens-français dans la France en guerre (1915–1919).* Montreal: Athéna 2003

McClintock, Anne. *Imperial Leather: Race, Gender, and Sexuality in the Colonial Contest.* London: Routledge 1995

McCullough, David. *The Path between the Seas: The Creation of the Panama Canal.* New York: Simon & Schuster 1977

Macdonald, Margaret. "Army Nursing." *Canadian Nurse* 9 (June 1913): 357–9

McGee, Anita Newcomb. "Women Nurses in the American Army." *Proceedings of the 8th Annual Meeting of the Association of Military Surgeons.* September 1899

Mackenzie, Midge. *Shoulder to Shoulder.* New York: Knopf 1975

MacLean, R.A. *Bishop John Cameron, Piety and Politics.* Antigonish: Casket Printing and Publishing 1991

Macphail, Andrew. *In Flanders Fields.* Toronto: Briggs 1919

– *Official History of the Canadian Forces in the Great War, 1914–1919: Medical Services.* Ottawa: King's Printer 1925

McPherson, Kathryn. "Carving Out a Past: The Canadian Nurses' Association War Memorial." *Histoire sociale/Social History* 29 (November 1996): 417–29

Macpherson, William Grant. *History of the Great War: Medical Services. General History.* London: His Majesty's Stationery Office 1924

Mann, Susan. "Silence and Canadian Military Nursing, 1914–1918." Paper delivered at the McGill Centre for Research and Teaching on Women, 29 November 2001

– "Travel Lessons: Canadian Women 'Across the Pond,' 1865–1905." In *Women, Teaching, and Learning. Essays in Honour of Alison Prentice,* ed. Paula Bourne and Elizabeth Smyth. Forthcoming

– "Where Have All the Bluebirds Gone? On the Trail of Canada's Military Nurses." *Atlantis* 26 (Fall 2001): 35–43

– ed. *The War Diary of Clare Gass.* Montreal: McGill-Queen's University Press 2000

Marshall, Logan. *The Story of the Panama Canal.* London: Sampson-Low, Marston 1913

Martin, Thomas W. *Doctor William Crawford Gorgas of Alabama and the Panama Canal.* New York: Newcomen Society of England 1947

Meacham, J.H. & Co. *Illustrated Historical Atlas of Pictou County Nova Scotia* [1879]. Belleville: Mika (facsimile reproduction) 1972

Mears, James E. *The Triumph of American Medicine in the Construction of the Panama Canal*. Philadelphia: W.J. Dornan 1913

Melosh, Barbara. *"The Physician's Hand": Work, Culture, and Conflict in American Nursing*. Philadelphia: Temple University Press 1982

Miller, Carman. *Painting the Map Red: Canada and the South African War 1899–1902*. Montreal: McGill-Queen's University Press 1993

Morgan, Henry J., ed. *Canadian Men and Women of the Time*. Toronto: William Briggs 1898 and 1912

Morrison, Edward W. *With the Guns in South Africa*. Hamilton: Spectator Printing 1901

Morton, Desmond. *A Peculiar Kind of Politics: Canada's Overseas Ministry in the First World War*. Toronto: University of Toronto Press 1982

– *When Your Number's Up: The Canadian Soldier in the First World War*. Toronto: Random House 1993

Mottus, Jane. *New York Nightingales: The Emergence of the Nursing Profession at Bellevue and New York Hospitals 1850–1920*. Ann Arbor: UMI Research Press 1981

Musicant, Ivan. *Empire by Default. The Spanish American War and the Dawn of the American Century*. New York: Henry Holt 1998

Musolf, Karen J. *From Plymouth to Parliament: A Rhetorical History of Nancy Astor's 1919 Campaign*. New York: St Martin's Press 1999

Nicholson, Gerald W.L. *Canada's Nursing Sisters*. Toronto: Hakkert 1975

Norris, Marjorie Barron. *Sister Heroines: The Roseate Glow of Wartime Nursing 1914–1918*. Calgary: Bunker to Bunker Publishing 2002

Ouditt, Sharon. *Fighting Forces, Writing Women: Identity and Ideology in the First World War*. London: Routledge 1994

Place Names and Places of Nova Scotia. Halifax: Public Archives of Nova Scotia 1967

Pope, Georgina. "Army Nursing." *Canadian Nurse* 10 (October 1914): 597–601

– "Reminiscences of Service in South Africa during the Boer War." *Canadian Nurse* 21 (November 1925): 565–70

Prescott, John F. *In Flanders Fields: The Story of John McCrae*. Erin, ON: Boston Mills Press 1985

Quiney, Linda. "Assistant Angels: Canadian Women as Voluntary Aid Detachment Nurses during and after the Great War, 1914–1930." PHD thesis (history), University of Ottawa 2002

Rankin, Rev. D.J. *A History of the County of Antigonish, Nova Scotia*. Toronto: Macmillan 1929

Rawling, Bill. *Death Their Enemy: Canadian Medical Practitioners and War*. Ottawa 2001

Reverby, Susan. *Ordered to Care: The Dilemma of American Nursing 1850–1945*. Cambridge: Cambridge University Press 1987

Riegler, Natalie. "The Work and Networks of Jean Gunn, Superintendent of Nurses, Toronto General Hospital 1913–1941." PHD thesis (education), University of Toronto 1992

Sarnecky, Mary T. *A History of the U.S. Army Nurse Corps*. Philadelphia: University of Pennsylvania Press 1999

– "Nursing in the American Army from the Revolution to the Spanish-American War." *Nursing History Review* 5 (1997): 49–69

Scott, Eric, ed. *Nobody Ever Wins a War. The World War I Diaries of Ella Mae Bongard, R.N.* Ottawa: Janeric 1997

Shields, Carol. *Jane Austen*. London: Penguin 2001

Stimson, Julia. "Nursing in Government Services." *American Journal of Nursing* 22 (March 1922): 427–30

Summers, Anne. *Angels and Citizens: British Women as Military Nurses 1854–1914*. London: Routledge and Kegan Paul 1988

Thornton, Martin, ed. *Nancy Astor's Canadian Correspondence, 1912–1962*. Lewiston: Edwin Mellen Press 1997

Toman, Cynthia. "'Officers and Ladies': Canadian Nursing Sisters, Women's Work, and the Second World War." PHD thesis (history), University of Ottawa 2003

Vance, Jonathan. *Death So Noble: Memory, Meaning, and the First World War*. Vancouver: University of British Columbia Press 1997

Vennat, Pierre. *Les "Poilus" québécois de 1914–1918: histoire des militaires canadiens-français de la Première guerre mondiale*. Vol. 1. Montreal: Meridien 1999

Waite, Peter. *The Man from Halifax: Sir John Thompson, Prime Minister*. Toronto: University of Toronto Press 1985

Wilkinson, Maude. "Four Score and Ten." *Canadian Nurse* 73 (October 1977): 26–9; (November 1977): 14–22; (December 1977): 16–23

Wilson-Simmie, Katherine M. *Lights Out! A Canadian Nursing Sister's Tale*. Belleville: Mika 1981

Woodward, Llewellyn. *Great Britain and the War of 1914–1918*. London: Methuen 1967

Index

QUEBEC
OTTAWA
HALIFAX
NEW YORK

30°

Tropic of Capricorn

ANCON

uator

THE NURSING WORLD OF
MARGARET MACDONALD

Tropic of Cancer

30°

60°